T0332534

Arithmetic Optimization Techniques for Hardware and Software Design

Obtain better system performance, lower energy consumption, and avoid hand-coding arithmetic functions with this concise guide to automated optimization techniques for hardware and software design. High-level compiler optimizations and high-speed architectures for implementing FIR filters are covered, which can improve performance in communications, signal processing, computer graphics, and cryptography. Clearly explained algorithms and illustrative examples throughout make it easy to understand the techniques and write software for their implementation. Background information on the synthesis of arithmetic expressions and computer arithmetic is also included, making the book ideal for new-comers to the subject. This is an invaluable resource for researchers, professionals, and graduate students working in system level design and automation, compilers, and VLSI CAD.

Ryan Kastner is an Associate Professor in the Department of Computer Science and Engineering at the University of California, San Diego. He received his Ph.D. in Computer Science from UCLA in 2002 and has since published over 100 technical papers and three books. His current research interests are in embedded system design, particularly the use of reconfigurable computing devices for digital signal processing.

Anup Hosangadi is an R&D Engineer in the Emulation Group at Cadence Design Systems, Inc. He received his Ph.D. in Computer Engineering from the University of California, Santa Barbara, in 2006 and his research interests include high-level synthesis, combinatorial optimization, and computer arithmetic.

Farzan Fallah is currently a visiting scholar at Stanford University, Stanford. He received his Ph.D. in Electrical Engineering and Computer Science from MIT in 1999, after which he worked as a Project Leader at Fujitsu Laboratories of America in Sunnyvale until 2008. Farzan has published over 60 papers and has 20 patents granted or pending. He has received a Best Paper Award at the Design Automation Conference in 1998 and a Best Paper Award at the VLSI Design Conference in 2005. He is currently the cochair of the Low Power Technical Committee of ACM SIGDA and an associate editor of the *ACM Transactions on Design Automation of Electronic Systems*.

Arithmetic Optimization Techniques for Hardware and Software Design

RYAN KASTNER

Univercity of California, San Diego

ANUP HOSANGADI

Cadence Design Systems, Inc.

FARZAN FALLAH

Stanford University

Shaftesbury Road, Cambridge CB2 8EA, United Kingdom

One Liberty Plaza, 20th Floor, New York, NY 10006, USA

477 Williamstown Road, Port Melbourne, VIC 3207, Australia

314–321, 3rd Floor, Plot 3, Splendor Forum, Jasola District Centre, New Delhi – 110025, India

103 Penang Road, #05–06/07, Visioncrest Commercial, Singapore 238467

Cambridge University Press is part of Cambridge University Press & Assessment,
a department of the University of Cambridge.

We share the University's mission to contribute to society through the pursuit of
education, learning and research at the highest international levels of excellence.

www.cambridge.org
Information on this title: www.cambridge.org/9780521880992

First published 2010

A catalogue record for this publication is available from the British Library

Library of Congress Cataloging-in-Publication data
Kastner, Ryan.
    Arithmetic optimization techniques for hardware and software design / Ryan Kastner,
Anup Hosangadi, Farzan Fallah.
        p.   cm.
    ISBN 978-0-521-88099-2 (Hardback)
    1. Computer arithmetic.   2. Electronic digital computers–Design and construction.
3. Computer software–Development.   4. Mathematical optimization.   I. Hosangadi, Anup.
II. Fallah, Farzan.   III. Title.
    QA76.9.C62K37 2010
    004.01′5196–dc22

                                                                    2009050372

ISBN   978-0-521-88099-2   Hardback

Contents

Abbreviations

ACU	address calculation units
ADPCM	adaptive differential pulse-code modulation
AE	address expression
AEB	available expression blocks
ALAP	as late as possible
ALU	arithmetic logic unit
ASAP	as soon as possible
ASIC	application specific integrated circuit
AST	abstract syntax tree
BSC	binary-stored carry
CAX	concurrent arithmetic extraction
CDFG	control data flow graph
CFG	control flow graph
CIM	cube intersection matrix
CLA	carry look-ahead adder
CLB	configurable logic block
CLG	carry look-ahead generator
CNF	conjunctive normal form
CPA	carry propagate adder
CSA	carry save adder
CSD	canonical signed digits
CSE	common subexpression elimination
DAG	directed acyclic graph
DCT	discrete cosine transform
DFG	data flow graph
DFT	discrete Fourier transform
DHT	discrete Hartley transform
DSP	digital signal processor/processing
DST	discrete sine transform
DU	define use
DWT	discrete wavelet transform
FDS	force directed scheduling
FF	flip flop

FFT	finite Fourier transform
FIR	finite impulse response
FPGA	field programmable gate array
FX	fast-extract
HDL	hardware description language
IDCT	inverse discrete cosine transform
IIR	infinite impulse response
ILP	integer linear programming
IMDCT	inverse modified discrete cosine transform
IP	intellectual property
KCM	kernel-cube matrix
LUT	look up table
MAC	multiply accumulate
MCM	multiple-constant multiplication
MDCT	modified discrete cosine transform
MSPS	million samples per second
NP	non-deterministic polynomial
PDA	parallel distributed arithmetic
PDG	program dependence graph
PRE	partial redundancy elimination
RCA	ripple carry adder
RCS	resource constrained scheduling
RDFT	real discrete Fourier transform
RTL	register transfer level
SA	simulated annealing
SOP	sum of products
SSA	static single assignment
TCS	timing constrained scheduling
THR	tree height reduction
WHT	Walsh–Hadamard transform

Preface

The purpose of the book is to provide an understanding of the design methodologies and optimizations behind the hardware synthesis and software optimization of arithmetic functions. While we have provided a discussion on the fundamentals of software compilation, hardware synthesis and digital arithmetic, much of the material focuses on the implementation of linear systems and polynomial functions in hardware or software. It is therefore intended for students and researchers with a solid background in computing systems.

The three of us started looking into this topic in 2003, back when Anup was a graduate student of Ryan's at the University of California, Santa Barbara; Farzan was a researcher at Fujitsu at that time. Our initial research focused on the optimizations of polynomial functions, attempting to understand the optimal method for synthesizing these as a digital circuit. While developing the model for this synthesis process, we noticed that this same model could be used to describe linear systems. Therefore, the algorithms we developed to optimize polynomials were applicable to linear systems as well. Around this time we received additional funding from the UC Discovery grant and Fujitsu to further study these optimizations. The resulting research was published as numerous journal, conference and workshop papers, and was a basis for Anup's Ph.D. thesis. We noticed the significant lack of published material in this topic area and approached Cambridge University Press with the idea of writing a book on the topic; the obvious result of this lies in the following pages.

This book would not be possible without the help of many people. We would like to thank Fujitsu Laboratories of America and the UC Discovery Grant Program for their support of our research over the years. We would like to thank Cambridge University Press for the help in developing this book. We are particularly thankful for the editors' immense amount of patience. Ryan would further like to acknowledge support from the National Science Foundation Grants CNS-0839944 and CNS-0411321.

1 Introduction

1.1 Overview

Arithmetic is one of the old topics in computing. It dates back to the many early civilizations that used the abacus to perform arithmetic operations. The seventeenth and eighteenth centuries brought many advances with the invention of mechanical counting machines like the slide rule, Schickard's Calculating Clock, Leibniz's Stepped Reckoner, the Pascaline, and Babbage's Difference and Analytical Engines. The vacuum tube computers of the early twentieth century were the first programmable, digital, electronic, computing devices. The introduction of the integrated circuit in the 1950s heralded the present era where the complexity of computing resources is growing exponentially. Today's computers perform extremely advanced operations such as wireless communication and audio, image, and video processing, and are capable of performing over 10^{15} operations per second.

Owing to the fact that computer arithmetic is a well-studied field, it should come as no surprise that there are many books on the various subtopics of computer arithmetic. This book provides a focused view on the optimization of polynomial functions and linear systems. The book discusses optimizations that are applicable to both software and hardware design flows; e.g., it describes the best way to implement arithmetic operations when your target computational device is a digital signal processor (DSP), a field programmable gate array (FPGA) or an application specific integrated circuit (ASIC).

Polynomials are among the most important functions in mathematics and are used in algebraic number theory, geometry, and applied analysis. Polynomial functions appear in applications ranging from basic chemistry and physics to economics, and are used in calculus and numerical analysis to approximate other functions. Furthermore, they are used to construct polynomial rings, a powerful concept in algebra and algebraic geometry.

One of the most important computational uses of polynomials is function evaluation, which lies at the core of many computationally intensive applications. Elementary functions such as sin, cos, tan, $\sin^{-1}$, $\cos^{-1}$, sinh, cosh, tanh, exponentiation and logarithm are often approximated using a polynomial function. Producing an approximation of a function with the required accuracy in a rather large interval may require a polynomial of a large degree. For instance, approximating the function $\ln(1 + x)$ in the range $[-1/2, 1/2]$ with an error less than 10^{-8}

requires a polynomial of degree 12. This requires a significant amount of computation, which without careful optimization results in unacceptable runtime.

Linear systems also play an important role in mathematics and are prevalent in a wide range of applications. A linear system is a mathematical model based on linear operators. Linear systems typically exhibit features and properties that are much simpler and easier to understand and manipulate than the more general, nonlinear case. They are used for mathematical modeling or abstraction in automatic control theory, signal processing, and telecommunications.

Perhaps the foremost computational use of linear systems is in signal processing. A typical signal processing algorithm takes as input a signal or a set of signals and outputs a transformation of them that highlights specific aspects of the data set. For example, the Fourier transform takes as the input the value of a signal over time and returns the corresponding signal transformed into the frequency domain. Such linear transforms are prevalent in almost any form of DSP and include the aforementioned discrete Fourier transform (DFT), as well as the discrete cosine transform (DCT), finite impulse response (FIR) filters, and discrete wavelet transform (DWT).

Polynomials and linear systems lie at the heart of many of the computer intensive tasks in real-time systems. For example, radio frequency communication transceivers, image and video compression, and speech recognition engines all have tight constraints on the time period within which they must compute a function; the processing of each input, whether it be an electromagnetic sample from the antenna, a pixel from a camera or an acoustic sample from a microphone, must be performed within a fixed amount of time in order to keep up with the application's demand. Therefore, the processing time directly limits the real-time behavior of the system.

The bulk of the computation in these applications is performed by mathematical functions. These functions include many of the aforementioned elementary functions (sin, cos, tan, exponentiation, and logarithm) as well as linear transforms (DFT, DCT, DWT, and FIR filters). Application developers often rely on hand-tuned hardware and software libraries to implement these functions. As these are typically a bottleneck in the overall execution of the application, the sooner they finish, the faster the applications run. However, small changes in the parameters of the function (e.g., moving from 16-bit to 32-bit data, changing the coefficients of a filter, adding more precision to the linear transform) require significant redesign of the library elements, perhaps even starting from scratch if the library does not support the exact specification that is required. Further, as the underlying computing platform changes, the libraries should ideally be ported to the new platform with minimal cost and turnaround time. Finally, designers require the ability to tradeoff between different performance metrics including speed, accuracy, and resource usage (i.e., silicon area for hardware implementation and the number of functional units and the amount of memory for software implementations). Therefore, methods to ease the design space exploration over these points are invaluable.

Many of the applications that we consider lie in the realm of embedded computing. These are nontraditional computing systems where the processor is a component of a larger system. Unlike desktops, laptops, and servers, embedded systems are not thought of as primarily computing devices. Example applications include anti-lock braking systems and navigation controls in automobiles, the Mars Rover and robotic surgical systems (along with many other robotics applications), smart phones, MP3 players, televisions, digital video recorders and cameras; these are just some of the devices that can be classified as embedded systems.

There has been an explosive growth in the market for embedded systems primarily in the consumer electronics segment. The increasing trend towards high performance and portable systems has forced researchers to come up with innovative techniques and tools that can achieve these objectives and meet the strict time to market requirements. Most of these consumer applications, such as smart phones, digital cameras, portable music and video players, perform some kind of continuous numerical processing; they constantly process input data and perform extensive calculations. In many cases, these calculations determine the performance and size of the system implemented. Furthermore, since these calculations are energy intensive, they are the major factors determining the battery life of the portable applications.

Embedded system designers face a plethora of decisions. They must attempt to delicately balance a number of often conflicting variables, which include cost, performance, energy consumption, size, and time to market. They are faced with many questions; one of the most important is the choice of the computational device. Microprocessors, microcontrollers, DSPs, FPGAs and ASICs are all appropriate choices depending on the situation, and each has its benefits and drawbacks. Some are relatively easy to program (microprocessors, microcontrollers, DSPs), while others (ASICs, FPGAs) provide better performance and energy consumption. The first three choices require a software design flow, while the last two (ASICs and FPGAs) require hardware design tools. Increasingly, computing devices are "system-on-chip" and consist of several of the aforementioned computational devices. For example, cell phones contain a mix of DSPs, microcontrollers, and ASICs – all on the same physical silicon die. This necessitates a mixed hardware/software design flow, which we discuss in more detail in the following.

Figure 1.1 illustrates a typical design flow for computationally intensive embedded system applications. The application is described using a specification language that expresses the functional requirements in a systematic manner. Additionally, the designer provides constraints, which include the available resources, timing requirements, error tolerance, maximum area, power consumption. The application specification is then analyzed and an appropriate algorithm is selected to implement the desired functionality. For example, signal processing applications must choose the appropriate transforms. Computer graphics applications must select the polynomial models for the surfaces, curves, and textures. An important step is the conversion of floating point representation

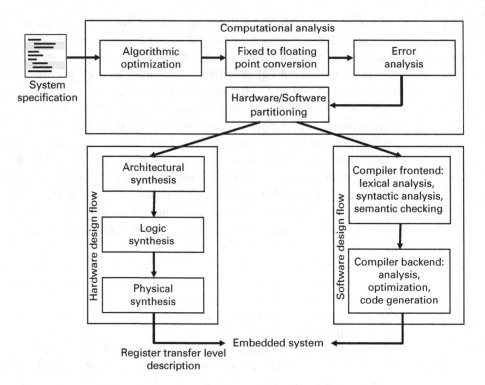

Figure 1.1 Embedded system design flow.

to fixed point representation. Though floating point representation provides greater dynamic range and precision than fixed point, it is far more expensive to compute. Most embedded system applications tolerate a certain degree of inaccuracy and use the much simpler fixed point notation to increase throughput and decrease area, delay, and energy. The conversion of floating point to fixed point produces some errors [1]. These errors should be carefully analyzed to see if they reside within tolerable limits [2, 3].

At this point, the application is roughly divided between hardware and software. The designer, perhaps with the help of automated tools, determines the parts of the system specification that should be mapped onto hardware components and the parts that should be mapped to software. For real-time applications with tight timing constraints, the computation intensive kernels are often implemented in hardware, while the parts of the specification with looser timing constraints are implemented in software. After this decision, the architecture of the system and the memory hierarchy are decided. The custom hardware portions of the system are then designed by means of a behavioral description of the algorithm using a hardware description language (HDL). Hardware synthesis tools transform these hardware descriptions into a register transfer level (RTL) language description by means of powerful hardware synthesis tools. These synthesis tools mainly perform scheduling, resource allocation, and binding of the various operations obtained from an intermediate representation of the behavior represented in the HDL [4]. In addition the tools perform optimizations such as redundancy elimination (common subexpression elimination (CSE) and value numbering) and critical path minimization. The constant multiplications in the linear systems and polynomials can be decomposed into shifts and additions and the resulting complexity can be further reduced by eliminating common subexpressions [5–8]. Furthermore, there are some numeric transformations of the constant coefficients that can be applied to linear transforms to reduce the strength of the operations [9, 10]. This book provides an in-depth discussion of such transforms. The order and priorities of the various optimizations and transformations are largely application dependent and are the subject of current research. In most cases, this is done by evaluating a number of transformations and selecting the one that best meets the constraints [11]. The RTL description is then synthesized into a gate level netlist, which is subsequently placed and routed using standard physical design tools.

For the software portion of the design, custom instructions tuned to the particular application may be added [12–14]. Certain computation intensive kernels of the application may require platform dependent software in order to achieve the best performance on the available architecture. This is often done manually by selecting the relevant functions from optimized software libraries. For some domains, including signal processing applications, automatic library generators are available [11]. The software is then compiled using various transformations and optimization techniques [15]. Unfortunately, these compiler optimizations perform limited transformations for reducing the complexity of polynomial expressions and linear systems. For some applications, the generated assembly code is optimized (mostly manually) to improve performance, though it is not practical for large and complex programs. An assembler and a linker are then used to generate the executable code.

Opportunities for optimizing polynomial expressions and linear systems exist for both the hardware and the software implementations. These optimizations have the potential for huge impact on the performance and power consumption of the embedded systems. This book presents techniques and algorithms for performing such optimizations during both the hardware design flow and the software compilation.

1.2   Salient features of this book

The unique feature of this book is its treatment of the hardware synthesis and software compilation of arithmetic expressions. It is the first book to discuss automated optimization techniques for arithmetic expressions. The previous literature on this topic, e.g., [16] and [17], deals only with the details of implementing arithmetic intensive functions, but stops short of discussing techniques to optimize them for different target architectures. The book gives a detailed introduction to the kind of arithmetic expressions that occur in real-life applications, such as signal processing and computer graphics. It shows the reader the importance of optimizing arithmetic expressions to meet performance and resource constraints and improve the quality of silicon. The book describes in detail the different techniques for performing hardware and software optimizations. It also describes how these techniques can be tuned to improve different parameters such as the performance, power consumption, and area of the synthesized hardware. Though most of the algorithms described in it are heuristics, the book also shows how optimal solutions to these problems can be modeled using integer linear programming (ILP). The usefulness of these techniques is then verified by applying them on real benchmarks.

In short, this book gives a comprehensive overview of an important problem in the design and optimization of arithmetic intensive embedded systems. It describes in detail the state of the art techniques that have been developed to solve this problem. This book does not go into detail about the mathematics behind the arithmetic expressions. It assumes that system designers have performed an analysis of the system and have come up with a set of polynomial equations that describe the functionality of the system, within an acceptable error. Furthermore, it assumes that the system designer has decided what is the best architecture (software, ASIC or FPGA or a combination of them) to implement the arithmetic function. The book does not talk about techniques to verify the precision of the optimized arithmetic expressions. Techniques such as those discussed in [2] and [18] can be used to verify if the expressions produce errors within acceptable limits.

1.3   Organization

- Chapter 2 illustrates the different applications that require arithmetic computation. It shows how polynomial expressions and linear computations reside in a number of applications that drive embedded systems and high-performance computing markets. The chapter discusses how polynomials are employed in computer graphics applications and describes the use of linear systems in DSP, cryptography, and address calculation.
- Chapter 3 presents an overview of the software compilation process and shows opportunities to optimize linear systems and polynomial expressions.
- Chapter 4 provides a high-level description of the hardware synthesis design flow. It explains the major steps in this design flow including input specification, algorithm optimization, scheduling, binding, and resource allocation. The chapter illustrates these concepts with a case study of an FIR filter.
- Chapter 5 gives a brief introduction to the concepts in digital arithmetic. It explains number representations including fixed and floating point representations. Also, it presents different architectures to perform two-operand and multiple-operand addition. These concepts are important in order to gain an understanding of the optimizations described in Chapters 6 and 7.

- Chapter 6 presents algebraic optimization techniques for polynomial expressions. It describes representations of polynomial expressions as well as various algorithms to optimize polynomials for both hardware and software implementation. The chapter concludes with experimental results showing the relative benefits of the various optimization techniques.
- Chapter 7 describes algebraic techniques for the optimization of linear arithmetic computations such as FIR filters and other linear transforms. Algorithms to optimize multiple-operand addition are also presented. Finally, the chapter presents experimental results where the usefulness of these techniques is demonstrated using real-life examples.

1.4 Target audience

When writing this book we had several audiences in mind. Much of the material is targeted towards specialists, whether they be researchers in academia or industry, who are designing both software and hardware for polynomial expressions and/or linear systems. The book also provides substantial background of the state of the art algorithms for the implementation of these systems, and serves as a reference for researchers in these areas. This book is designed to accommodate readers with different backgrounds, and the book includes some basic introductory material on several topics including computer arithmetic, software compilation, and hardware synthesis. These introductory chapters give just enough background to demonstrate basic ideas and provide references to gain more in-depth information. Most of the book can be understood by anyone with a basic grounding in computer engineering. The book is suitable for graduate students, either as a reference or as textbook for a specialized class on the topics of hardware synthesis and software compilation for linear systems and polynomial expressions. It is also suitable for an advanced topics class for undergraduate students.

References

[1] C. Shi and R.W. Brodersen, An automated floating-point to fixed-point conversion methodology, *IEEE International Conference on Acoustics, Speech, and Signal Processing, 2003*. Washington, DC: IEEE Computer Society, 2003.

[2] C.F. Fang, R.A. Rutenbar, and T. Chen, Fast, accurate static analysis for fixed-point finite-precision effects in DSP designs, *International Conference on Computer Aided Design (ICCAD), San Jose, 2003*. Washington, DC: IEEE Computer Society, 2003.

[3] D. Menard and O. Sentieys, Automatic evaluation of the accuracy of fixed-point algorithms, *Design, Automation and Test in Europe Conference and Exhibition, 2002*. Washington, DC: IEEE Computer Society, 2002.

[4] G.D. Micheli, *Synthesis and optimization of digital circuits*, New York, NY: McGraw-Hill, 1994.

[5] M. Potkonjak, M.B. Srivastava, and A.P. Chandrakasan, Multiple constant multiplications: efficient and versatile framework and algorithms for exploring common subexpression elimination, *IEEE Transactions on Computer Aided Design of Integrated Circuits and Systems*, **15**(2), 151–65, 1996.

[6] R. Pasko, P. Schaumont, V. Derudder, V. Vernalde, and D. Durackova, A new algorithm for elimination of common subexpressions, *IEEE Transactions on Computer Aided Design of Integrated Circuits and Systems*, **18**(1), 58–68, 1999.

[7] R. Pasko, P. Schaumont, V. Derudder, and D. Durackova, Optimization method for broadband modem FIR filter design using common subexpression elimination, *International Symposium on System Synthesis, 1997*. Washington, DC: IEEE Computer Society, 1997.

[8] A. Hosangadi, F. Fallah, and R. Kastner, Common subexpression elimination involving multiple variables for linear DSP synthesis, *IEEE International Conference on Application-Specific Architectures and Processors, 2004*. Washington, DC: IEEE Computer Society, 2004.

[9] A. Chatterjee, R.K. Roy, and M.A. D'Abreu, Greedy hardware optimization for linear digital circuits using number splitting and refactorization, *IEEE Transactions on Very Large Scale Integration (VLSI) Systems*, **1**(4), 423–31, 1993.

[10] H.T. Nguyen and A. Chatterjee, Number-splitting with shift-and-add decomposition for power and hardware optimization in linear DSP synthesis, *IEEE Transactions on Very Large Scale Integration (VLSI) Systems*, **8**, 419–24, 2000.

[11] M. Puschel, B. Singer, J. Xiong, *et al.*, SPIRAL: a generator for platform-adapted libraries of signal processing algorithms, *Journal of High Performance Computing and Applications*, **18**, 21–45, 2004.

[12] R. Kastner, S. Ogrenci-Memik, E. Bozorgzadeh, and M. Sarrafzadeh, Instruction generation for hybrid reconfigurable systems, *International Conference on Computer Aided Design*. New York, NY: ACM, 2001.

[13] A. Peymandoust, L. Pozzi, P. Ienne, and G. De Micheli, Automatic instruction set extension and utilization for embedded processors, *IEEE International Conference on Application-Specific Systems, Architectures, and Processors, 2003*. Washington, DC: IEEE Computer Society, 2003.

[14] Tensilica Inc., http://www.tensilica.com.

[15] S.S. Muchnick, *Advanced Compiler Design and Implementation*, San Francisco, CA: Morgan Kaufmann Publishers, 1997.

[16] J.P. Deschamps, G.J.A. Bioul, and G.D. Sutter, *Synthesis of Arithmetic Circuits: FPGA, ASIC and Embedded Systems*, New York, NY: Wiley-Interscience (2006).

[17] U. Meyer-Baese, *Digital Signal Processing with Field Programmable Gate Arrays*, third edition. Springer, 2007.

[18] C. Fang Fang, R.A. Rutenbar, M. Puschel, and T. Chen, Toward efficient static analysis of Finite-Precision effects in DSP applications via affine arithmetic modeling, *Design Automation Conference*. New York, NY: ACM, 2003.

2 Use of polynomial expressions and linear systems

2.1 Chapter overview

Polynomial expressions and linear systems are found in a wide range of applications: perhaps most fundamentally, Taylor's theorem states that any differentiable function can be approximated by a polynomial. Polynomial approximations are used extensively in computer graphics to model geometric objects. Many of the fundamental digital signal processing transformations are modeled as linear systems, including FIR filters, DCT and H.264 video compression. Cryptographic systems, in particular, those that perform exponentiation during public key encryption, are amenable to modeling using polynomial expressions. Finally, address calculation during data intensive applications requires a number of add and multiply operations that grows larger as the size and dimension of the array increases. This chapter describes these and other applications that require arithmetic computation. We show that polynomial expressions and linear systems are found in a variety of applications that are driving the embedded systems and high-performance computing markets.

2.2 Approximation algorithms

Polynomial functions can be used to approximate any differentiable function. Given a set of points, the unisolvence theorem states that there always exists a unique polynomial, which precisely models these points. This is extremely useful for computing complex functions such as logarithm and trigonometric functions and forms the basis for algorithms in numerical quadrature and numerical ordinary differential equations. More precisely, the unisolvence theorem states that, given a set of $n + 1$ unique data points, a unique polynomial with degree n or less exists.

As an example, consider the Taylor expansion of $\sin(x)$ approximated to four terms:

$$\sin(x) = x - \frac{x^3}{3!} + \frac{x^5}{5!} - \frac{x^7}{7!}. \tag{2.1}$$

This is a polynomial of degree 7 that approximates the sine function. Assuming that the terms $1/3!$, $1/5!$, and $1/7!$ are precomputed (these will be denoted as S_3, S_5, and S_7, respectively), the naïve evaluation of this polynomial representation requires 3 additions/subtractions, 12 variable multiplications, and 3 constant multiplications. However, it is possible to optimize this polynomial to reduce the number of operations needed for its computation. For example, the techniques described in this book produce the following set of equations, which are equivalent to the four-term Taylor expansion of sin (x):

$$d_1 = x \cdot x,$$
$$d_2 = S_5 - S_7 \cdot d_1,$$
$$d_3 = d_2 \cdot d_1 - S_3,$$
$$d_4 = d_3 \cdot d_1 + 1,$$
$$\sin(x) = x \cdot d_4.$$

Here, only three additions/subtractions, four variable multiplications, and one constant multiplication are needed.

It is noteworthy that computing these expressions, even in their optimized form, is expensive in terms of hardware, cycle time, and power consumption. If the arguments to these functions are known beforehand, the functions can be pre-computed and stored in lookup tables in memory. However, in cases where these arguments are not known or the memory size is limited, these expressions must be computed during the execution of the application that uses them.

2.3   Computer graphics

Computer graphics is a prime example of an application domain that uses polynomials to approximate complex functions. The use of computer graphics is widespread and includes applications such as video games, animated movies, and scientific modeling. In general, these applications are computationally expensive. Advanced graphics is increasingly being integrated into embedded devices due to the consumer demand and improvements in technology. Therefore, techniques that optimize computation time, power, energy, and throughput for graphics applications are of utmost importance.

Polynomials are the fundamental model for approximating arcs, surfaces, curves, and textures. In fact, most geometric objects are formulated in terms of polynomial equations, thereby reducing many graphic problems to the manipulation of polynomial systems [1]. Therefore, solving polynomial systems is an elementary problem in many geometric computations. As an example, consider the process of spline interpolation, which is used to model textures and surfaces. A spline is a method of approximation, in which a function is divided piecewise into a set of polynomials, i.e., each piece of the function is approximated using a polynomial. More formally, given a set of $n+1$ distinct points, a k-spline function is a set of n polynomial functions with degree less than or equal to k. This interpolation allows each polynomial to have a low degree, as opposed to having one high-degree polynomial approximation for the entire curve. In general, the spline interpolation yields similar accuracy to modeling the same curve using one higher-degree polynomial. Therefore, splines are less computationally complex.

Consider a quartic spline – a spline where the polynomials have degree less than or equal to 4, i.e., $k = 4$. A quartic spline is smooth in both first and second derivatives and continuous in the third derivative. The unoptimized polynomial expression representing a quartic spline is

$$P = zu^4 + 4avu^3 + 6bu^2v^2 + 4uv^3w + qv^4. \tag{2.2}$$

The straightforward implementation requires 23 multiplications and 4 additions. The number of operations can be reduced using two-term common subexpression elimination (CSE), a common software compiler technique used in most optimizing compilers [2]. CSE is an iterative algorithm where two-term common subexpressions are extracted and eliminated. The result of the two-term CSE algorithm depends on the ordering of the operations in the parse tree of the expression. The results using the ordering that produces the least number of operations for the CSE algorithm are

$$d_1 = u^2; d_2 \; H = v^2; d_3 = uv;$$
$$P = d_1^2 z + 4ad_1 d_3 + 6bd_1 d_2 + 4wd_2 d_3 + qd_2^2. \tag{2.3}$$

Note that three two-term common subexpressions were extracted: u^2, v^2, and uv. This form requires 16 multiplications and 4 additions, reducing the number of multiplications by seven from the straightforward implementation. Alternatively, the Horner form can be used to reduce the number of operations. The Horner form is a way of efficiently computing a polynomial by viewing it as a linear combination of monomials. In the Horner form, a polynomial is converted into a nested sequence of multiplications and additions, which is very efficient to compute with multiply accumulate (MAC) operations; it is a popular form for evaluating many polynomials in signal processing libraries including the GNU C library [3]. The Horner form of the quartic spline polynomial is

$$P = zu^4 + v \cdot (4au^3 + v \cdot (6bu^2 + v \cdot (4uw + qv))). \tag{2.4}$$

It uses 17 multiplications and 4 additions. The Horner form produces a good representation for a univariate polynomial, e.g., the Taylor series form for sine, but it often performs poorly on multivariate polynomials such as the quartic spline example. It is not always clear which of the variables should be factored in the Horner form to get the best result.

The quartic spline polynomial optimized using the algebraic techniques discussed in this book is

$$d_1 = v^2; d_2 = 4v;$$
$$P = u^3 \cdot (uz + ad_2) + d_1 \cdot (qd_1 + u \cdot (wd_2 + 6bu)). \tag{2.5}$$

It uses 13 multiplications and 4 additions. This implementation produces three fewer multiplications than the two-term CSE algorithm and four fewer multiplications than the Horner form. The algebraic techniques presented later in this book can optimize more than one expression at a time and can optimize expressions consisting of any number of variables. These algorithms use a canonical form to represent the arithmetic expressions and consider the detection of any common subexpression or algebraic factorization.

2.4   Digital signal processing (DSP)

DSP is an increasingly important form of computation found in applications including audio, image, video, speech, and/or communications. Therefore, most of the techniques described in this book are focused on the general area of signal processing. In this chapter, we focus on two of the more commonly used functions – FIR filters and linear transforms. These functions are ubiquitous in signal processing applications. There are many other uses of optimizations for DSP, which will be discussed in this book.

2.4.1   Finite impulse response (FIR) filters

Filtering is perhaps the most common computation in signal processing. Filters are often major determinants of the performance of the entire system. Therefore, it is important to have good tools for optimizing these functions.

The FIR filter is a common form of digital filter. It is preferred to other alternatives, e.g., infinite impulse response (IIR), due to its lack of feedback and phase distortion. Furthermore, FIR filters are relatively simple to implement; most digital signal processors have specialized functional units (e.g., MAC) for efficient FIR filter computation.

An *L-tap* FIR filter involves a convolution of the L most recent input samples with a set of constants. This is typically denoted as:

$$y[n] = \sum h[k] \cdot x[n-k], \quad k = 0, 1, \ldots, L-1. \tag{2.6}$$

The output value $y[n]$ is computed by multiplying the L most recent input samples from the input vector x by a set of constant coefficients stored in the h vector, where $|h| = L$. Equivalently, $h[k]$ represents the kth constant coefficient of the filter, $x[n]$ represents the input time series, and $y[n]$ is the output time series. The constants vary depending on the type of filter (e.g., low-pass, high-pass, Butterworth).

There are many different implementations for an FIR filter. The conventional tapped delay-line realization of this inner product is shown in Figure 2.1. The computation of each output sample consists of L constant multiplications and $L-1$

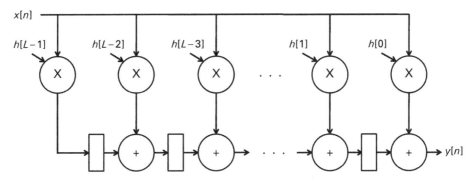

Figure 2.1 The tapped delay line representation of an FIR filter with L taps. Each output sample requires L constant multiplications and $L - 1$ additions.

additions. A fully parallel implementation uses $O(L)$ constant multipliers, $O(L)$ adders, and $O(L)$ registers. As one can see, this requires a substantial amount of resources, but results in a high throughput. A serial version of the FIR filter can be realized using a single MAC block. This reduces both the resource requirement and the throughput by $O(L)$.

The methods described in this book can be used to optimize the FIR filter computation. In particular, we describe a number of optimizations, including the aforementioned tapped delay line, distributed arithmetic, and arithmetic optimizations. We compare various implementations and show several new methods that outperform the conventional ones.

2.4.2 Linear transforms

A linear transform is a set of linear functions that define a relationship between input and output variables. A linear transform is often preferable to nonlinear transforms due to its simplistic model and subsequent relative ease of computation. Linear transforms are used in a range of applications including control theory and signal processing. While we focus primarily on the latter in this section of the book, the presented techniques are generally applicable for the optimization of any linear system.

In general, a linear system can be expressed as a multiplication of a constant matrix C with a vector of input samples X, where each output signal $Y[i]$ is of the form

$$Y[i] = \sum_{j=0}^{N-1} C_{i,j} \cdot X[j]. \tag{2.7}$$

As an example, consider the DCT [4], which is commonly used for compression in many signal processing systems. For example, the DCT is used in both JPEG and MPEG compression [5]. The DCT expresses data as a sum of sinusoids, in a

$$
C = \begin{bmatrix}
\cos(0) & \cos(0) & \cos(0) & \cos(0) \\
\cos(\pi/8) & \cos(3\pi/8) & \cos(5\pi/8) & \cos(7\pi/8) \\
\cos(\pi/4) & \cos(3\pi/4) & \cos(5\pi/4) & \cos(7\pi/4) \\
\cos(3\pi/8) & \cos(7\pi/8) & \cos(\pi/8) & \cos(5\pi/8)
\end{bmatrix}
= \begin{bmatrix}
A & A & A & A \\
B & C & -C & -B \\
D & -D & -D & D \\
C & -B & B & -C
\end{bmatrix}
$$

Figure 2.2 The constant matrix for a four-point DCT. The matrix on the right provides a simple substitution of the variables A, B, C, and D for the constants $\cos(0)$, $\cos(\pi/8)$, $\cos(3\pi/8)$, and $\cos(\pi/4)$, respectively.

(a)

$$
\begin{bmatrix}
y_0 \\
y_1 \\
y_2 \\
y_3
\end{bmatrix}
= \begin{bmatrix}
A & A & A & A \\
B & C & -C & -B \\
D & -D & -D & D \\
C & -B & B & -C
\end{bmatrix}
\begin{bmatrix}
x_0 \\
x_1 \\
x_2 \\
x_3
\end{bmatrix}
$$

(b)

$$y_0 = Ax_0 + Ax_1 + Ax_2 + Ax_3$$

$$y_1 = Bx_0 + Cx_1 - Cx_2 - Bx_3$$

$$y_2 = Dx_0 - Dx_1 - Dx_2 + Dx_3$$

$$y_3 = Cx_0 - Bx_1 + Bx_2 - Cx_3$$

Figure 2.3 (a) A four-point DCT represented as a multiplication of input vector with a constant matrix and (b) the corresponding set of equations.

similar manner to Fourier transform. In fact, it is a special case of the DFT [6], but uses only real numbers (corresponding to the cosine values of complex exponentials, hence, the name). DCT has a strong energy compaction, which is ideal for compression of image and video data, where most of the signal information is found in the lower-frequency components.

DCT can be modeled according to Equation (2.7), where the constant matrix (C) and a vector of input samples (X) are multiplied to compute the output vector Y. The constant matrix for a four-point DCT is shown in Figure 2.2. The matrix multiplication with a vector of input samples is shown in Figure 2.3. In the figures, A, B, C and D can be viewed as distinct constants. The straightforward computation of this matrix multiplication requires 16 multiplications and 12 additions/subtractions. In general $O(N^2)$ operations are required for an N-point DCT. However, by extracting common factors, these expressions can be rewritten as shown in Figure 2.4. This implementation is cheaper than the original implementation by ten multiplications and four additions/subtractions. In general, factorization of DCT equations can reduce the number of operations to $O(N \log N)$. However, these optimizations are typically done manually in hand-coded signal processing libraries; the methods discussed in this book can extract these common factors and common subexpressions automatically.

The 4×4 linear integer transform used in H.264 [5] is another example of a linear system found in signal processing. It is a digital video codec that achieves a very high data compression rate. The integer transform for the video encoding

$d_1 = x_0 + x_3$

$d_2 = x_1 + x_2$

$d_3 = x_1 - x_2$

$d_4 = x_0 - x_3$

$y_0 = A \cdot (d_1 + d_2)$

$y_1 = B \cdot d_4 + C \cdot d_3$

$y_2 = D \cdot (d_1 - d_2)$

$y_3 = C \cdot d_4 - B \cdot d_3$

Figure 2.4 The four-point DCT after using techniques to eliminate common subexpressions.

and the translation of the constant values 1 and 2 to A and B, respectively, is shown in

$$
\begin{bmatrix} Y_0 \\ Y_1 \\ Y_2 \\ Y_3 \end{bmatrix} = \begin{bmatrix} 1 & 1 & 1 & 1 \\ 2 & 1 & -1 & -2 \\ 1 & -1 & -1 & 1 \\ 1 & -2 & 2 & -1 \end{bmatrix} \begin{bmatrix} X_0 \\ X_1 \\ X_2 \\ X_3 \end{bmatrix} = \begin{bmatrix} A & A & A & A \\ B & A & -A & -B \\ A & -A & -A & A \\ A & -B & B & -A \end{bmatrix} \begin{bmatrix} X_0 \\ X_1 \\ X_2 \\ X_3 \end{bmatrix}
\tag{2.8}
$$

The first thing to note about the above transform is its similarity to the DCT transform. Careful inspection of the matrices shows that this instance of the linear transform is a special case of the four-point DCT.[1] Using the optimization techniques on the above transform gives the same set of extracted subexpressions as DCT after substituting the H.264's constant value A for the DCT constant values C and D (see Figure 2.2). Another notable difference is the simplicity of the constant values in the 4×4 linear integer transform of H.264. In fact, we can exploit this using strength reduction to optimize the final implementation. Multiplication by 1 and -1 is obviously trivial; similarly multiplication by constant value 2 is simply a left shift by one bit.

Many DSP algorithms contain a large number of multiplications with constants [7]. Careful decomposition of constant multiplications into shifts and additions leads to tremendous benefits with respect to execution time, area, throughput, and power/energy. Arithmetic optimizations can handle and exploit constant multiplications as a set of shifts and additions. This is particularly beneficial for hardware optimization. We will discuss this issue in further detail in the following. First, consider Figure 2.5, which shows optimizations on the H.264 example [8]. The number of additions is 8, which is less than the 12 required in the naïve method.

There are several things to notice about this figure. First, the "$-$" symbols denote negation of the number. These negations could just as easily have been denoted as a subtraction on the subsequent addition operation. The "$\ll 1$" indicates a left shift by one bit. This is a result of the strength reduction of the constant multiplication by 2. Any multiplication by a constant value can be substituted by a set of shifts and

---

[1] Let DCT A = H.264 A, DCT B = H.264 B, DCT C = H.264 A, DCT D = H.264 A.

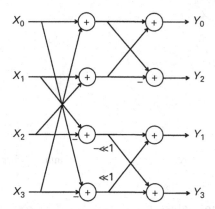

Figure 2.5 H.264 integer transform after extracting common subexpressions and applying strength reduction on the constant multiplications.

additions. Therefore, the constant multiplications in the DCT example could be similarly translated into a set of shift and add operations, albeit a much more complicated one than the rather simple H.264 example.

Multipliers are expensive in terms of area, delay, and power/energy consumption. When considering hardware implementations, the full flexibility of a general-purpose multiplier is not required in some cases. For example, the constant multiplication can be implemented using a sequence of additions and shift operations. In a hardware implementation, the shift operation is "free" as it involves simple rewiring. Therefore, the complexity of the constant multiplication is directly related to the number of additions. There are many techniques that convert a constant multiplication into a set of shift and add operations. Most techniques revolve around the use of signed digit representation [9] for the constant value and attempt to extract common bit patterns within a single constant value. The techniques presented in this book are also capable of such optimizations. Furthermore, the techniques presented in this book can optimize the shift and add conversion among groups of constant values. For example, we may find similar bit patterns in constants C and D in the DCT example.

2.5   Cryptography

Cryptography is the study of hiding information from an adversary that wishes to steal the information. It is a fundamental concern in computer and network security. It is found in a variety of everyday applications including email, web browsing, banking, and electronic commerce.

A major problem in the early history of cryptography was the requirement that each user has the same secret key. This key had to be exchanged using a nonencrypted method, e.g., through a personal meeting of the users or by a trusted courier. This symmetric key was then used to encrypt and decrypt the message. As one can imagine, key distribution posed a significant hurdle in the early adoption of cryptographic systems.

Public key cryptography solved this problem through the use of asymmetrical encryption. Each user in a public key cryptographic system has two keys – one public and one private. Only the user knows the private key, while everyone knows the public key. The keys are generated using a one-way function – a function that is easily computed, yet it is very difficult to perform the "reverse" computation. For example, it is easy to multiply two prime numbers; however, it is quite difficult to factor the product into two prime numbers.

RSA [10] is a common algorithm for public key encryption. It involves a substantial amount of arithmetic computation during encryption and decryption. The system is based on a public key pair (n,e) and a private key pair (n,d), where n is the product of two large prime numbers $(n = p \times q)$. When a message m has to be transmitted, it is encrypted using the public key of the recipient as $c = m^e$ mod n. The original message is decrypted at the receiver using his private key as $m = c^d$ mod n. The computation for both encryption and decryption is dominated by the exponentiation, m^e for encryption and c^d for decryption. Exponentiation is very expensive as the size of the exponents are of the order of 1024 bits in modern implementations [11]. Therefore, fast public key encryption relies on the ability to compute numbers with large exponents quickly.

The most popular method for performing exponentiation is using the method of squaring, though there are some methods which use the concept of addition chains and claim to reduce the number of multiplications by an average of 22% over the squaring method [12]. Finding common bit patterns in the exponent can also reduce the number of multiplications. For example consider the exponentiation x^{2925}. Note that $2925 = (101101101101)_2$. Using the method of squaring, x^{2925} can be computed as shown in Figure 2.6. By eliminating the common digit pattern $d_1 = 101$ in the exponent P, it can be rewritten as $P = d_1 + d_1 \ll 3 + d_1 \ll 6 + d_1 \ll 9$ (the $\ll$ represents the left shift operator). By further extracting the common part $d_2 = d_1 + d_1 \ll 3$, P can be rewritten as $P = d_2 + d_2 \ll 6$. Using this property, the integer exponentiation is rewritten as shown in Figure 2.6. This takes three fewer multiplications than the method of squaring. Therefore, it can be seen that further reduction in the number of operations over conventional methods is possible by extracting common patterns to eliminate redundant operations.

2.6   Address calculation in data intensive applications

Data transfer intensive applications often consist of a number of memory accesses, and therefore involve many arithmetic operations during the

(a)

$t_1 = x \cdot x = x^2$	10
$t_2 = t_1 \cdot t_1 = x^4$	100
$t_3 = t_2 \cdot x = x^5$	101
$t_4 = t_3 \cdot t_3 = x^{10}$	1010
$t_5 = t_4 \cdot x = x^{11}$	1011
$t_6 = t_5 \cdot t_5 = x^{22}$	10110
$t_7 = t_6 \cdot t_6 = x^{44}$	101100
$t_8 = t_7 \cdot x = x^{45}$	101101
$t_9 = t_8 \cdot t_8 = x^{90}$	1011010
$t_{10} = t_9 \cdot x = x^{91}$	1011011
$t_{11} = t_{10} \cdot t_{10} = x^{182}$	10110110
$t_{12} = t_{11} \cdot t_{11} = x^{364}$	101101100
$t_{13} = t_{12} \cdot x = x^{365}$	101101101
$t_{14} = t_{13} \cdot t_{13} = x^{730}$	1011011010
$t_{15} = t_{14} \cdot x = x^{731}$	1011011011
$t_{16} = t_{15} \cdot t_{15} = x^{1462}$	10110110110
$t_{17} = t_{16} \cdot t_{16} = x^{2924}$	101101101100
$t_{18} = t_{17} \cdot x = x^{2925}$	101101100101

(b)

$P = 101101101101 = 2925$	
$d_1 = 101$	
$d_2 = d_1 + d_1 \ll 3$	
$P = d_2 + d_2 \ll 6$	
$t_1 = x \cdot x = x^2$	10
$t_2 = t_1 \cdot t_1 = x^4$	100
$t_3 = t_2 \cdot x = x^5$	101 (d_1)
$t_4 = t_3 \cdot t_3 = x^{10}$	1010
$t_5 = t_4 \cdot t_4 = x^{20}$	10100
$t_6 = t_5 \cdot t_5 = x^{40}$	101000
$t_7 = t_6 \cdot t_3 = x^{45}$	101101 (d_2)
$t_8 = t_7 \cdot t_7 = x^{90}$	1011010
$t_9 = t_8 \cdot t_8 = x^{180}$	10110100
$t_{10} = t_9 \cdot t_9 = x^{360}$	101101000
$t_{11} = t_{10} \cdot t_{10} = x^{720}$	1011010000
$t_{12} = t_{11} \cdot t_{11} = x^{1440}$	10110100000
$t_{13} = t_{12} \cdot t_{12} = x^{2880}$	101101000000
$t_{14} = t_{13} \cdot t_7 = x^{2985}$	101101101101

Figure 2.6 Exponentiation: (a) using the method of squaring, and (b) eliminating common computations. The number next to the equations denotes the binary representation of the current exponent.

computation of the memory access pointers. Consider an indexed linear array of elements $A[I_1][I_2]\cdots[I_n]$ with the maximal number of array entries in each dimension represented by S_j, for each dimension j. Assuming a row-major type organization for the array A, the address expression (AE) for an element of the array is $AE = (((I_1 \times S_2 + I_2) \times S_3 + I_3) \times S_4 + \cdots) \times S_n + I_n$. The values of the array sizes $\{S_j\}$ are known a priori for statically allocated arrays. In this case, the address expression becomes an affine form of the type $AE = C_1 \times I_1 + C_2 \times I_2 + C_3 \times I_3 + \cdots + I_n$.

These computations are very often on the critical paths in loops and are good candidates for optimization. The work in [13] addressed this issue and presented various algebraic transformations for optimizing these address calculations. The authors targeted the hardware synthesis of custom address calculation units (ACUs). A number of transformations were investigated including splitting and clustering the address expressions. The optimizations were designed to break the individual AE into smaller pieces and then recombine these pieces into an optimized arithmetic expression. Induction variable analysis (a well-known compiler optimization that transforms an array index into a pointer that is incremented by a constant value [2]) and global algebraic transformations, such as CSE and constant propagation were also investigated.

2.7   Summary

This chapter looked at a number of application domains that use polynomial expressions and linear systems, and therefore would benefit from the optimizations presented in this book. We discussed how polynomial functions can approximate any differentiable function, making them attractive to provide estimates for complex functions. For example, computer graphics often approximate arcs, surfaces, curves, and textures using simple polynomial functions. Furthermore, we described how linear systems are prevalent in DSP, which permeates audio, speech, image and communications applications. Finally, we described how to use polynomial functions to model exponentiation required for public key cryptography, as well as address calculation for data intensive applications, making their optimization important for both of these applications.

References

[1] R. H. Bartels, J. C. Beatty, and B. A. Barsky, *An Introduction to Splines for Use in Computer Graphics and Geometric Modeling*. San Franciso, CA: Morgan Kaufmann Publishers, Inc., 1987.

[2] S. S. Muchnick, *Advanced Compiler Design and Implementation*. San Francisco, CA: Morgan Kaufmann Publishers, 1997.

[3] M. K. Johnson, Introduction to the GNU C Library, *Linux Journal*, **1994**, 5, 1994.

[4] K. R. Rao and P. Yip, Discrete Cosine Transform: Algorithms, Advantages, Applications. New York, NY: Academic Press Professional, Inc., 1990.

[5] I. E. G. Richardson, *H.264 and MPEG-4 Video Compression*. New York, NY: John Wiley and Sons, 2003.

[6] R. Tolimieri, M. An, and C. Lu, *Algorithms for Discrete Fourier Transforms and Convolution*. Springer, 1997.

[7] M. Potkonjak, M. B. Srivastava, and A. P. Chandrakasan, Multiple constant multiplications: efficient and versatile framework and algorithms for exploring common subexpression elimination, *IEEE Transactions on Computer Aided Design of Integrated Circuits and Systems*, **15** (2), 151–56, 1996.

[8] H. S. Malvar, A. Hallapuro, M. Karczewicz, and L. Kerofsky, Low-complexity transform and quantization in H.264/AVC, *IEEE Transactions on Circuits and Systems for Video Technology*, **13**, 598–603, 2003.

[9] M. D. Ercegovac and T. Lang, *Digital Arithmetic*. San Francisco, CA: Morgan Kaufmann Publishers, 2004.

[10] R. L. Rivest, A. Shamir, and L. Adleman, On digital signatures and public-key cryptosystems, *IEEE International Symposium on Information Theory*, p. 41. Washington, DC: IEEE Computer Society, 1977.

[11] B. Schneier, *Applied Cryptography: Protocols, Algorithms and Source Code in C*, second edition. New York, NY: John Wiley and Sons Inc, 1996.

[12] P. Downey, B. Leong, and R. Sethi, Computing sequences with addition chains, *SIAM Journal of Computing*, **10**, 638–46, 1981.

[13] M. A. Miranda, F. V. M. Catthoor, M. Janssen, and H. J. De Man, High-level address optimization and synthesis techniques for data-transfer-intensive applications, *IEEE Transactions on Very Large Scale Integration (VLSI) Systems*, **6**, 677–86, 1998.

3 Software compilation

3.1 Chapter overview

To further motivate the techniques described in this book, we demonstrate the situations in which they are useful and the manner in which they fit into the design flow. Arithmetic optimizations are applicable when writing software as well as during the design of hardware components. This chapter gives a high-level overview of the software compilation process. We start by describing the basic structure of a modern compiler. Then we provide more detail about the compilation process including the place where arithmetic optimizations can be implemented. Finally, we describe the algebraic transformations that are used in current compilers. These include dataflow optimization, CSE, value numbering, loop invariant code motion, partial redundancy elimination (PRE), operator strength reduction, and the Horner form.

3.2 Basic software compiler structure

A compiler is used to reduce the complexity of designing digital systems. Quite simply, it transforms an input specification written in some high-level language into another language which is almost always at a lower level of abstraction. Perhaps the most common example is a software compiler, which takes source code written in some high-level programming language (e.g., C/C++, Java) into object code specified by an assembly or machine language for programming a microprocessor (e.g., Intel x86, SPARC, MIPS).

A compiler provides several benefits including:

(1) Raising the level of abstraction to allow the programmer to reason about the problem in a high-level language, which is often more efficient.
(2) Performing trivial and/or tedious transformations, e.g., converting assembly code into binary code.
(3) Finding obvious semantic and syntactic mistakes in the specification.
(4) Performing a set of complex optimizations that may not be obvious to the programmer.

Figure 3.1 provides a visual description of the basic steps during compilation. A source program is given as input to the compiler, which performs a number of

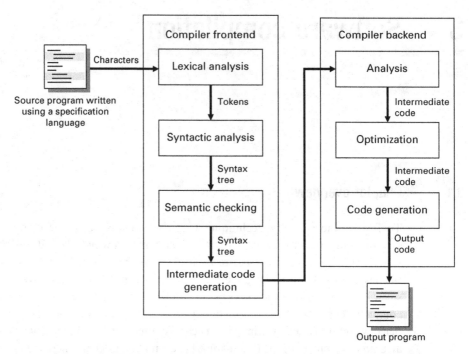

Figure 3.1 The basic structure of a compiler. Compilers are divided into two stages: a frontend and a backend. The goal is to translate a source program into an output program; this requires many different optimizations.

steps to transform that program into an output program. We briefly describe each of these steps in further detail.

Lexical analysis is the first step in compilation; it is often called "lexing" or "scanning." This is the act of breaking the input into a set of words or tokens. A token is an atomic unit in the programming language and commonly includes variable names, operations, type identifiers, keywords, numbers, and symbols. One can draw a parallel between lexical analysis and converting letters to words.

Most specification languages specify the token syntax using a regular language, and, therefore, valid tokens can be represented using a set of regular expressions. Since every regular expression has an equivalent finite automaton, we can recognize tokens by scanning the input program one character at a time, following the appropriate transitions in the finite automaton, and outputting valid tokens when we reach certain specified states. This stage can find only limited types of errors, more specifically errors involved in creating tokens. For example, it can determine that the characters "12abc" are not valid in the C language since C specifies that variables must start with an alphabetic character.

Syntactic analysis takes the set of tokens from the lexical analysis stage and groups them into meaningful phrases. This is most often done by creating a tree of tokens, a parse tree, which specifies the relationship between the tokens. The tree is built according to the rules of the formal grammar as denoted in the input language specification. The parse tree is used in the subsequent stages for analysis and optimization. In some sense, this stage can be viewed as grouping words (tokens) into sentences (valid structures in the language). This stage is also often referred to as "parsing."

Semantic checking analyzes the parse tree to verify that the input program abides by the requirements of the specification language. Several properties are confirmed. For example, object binding associates the use of every variable/function to its definition. Definite assignment verifies that every variable is defined before it is used. Type checking is performed on expressions to insure that operations are being performed on variables of the appropriate type. A symbol table, which stores each variable's type and location, is built during this stage and used for checking as well as in the later stages of compilation.

The frontend of the compiler ends with the *intermediate code generation*. This stage transforms the syntax tree into another representation. This representation varies from compiler to compiler and depends on the input specification language(s) that the compiler accepts as well as the target output language(s) that the compiler produces. Optimizing compilers often use more than one intermediate representation. In general, the representation is the starting point of the transformation into the final output program. Therefore, the intermediate code often looks somewhat similar to the output code. The proceeding optimizations perform transformations on this intermediate code; hence, the representation must be easy to change. Furthermore, it should retain the important features of the input code, while simplifying the code by removing the unimportant features.

We now discuss two common models of computation used for intermediate representations – the data flow graph (DFG) and the control flow graph (CFG). These graphs show the dependencies between operations in the code. Figure 3.2 displays the CFG for an implementation of a factorial function. The function is broken into a set of basic blocks, which are the nodes of a CFG. A basic block is a sequence of consecutive intermediate language statements in which flow of control can only enter at the beginning and leave at the end. In other words, a basic block is an atomic sequence of statements, i.e., if one of the statements is executed it means that all other statements will also be executed. The arrows in the CFG define control dependencies amongst the basic blocks. More formally, a *CFG* is a directed multigraph in which: (1) the nodes are basic blocks and (2) the edges represent flow of control (branches or fall-through execution). Note that the CFG is formed statically; therefore, we have no information about the values of the data. Hence, an edge in the CFG simply means there is a possibility to take that path. Many arithmetic optimizations are performed on a CFG as we discuss in Section 3.3.

A *DFG* is a directed acyclic graph where each node is a single instruction or operation and each edge denotes a direct data dependency between the output of one node and the input of another. Figure 3.2 shows a simple two-node DFG

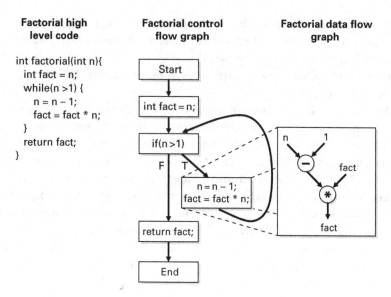

Figure 3.2 CFG and DFG representations of the factorial function. The CFG displays the control dependencies in the function while the DFG exhibits the data dependencies for the statements within the function.

corresponding to the two statements in one of the basic blocks of the factorial function. There are two operations in this basic block and equivalently two nodes in the DFG. The subtract operation produces a data value n that is used by the subsequent operation. Hence there is an edge from the subtract node to the multiply node.

Most intermediate representations use some sort of CFG and DFG to model dependencies. Of course, there are intermediate representations which use other models of computation. This book focuses primarily on the CFG and the DFG. We refer the interested reader to more advanced compiler books [1, 2] for further information.

The development of a compiler frontend is a fairly straightforward process. There are a number of standard tools (e.g., lex, yacc [3]) to perform each of the steps and the methodology is quite mature. On the other hand, most compiler research is focused on the backend, which is still evolving. The backend may vary significantly across optimizing compilers. As such, we will discuss the backend stages at a high level, and focus our discussion on the portions that are pertinent to this book. Referring again to Figure 3.1, we can see there are three stages in the backend: analysis, optimization, and code generation.

The *analysis* stage gathers general information about the program structure. Some typical analyses include deriving information about the data flow, control flow, function calls, pointers, etc. The previously discussed CFG and DFG are usually built during this stage. In addition, the call graph, which models function calls, is often created at this time.

The *optimization* stage performs transformations on the intermediate code such that the resulting code is better (according to some optimization function), yet is functionally equivalent to the initial code. There are probably thousands (if not more) of optimizations that can be performed. Some of the more popular include copy propagation, constant propagation, loop unrolling, dead code elimination, code hoisting, induction variable removal, partial redundancy elimination, inline expansion, tail merging, data prefetching, branch prediction, and software pipelining, to name just a few. Again, we refer the interested reader to advanced books on compiler optimization, e.g., [1, 2]. We discuss the compiler techniques relevant to arithmetic optimization in the following sections of the book.

The final stage of the backend is *code generation*. This transforms the intermediate representation into the final output program. For a software compiler, this is the native machine language of the targeted microprocessor. This stage requires decisions about resource usage, e.g., how to schedule the operations onto the functional units, how to assign data to memory (e.g., which data go into what register, what is stored in main memory). This stage is, of course, quite dependent on the language of the target program.

3.3   Algebraic transformations in optimizing software compilers

This section presents some related work on the optimization of arithmetic computations used in modern software compilers. The presented techniques are applied to general purpose programs and arithmetic expressions. In particular, the discussion focuses on various techniques for redundancy elimination used in modern software compilers.

3.3.1   Dataflow optimizations in modern software compilers

This subsection introduces common dataflow optimizations performed in most modern optimizing software compilers. The optimization process begins with dataflow analysis, which provides global information on how a procedure or a larger segment of a program manipulates data. The information provided by the dataflow analysis enables the application of optimizations such as local and global CSE, constant propagation, strength reduction, and loop invariant code motion, each of which is described briefly in this section. For example, constant propagation analysis determines if all assignments to a particular variable evaluate to the same constant value at all times.

The dataflow analysis result is stored in data structures such as define use (DU) chains to hold information about the definitions and uses of all variables in the procedure. This chapter presents some of the main dataflow optimizations. A detailed description of these data structures and the procedure for performing dataflow analysis can be found in compiler texts such as [1]. The transformations

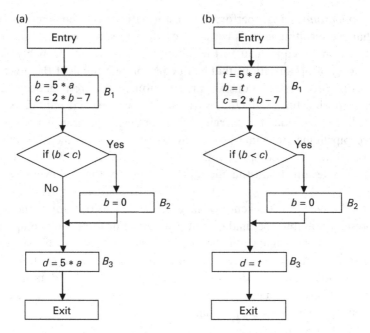

Figure 3.3 An example of applying CSE: (a) the original flowgraph, and (b) the flowgraph after eliminating common subexpression $5*a$.

are typically performed on an intermediate form of the code such as the flowgraph shown in Figure 3.3.

3.3.2   Common subexpression elimination (CSE)

An expression in a program is a common subexpression if there is another occurrence of the same expression whose evaluation always precedes this one in execution order and if the operands of the expression remain unchanged between the two evaluations. It is possible to calculate the value of a common subexpression once and use this precalculated value the next time(s) the expression is computed. This can be beneficial in terms of computation time if the expression is complex and the two occurrences happen close to each other. The process of finding common subexpressions and rewriting a program to calculate them once is called *common subexpression elimination (CSE)*.

CSE can be performed both locally within the basic blocks and globally across the CFG. The global CSE procedure can detect the local common subexpressions as well as common subexpressions found between basic blocks. However, it requires more computation time. The algorithm for local CSE works within single basic blocks and keeps track of *available expressions blocks* (AEBs), i.e., the expressions which have been computed within the block and whose operands have not been changed since the computation. The algorithm then iterates through the basic block, adding entries to and removing them from the list of AEBs as appropriate, inserting instructions to save the expressions' values in temporary variables, and modifying existing instructions to use the values saved in temporary variables. The iteration stops when no further common subexpression exists.

The global CSE procedure operates on the entire function, or equivalently the CFG, and finds the available expressions. An expression *exp* is said to be available at the entry to a basic block if there is an evaluation of *exp* on every control path from the entry to this block that is not killed before the entry to the basic block (an expression is killed if one or more of its operands is assigned a new value). The set of available expressions can be found as follows. Assume that $EVAL(i)$ is the set of expressions evaluated in block i available at the block's exit. Further, assume $KILL(i)$ denotes the set of expressions killed by block i. $EVAL(i)$ is computed by scanning block i from the beginning to the end, accumulating the expressions evaluated in it, and deleting those expressions whose operands are later assigned new values inside the block. $AEin(i)$ and $AEout(i)$ represent the sets of available expressions on entry to and exit from block i, respectively, as shown in the data-flow equations in

$$AEin(i) = \bigcap_{j \in \mathrm{Pr}ed(i)} AEout(j)$$

$$AEout(i) = EVAL(i) \cup (AEin(i) - KILL(i)). \tag{3.1}$$

$AEin(i)$ can be computed by finding the intersection of all expressions available at the exit of blocks preceding block i, i.e., $Pred(i)$; $AEout(i)$ is the union of all expressions evaluated at block i that are available at the exit of the block, and the expressions available at the entry of block i that are not killed in the block.

3.3.3 Value numbering

Another useful method for redundancy elimination is called value numbering [4]. Value numbering is based on symbolic evaluation of expressions. It associates a symbolic value with each computation without interpreting the operation performed by the computation, but in such a way that any two computations with the same symbolic value always compute the same value.

In the code in Figure 3.4(a), value numbering assigns the same value number to x and y and the same value number to z and w. As a result the code may be rewritten as shown in Figure 3.4(b). Later references to y and w can be replaced with x and z, respectively. Thus, the code can be simplified as shown in Figure 3.4(c).

While value numbering has the same effect as CSE for basic blocks, there are differences for global transformations, as shown in Figure 3.5. In the code of Figure 3.5(a), variables b and d are found to be equal by value numbering. The same result cannot be obtained by applying the CSE technique because there is no common subexpression in the expressions. This is because CSE performs only a

(a)   (b)   (c)
x = 2   x = 2   x = 2
y = 2   y = x   z = x + 1
z = x + 1   z = x + 1
w = y + 1   w = z

Figure 3.4 An example of value numbering: (a) the original code, (b) the code transformed using value numbering, and (c) the simplified code.

(a)   (b)
b = a + 3   b = 5 * a
c = a   if (a > 0)
d = c + 3   c = 5 * a

Figure 3.5 Examples showing the difference between value numbering and CSE's capabilities: (a) an example which can be simplified using value numbering, but not CSE, and (b) an example which can be simplified using CSE, but not value numbering.

simple lexicographic search. On the other hand, Figure 3.5(b) shows an example where global CSE is able to determine that expression $(5 * a)$ appears twice, but value numbering cannot detect it because variables b and c are not always equal. For example, if the value of a is not greater than 0, then $c = 5 * a$ will not be executed, therefore, b and c may have different values.

The original formulation of value numbering operates on individual basic blocks, but has been extended to a global form [5, 6]. To use value numbering for basic blocks, hashing is used to partition expressions into classes. Upon encountering an expression, its hash value is computed. If it is not already among the expressions with that hash value, it is added to them. The hash function and the expression matching function are defined to take commutativity of the operators into account.

3.3.4   Loop invariant code motion

Loop invariant code motion finds computations inside a loop that produce the same value at every iteration, and subsequently moves these computations outside of the loop. This happens frequently in address calculation for accessing elements of arrays. Identifying loop invariant computations is fairly simple. After performing control flow analysis and identifying loops, the loop invariant instructions can be found inductively as follows. An instruction is a loop invariant if for each of its operands one of the followings is true:

(i)   the operand is a constant, or
(ii) all definitions of the operand reaching this use of the operand are located outside the loop, or
(iii) there is exactly one definition of the operand reaching the instruction and that definition is loop invariant.

```
(a)                              (b)
for i = 1, 100 {                 a1 =  10 * (n + 1)
    a = i * (n + 1)              a2 =  100 * n
    for j = 1, 100               for i = 1, 100 {
        b(i, j) = 100 * n + 10 * a + j      a3 = a1 * i + a2
}
                                     for j = 1, 100
                                         b(i, j) = a3 + j
                                 }
```

Figure 3.6 (a) An example of code having loop invariant computations and (b) the code after transformation.

Figure 3.6(a) shows a piece of code in which there are several loop invariant expressions. Figure 3.6(b) shows the code after moving the loop invariant expressions outside of the loops. The original code performs two multiplications and two additions per iteration of the inner loop. The outer loop performs 201 multiplications and 201 additions during each iteration. Overall, the code executes 20 100 multiplications and 20 100 additions.

The modified code performs one addition at each iteration of the inner loop. The outer loop requires 1 multiplication and 101 additions for each iteration, resulting in a total of 102 multiplications and 10 101 additions. In this example, loop invariant code motion saves 19 998 multiplications and 9 999 additions. This can have a significant impact on the execution time of the code and the energy consumption of the processor executing it. Further improvement can be achieved by modifying the ranges of i and j in the FOR loops, e.g., instead of using 1 and 100 as the lower and upper bounds for variable j, $a3 + 1$ and $a3 + 100$ can be used, respectively.

3.3.5 Partial-redundancy elimination (PRE)

PRE is a combination of global CSE and loop invariant code motion with some additional code improvements. An expression is *partially redundant* at point p if it is redundant along some, but not all, paths that reach p. PRE converts partially redundant expressions into redundant expressions. To do this, it first uses data-flow analysis to discover which expressions are partially redundant. Next, it determines where to insert copies of a computation to convert a partial redundancy into a full redundancy. Finally, it inserts the appropriate code and deletes the redundant copy of the expression.

In Figure 3.7(a), the expression $c + d$ is available only along the branch on the right, and is, therefore, only partially redundant at the join of the two branches. Inserting another copy of the expression on the other branch makes the computation redundant and allows its elimination, as shown in Figure 3.7(b).

Loop invariant expressions are also partially redundant, as illustrated in Figure 3.8. In Figure 3.8(a), $c + d$ is partially redundant since it is available from one predecessor (along the back edge of the loop), but not the other. Inserting an evaluation of $c + d$ before the loop allows it to be eliminated from the loop body. Figure 3.8(b) shows the code after transformation.

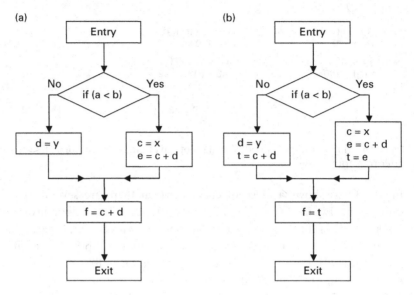

Figure 3.7 An example of the benefit of PRE: (a) the original partially redundant code, and (b) the simplified code.

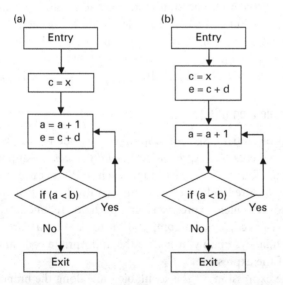

Figure 3.8 PRE can move loop invariant computations to reduce the number of operations: (a) the original loop, and (b) the loop after moving the loop invariant computation outside the loop.

3.3.6   Operator strength reduction

Operator strength reduction is the process of replacing costly (strong) operations with cheaper (weaker) ones. There are two types of strength reduction, weak and strong. In the weak form of strength reduction, an expression such as

(a)
```
for j = 1, 100
   a(5 * j + 2) = 1
```

(b)
```
t = 2
for j = 1, 100 {
   t = t + 5
   a(t) = 1
}
```

Figure 3.9 An example showing the benefits of strong strength reduction: (a) the original loop and (b) the loop after performing strong strength reduction.

$2 \times x$ is replaced with either $x + x$ or $x \ll 1$. In most processors performing multiplication is more costly than performing addition or shift. Therefore, this will reduce the program execution time. Furthermore, in many processors the number of multiplier units is smaller than the number of addition and shift units. Thus, using addition or shift instead of multiplication has the additional advantage that it allows the instruction to be scheduled earlier. This again helps to reduce the program execution time. In terms of energy consumption, using addition or shift instead of multiplication is similarly beneficial as multiplication typically consumes more energy than addition and shift [7]. Further reduction in the energy occurs due to the decrease in the execution time of the program.

Strong reduction is a more powerful form of strength reduction. In this case, an iterated series of strong computations is replaced with an equivalent series of weaker computations. For example, multiplications can be replaced with additions in array address calculations inside loops. The code in Figure 3.9(a) performs one multiplication and one addition at each iteration in order to calculate the address of array a. Figure 3.9(b) shows the code after transformation using strong strength reduction. In the transformed code, one addition is performed to compute the address of array a at each iteration. The original code performs a total of 100 multiplications and 100 additions in order to calculate the addresses for accessing array a, while in the modified code only 100 additions are performed. This significantly reduces the execution time of the code.

3.3.7 Implementing polynomials in the Horner form

Using the Horner form is one of the most popular methods of evaluating polynomial approximations of trigonometric functions, and is the default method in many libraries including the GNU C library [8]. In the Horner form, a polynomial is written as a sequence of nested multiplications and additions. For example, a polynomial in variable x, $P(x) = a_0 x^n + a_1 x^{n-1} + a_2 x^{n-2} + a_3 x^{n-3} + \cdots + a_n$ is written as, $P(x) = (\cdots ((a_0 x + a_1)x + a_2)x + \cdots + a_{n-1})x + a_n$

The Horner form has the following advantages:

(1) It reduces the number of multiplications required to calculate a polynomial. In the above example, calculating the polynomial in the original form requires

$n(n+1)/2$ multiplications and n additions,[1] while the Horner form uses n multiplications and n additions. This substantially reduces the number of multiplications if n is large. Since multiplication is an expensive operation in terms of cycle time and energy consumption, transforming to the Horner form is an effective way of reducing execution time and energy consumption of software programs. In [9], the authors report an average 55% reduction in the number of multiplications when the Horner form is used instead of unoptimized expressions for a set of applications.

(2) The special form of the resulting polynomial eases the use of MAC operations, which exist in many processors especially digital signal processors. The polynomial can be calculated by first computing $P_0 = a_0 x + a_1$ using a MAC operation, then calculating $P_1 = P_0 x + a_2$ and so on. This means the calculation can be done using n MAC operations. Again, this significantly reduces the execution time and the energy consumption.

(3) The Horner form increases the numerical stability. In the original form, even when the value of $P(x)$ is small, the intermediate values (e.g., x^n, $a_0 x^n$, $a_0 x^n + a_1 x^{n-1}$) can be prohibitively large. Thus, it may not be possible to represent them directly in a 32-bit or a 64-bit processor.[2] On the other hand, in the Horner form, intermediate values $P_0, P_1, \ldots, P_{n-1}$ can be small if for example a_0 and a_1 have different signs.

(4) It is easy to write polynomials in the Horner form. Therefore, it can be integrated into a compiler with little effort. Furthermore, the transformation of polynomials into the Horner form can be done quickly, which means it will not have a major impact on the compilation time which is very important in general purpose compilers.

The disadvantages of the Horner form are the following:

(1) It optimizes only a single polynomial at a time; it does not look for common subexpressions among a set of polynomials. Furthermore, it is not good at optimizing multivariate polynomials, used for example in computer graphics applications [10]. Equation (2.2) shows the quartic polynomial used in three-dimensional computer graphics for modeling textures. The original polynomial consists of 23 multiplications or 21 multiplications and 2 shift operations. The polynomial in the Horner form (shown in Equation (2.4)) has 17 multiplications or 15 multiplications and 2 shifts. Using algebraic methods [9], the polynomial can be optimized to a form which requires 13 multiplications or 12 multiplications and 1 shift.

(2) The Horner form may not give the best result if some coefficients of the polynomial are zero. For $P(x) = a_0 x^6 + a_2 x^4 + a_4 x^2 + a_6$ the Horner method

---

[1] Calculating term $a_i x^{n-i}$ requires $n-i$ multiplications. Therefore, the total number of necessary multiplications is $n + (n-1) + \cdots + 1 = n(n+1)/2$.

[2] It is possible to use several words to represent a large number on a processor, but this significantly reduces the performance.

(a)　　　　　(b)　　　　(c)
$P_1 = x^2 + xy$　　$z = x + y$　　$z = xy$
$P_2 = xy + y^2$　　$P_1 = xz$　　　$P_1 = x^2 + z$
　　　　　　　　$P_2 = yz$　　　$P_2 = z + y^2$

Figure 3.10 An example illustrating the power of algebraic techniques: (a) the original equations, (b) the equations optimized using an algebraic technique, and (c) the equations optimized using CSE.

results in $P(x) = (((((a_0x + 0)x + a_2)x + 0)x + a_4)x + 0)x + a_6$ which requires six MAC operations or six multiplications and three additions, while it is easy to write the polynomial using $y = x \times x$ as $P(x) = a_0y^3 + a_2y^2 + a_4y + a_6 = ((a_0y + a_2)y + a_4)y + a_6$. In this case, a total of four MAC operations or four multiplications and three additions are necessary.

3.3.8　Drawbacks of conventional techniques

While CSE, value numbering, loop-invariant code motion, PRE, operator strength reduction and the Horner transform are useful, they fail to find many optimization opportunities existing in polynomial expressions. In fact, other than operator strength reduction and the Horner transform, these techniques do not use properties specific to polynomial expressions during transformation.[3]

Consider the polynomials in Figure 3.10(a) and their optimized versions in Figure 3.10(b). The original form requires four multiplications and two additions to compute the polynomials; the optimized form requires only two multiplications and one addition. This is a 50% reduction in the number of multiplications and additions. The aforementioned transformations cannot find the solution presented in Figure 3.10(b); at best CSE can be used to eliminate $x \times y$ between the two polynomials. Figure 3.10(c) shows the result. This case requires three multiplications and two additions, which is obviously not optimum. The above example shows the power of algebraic methods, which use the properties of addition, subtraction and multiplication to better optimize arithmetic expressions.

3.4　Summary

This chapter presented some of the basic concepts in software design flows. We started by describing the fundamental steps for a software compiler including those in the frontend and the backend. Then we provided more detail on the compilation process including the place where arithmetic optimization can be

---

[3] Value numbering uses properties such as commutativity, but this is not specific to arithmetic operations.

implemented and described the algebraic transformations which are used in current compilers. As we will see in the next chapter, some of these optimizations can be used during hardware synthesis as well.

References

[1] S. S. Muchnick, *Advanced Compiler Design and Implementation*. San Francisco, CA: Morgan Kaufmann Publishers, 1997.

[2] K. Kennedy and J. R. Allen, *Optimizing Compilers for Modern Architectures: A Dependence-based Approach*. San Francisco, CA: Morgan Kaufmann Publishers, 2001.

[3] J. R. Levine, T. Mason, and D. Brown, *Lex & yacc*, second edition. Sebastopol, CA: O'Reilly & Associates, 1995.

[4] J. Cocke and J. T. Schwartz, Programming Languages and Their Compilers: Preliminary Notes, Technical Report, Courant Institute of Mathematical Sciences, New York University, 1970.

[5] J. R. Reif and H. R. Lewis, Symbolic evaluation and the global value graph, *Proceedings of the 4th ACM SIGACT-SIGPLAN Symposium on Principles of Programming Languages, Los Angeles, 1977*, pp. 104–18. New York, NY: ACM, 1977.

[6] B. Alpern, M. N. Wegman and F. K. Zadeck, Detecting equality of variables in programs, *Proceedings of the 15th ACM SIGPLAN-SIGACT Symposium on Principles of Programming Languages, San Diego, 1988*, pp. 1–11. New York, NY: ACM, 1988.

[7] A. Sinha and A. P. Chandrakasan, JouleTrack – a web based tool for software energy profiling, *Proceedings of the 38th Conference on Design Automation, Las Vegas, 2001.* pp. 220–225. New York, NY: ACM, 2001.

[8] http://www.gnu.org/software/libc/

[9] A. Hosangadi, F. Fallah and R. Kastner, Factoring and eliminating common subexpressions in polynomial expressions, *Proceedings of the 2004 IEEE/ACM International Conference on Computer-aided Design, San Jose, 2004*, pp. 169–174. Washington, DC: IEEE Computer Society, 2004.

[10] G. Nurnberger, J. W. Schmidt and G. Walz, *Multivariate Approximation and Splines*. Basel: Birkhäuser, 1997.

4 Hardware synthesis

4.1 Chapter overview

This chapter provides a brief summary of the stages in the hardware synthesis design flow. It is designed to give unfamiliar readers a high-level understanding of the hardware design process. The material in subsequent chapters describes different hardware implementations of polynomial expressions and linear systems. Therefore, we feel that it is important, though not necessarily essential, to have an understanding of the hardware synthesis process.

The chapter starts with a high-level description of the hardware synthesis design flow. It then proceeds to discuss the various components of this design flow. These include the input system specification, the program representation,[1] algorithmic optimizations, resource allocation, operation scheduling, and resource binding. The chapter concludes with a case study using an FIR filter. This provides a step-by-step example of the hardware synthesis process. Additionally, it gives insight into the hardware optimization techniques presented in the following chapters.

4.2 Hardware synthesis design flow

The initial stages of a hardware design flow are quite similar to the frontend of a software compiler. One of the biggest differences is that the input *system specification* languages are different. Hardware description languages must deal with many features that are unnecessary in software, which for the most part model execution in a serial fashion. Such features include the need to model concurrent execution of the underlying resources, define a variety of different data types specifically for different bit widths, and introduce some notion of time into the language. Figure 4.1 gives a high-level view of the different stages of hardware compilation.

Architectural synthesis is an automated design process that interprets an algorithmic representation of a behavior and creates hardware specification that

---

[1] We use the term "program representation," a common term in software compilation, due to the absence of a widely used term in hardware synthesis.

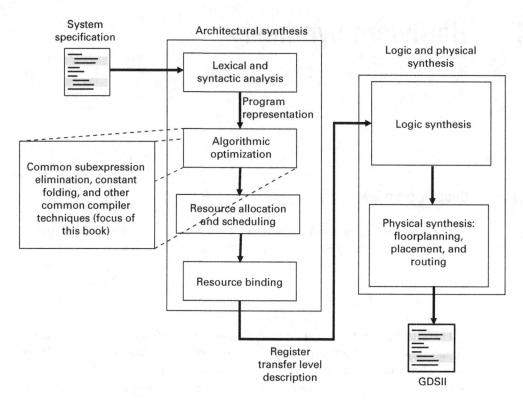

Figure 4.1 A high-level view of the stages of hardware compilation. These can be broadly broken down to architectural, logic, and physical synthesis. The optimizations described in this book are primarily focused on architectural synthesis, specifically on the algorithmic optimization.

executes the behavior. More formally, it is the process of creating a structural microarchitectural representation, or register transfer level (RTL) description, from a system specification of an application. A structural representation defines the exact interconnection between a set of architectural resources. An architectural resource is a storage element, functional unit, or interconnect logic. A storage element provides a method of saving the state of the circuit. A register is an example of a storage element. A functional unit performs an arithmetic or logic operation (e.g., addition, multiplication, shift). Interconnect logic is used to route data between memory and functional units. For example, a multiplexor propagates a particular piece of data (correspondingly a set of signals) depending on its input condition. A control unit (controller) issues control signals to direct the resources.

Architectural synthesis can be performed using any number of different design flows. Additionally, a designer typically adds constraints or optimization objectives. For example, the designer may want to produce a circuit that requires the least amount of area. In this case, the objective function would be to minimize the area. Many other constraints have been considered during architectural synthesis.

Throughput, power, clock frequency, and latency are some of the common optimization objectives.

The first step of architectural synthesis is *lexical and syntactic analysis*, which parses the input specification into a program representation. This step is very similar to that of software compilation and more details of this can be found in Section 3.2. The *program representation* is a description of the system specification that is easily amenable to analysis, optimization, and translation to a more refined specification, which in this case is the register transfer level description. There are many examples of program representations; we discuss some of them later in this chapter. The DFG is perhaps the most popular program representation for architectural synthesis. We formally describe this in Section 4.4. However, in order to progress our discussion to the next steps in the architectural synthesis process, we will now informally define it as a directed graph consisting of vertices that represent operations and directed edges that denote dependencies between operations.

The architectural synthesis problem can be defined in the following manner: given a system specification, a set of fully characterized architectural resources, a set of constraints, and an optimization function, determine a connected set of resources (a structural representation) that conforms to the given constraints and minimizes the objective function. The architectural synthesis problem can be split into the following subproblems: algorithmic optimization, resource allocation, operation scheduling, and operation binding.

Algorithmic optimization uses a set of techniques that transform the program representation to make it run faster, use fewer operations, expose parallelism, enable more accurate dependency analysis, improve memory usage, and so on. These techniques are very often similar to those found in software compilers and include optimizations such as CSE, loop unrolling, dead code elimination. The techniques that we present later in this book for polynomial and linear system optimization can be used in this stage.

Resource allocation is the act of choosing the appropriate number and type of components from a library. For example, you can choose to have two adders – one ripple carry and one carry look-ahead – one multiplier, one divider, etc. *Scheduling* determines the temporal ordering of the operations. Given a set of operations with execution delays and a partial ordering, the scheduling problem assigns a start time for each operation. The start times must follow the precedence constraints as specified in the system specification. Additional restrictions such as timing and area constraints may be added to the problem, depending on the target architecture. The scheduling affects the resource allocation and vice-versa. Therefore, the ordering of these two tasks is sometimes interchanged; some synthesis tools perform scheduling, then resource allocation, while others allocate the resources first, and then schedule the operations.

Resource binding is the assignment of each operation to a specific hardware component; it is an explicit mapping between operations and resources. The goal of resource binding is to minimize the area by allowing multiple operations to share a common resource. The scheduling limits the possible resource bindings.

For example, operations that are scheduled at the same time cannot share the same resource. To be more precise, any two operations can be bound to the same resource if they are not executed concurrently, i.e., are not scheduled in overlapping time steps. Some resources are capable of executing different operations, e.g., both an addition and subtraction can be bound to an arithmetic logic unit (ALU). The resource binding can greatly affect the area and latency of the circuit as it dictates the number of interconnect logic and storage elements of the circuit.

Logic synthesis is the act of taking the register transfer level description that is output from architectural synthesis and transforming it into a network of logic gates. There are a number of optimizations that are performed during this stage. The optimizations are generally grouped into two types – multi-level and two-level. The two-level optimizations have roots in Boolean minimization, which attempts to minimize the number of gates in a two-stage Boolean network. Multi-level optimizations often view the problem as a network of logic gates and attempt to minimize the number and the area of the gates as well as the critical path or the delay of the network. An interested reader can find a vast amount of literature on this topic. Reference [1] is a good introduction to the basic algorithms.

Physical synthesis or physical design looks at how the logical network can be transformed into an integrated circuit that can be fabricated. The output is essentially a set of planar geometric shapes that detail the size and the type of materials needed to make the transistors and wires in a circuit. GDSII is one common database format used to specify the layout of the integrated circuit. The primary tasks of physical synthesis are floorplanning, placement, and routing. *Floorplanning* creates a basic plan for the layout of the chip, indicating the general area where hard macros, power and ground planes, input/output (I/O) and other logic elements reside. *Placement* assigns an exact physical location for each of the logic gates, while *routing* determines the precise wiring of the required interconnections between the gates. Further information on the stages of physical synthesis, as well as the algorithms used to implement these stages, can be found in [2].

Now that we have given an overview of entire hardware synthesis process, we will go into detail on a few of the topics that are needed to fully understand the later chapters in this book. Specifically, we discuss the architectural synthesis process. The majority of the optimizations in this book occur in the algorithm optimization stage; however, it is important to understand the other stages in architecture synthesis, which we focus on in the remainder of the chapter.

4.3   System specification

A *system specification* is a representation that captures the aspects of the application that one wishes to synthesize and includes the architectural specification, functional specification, and desired performance metrics. The architectural specification describes the target technology that is finally used to implement the application. This can be a mix of intellectual property (IP) cores including microprocessors and parameterizable blocks (e.g., finite Fourier transforms (FFTs), FIR filters, matrix multiplication cores). Architectural specifications describe features such as the processing abilities of the IP cores, their interfaces, memory hierarchy, the number of IP cores available to the system, and so on. The functional specification precisely defines the computational relationship between the inputs and outputs of the IP core. Performance metrics describe the expected quality of the synthesized design and include things such as latency, throughput, clock frequency, area, and power or energy consumption.

Many system specifications use a design language that is an extended form of C. Spec C [3], System C [4], and Handel C [5] are a few examples of system design languages that extend C with additional language constructs needed for hardware synthesis. C provides a good method for describing the functional behavior and there are many methods for exploiting instruction level parallelism within C procedures. In fact, these methods are quite similar to the optimizations found in a software compiler backend. However, C often lacks the ability to provide the amount of task level parallelism needed for hardware design. Additionally, it has no methods for providing the timing constraints necessary in most system specifications. Some concepts in the C language, e.g., recursive functions and pointers, are extremely hard to implement in hardware. It may be possible to fully synthesize the full C language and there are methods for doing this [6–8]. However, most hardware synthesis tools employ a restricted form of C as an entry point into their design flow.

MATLAB® [9] is another popular system design language used for system specification. Tools such as Synplicity Synplify® DSP [10] and Xilinx AccelDSP™ accept MATLAB files as input. MATLAB is the prevalent language for many domains, e.g., communications, DSP, and controls. The MATLAB language is more abstract than C, and therefore suffers from many similar issues when used for hardware synthesis. An additional issue is the use of dynamic typing. Much like the tools that use C as an input, the majority of MATLAB hardware synthesis tools can only synthesize a subset of the MATLAB language. Additionally, these tools rely heavily on parameterized library elements, e.g., they will map operations such as matrix multiplication, matrix decomposition, and filters, directly to a library element designed specifically for these functions. Despite these limitations, hardware synthesis from MATLAB is popular with designers who lack intimate knowledge of hardware design. It is also useful for rapid prototyping.

4.4 Program representation

The first step of the architectural synthesis process translates the input system specification into a program representation. The *program representation* is a common view of the application that allows synthesis to a variety of IP cores, precisely describes coarse- and fine-grain parallelism, and allows a wide range of optimizations and transformations. It is finally converted into an output specification, which in the case of architectural synthesis is an RTL description. There are a number of common program representations including the abstract syntax tree (AST), CFG, DFG, static single assignment (SSA), and the program dependence graph (PDG). We briefly describe each of these in the following.

The *AST* [11, 12] is a high-level program representation that is typically used in the initial phases of optimization. Each node in the AST represents an operation and its children correspond to the operands. The AST is a translation of the parse tree from the first stage of architectural synthesis (lexical and syntactic analysis) with all but the terminal symbols removed. The AST stores all the necessary information to exactly reconstruct the input system specification. This information includes variable declarations, types of operations and control structures (e. g., loops, branches, and case statements), and a symbol table that maps variables to their types and vice-versa. The AST is often used to expose parallelism through transformations such as loop unrolling, loop merging, and function inlining. Then, it is typically translated into a more refined representation.

The *CFG* [11, 13] is a common program representation in both hardware synthesis and software compilation[2]. A CFG is a directed graph that expresses the control flow within a procedure. Each vertex in a CFG is a basic block – a sequential list of instructions with only one control transfer instruction. If control can potentially transfer from basic block i to basic block j, then there is a directed edge (i, j) from vertex i to vertex j. In a structured program, each CFG contains only one entry node, and one or more exit nodes. Figure 4.2 shows the CFG for a portion of code from an adaptive differential pulse-code modulation (ADPCM) encoder [14].

The CFG enables optimizations such as unreachable code elimination. This is done by making sure that there is a path from the entry node to every basic block. If no such path exists, we can remove the basic block, as it will never be executed. This often occurs with debugging code, when the condition to reach the code is defined through a static variable that is set to false.

The CFG exposes instruction level parallelism. Unfortunately, discovering more coarse-grain parallelism typically requires extensive data-flow and dependence analysis. The lack of a method to model hierarchy is another drawback of the CFG; the complexity of analysis increases as the design grows.

The *DFG* is probably the most common program representation used in hardware synthesis. It is derived from a basic block, which consists of a set of operations $O = \{o_1, o_2, \ldots, o_n\}$. A DFG $G(V, E)$ has a set of vertices $V = \{v_1, v_2, \ldots, v_n\}$ – one for each operation. A directed edge exists between two vertices v_i and v_j if the corresponding operations have direct data dependency. This means that operation o_j can start only after the completion of operation o_i. We use the notation $v_i \prec v_j$ to mean v_i precedes v_j. The DFG defines a partial ordering on the operations

---

[2] We also briefly described the CFG in Section 3.2.

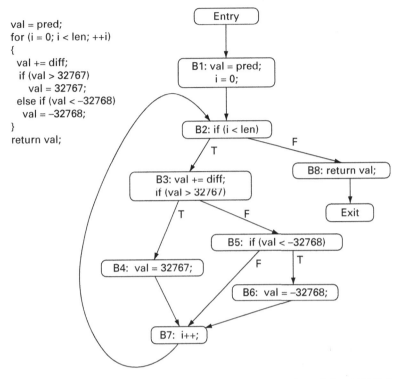

```
val = pred;
for (i = 0; i < len; ++i)
{
  val += diff;
  if (val > 32767)
    val = 32767;
  else if (val < -32768)
    val = -32768;
}
return val;
```

Figure 4.2 The C code and corresponding CFG for a portion of the ADPCM encoder application.

(vertices). Hence if $v_i \prec v_j$ and $v_j \prec v_k$, then $v_i \prec v_k$. Equivalently, if there exist two edges $e(v_i, v_j)$ and $e(v_j, v_k)$ then $v_i \prec v_k$. In other words, the transitive property holds. Since the basic block contains no internal control structures, a DFG is a directed acyclic graph (DAG). Typically, two virtual vertices v_s and v_e are added to the DFG. These are the start and end vertices, respectively. These vertices are included for convenience and defined such that v_s precedes all operations and all operations precede v_e. In other words, v_s is the only source vertex and v_e is the only sink vertex in the DFG. The virtual vertices correspond to null operations and have no effect on the function and incur no performance (delay, area, power, or energy) costs.

Figure 4.3 shows the DFG for a simple C function. The function takes as input four integer variables and computes the sum of the product of the variables a and b and c and d. The DFG includes the two virtual start and end nodes v_s and v_e.

The acyclic nature of the DFG limits its ability to model complicated timing constraints, e.g., it is impossible to describe feedback in pipelined hardware designs. Additionally, it is difficult to describe some scheduling constraints. For example, we often require that two operations be scheduled during the same clock cycle. This is naturally modeled using a cyclic dependency between the two operations, which cannot be done in a DFG.

```
1 int foo (int a, int b, int c, int d)
2 {
3     return a * b + c * d;
4 }
```

Figure 4.3 A simple C function and the corresponding DFG.

(a)	(b)
val += diff;	val_2 = val_1 + diff;
if (val > 32767)	if (val_2 > 32767)
val = 32767;	val_3 = 32767;
else if (val < –32768)	else if (val_2 < –32768)
val = –32768;	val_4 = –32768;
	val_5 = phi (val_2, val_3, val_4);

Figure 4.4 The ADPCM example (a) before and (b) after SSA conversion. The variable "val" is defined several times. Hence, it is renamed at each definition and phi-nodes are inserted at locations where multiple definitions of the original val variable exist.

SSA [15, 16] is an intermediate representation used to model data-flow dependencies. SSA insures that each variable is assigned exactly one time, and whenever a variable is used, it is referenced using the same name. Hence, SSA explicitly expresses define-use (def-use) chains[3] [12]. Special operations called phi-nodes must be inserted at join points in the CFG in cases when multiple definitions of the same variable are alive at that location. Figure 4.4 shows a small snippet of the ADCPM encoder application before and after translation into SSA form.

SSA eases the analysis of some optimizations. For example, dead code elimination is trivial since a variable that is defined yet never used can easily certainly be detected and eliminated in a program represented in SSA form. Additionally, SSA more easily exploits instruction level parallelism. While a program must be translated out of SSA form for software implementation due to the fact that the notion of a phi-node does not exist in the instruction set architecture, phi-nodes are easily synthesized in hardware [17, 18] since they are naturally expressed as multiplexers.

The *PDG* [19] explicitly expresses both control and data dependencies. It consists of both a control dependence subgraph and a data dependence subgraph. The PDG has four different types of nodes – entry, region, predicate, and

---

[3] Def-use chains are a representation of data-flow information for variables in a program. A def-use chain for a variable connects a definition of that variable to all its possible uses.

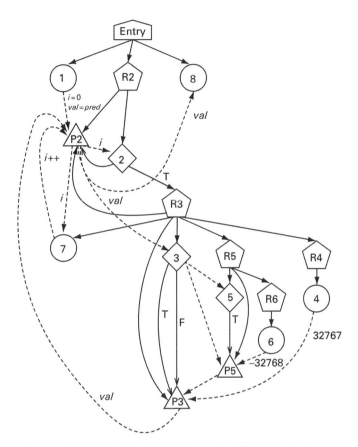

Figure 4.5 A PDG for the ADPCM encoder. The dashed edges correspond to data dependencies and solid ones denote control dependencies. The diamond nodes represent predicate nodes and the circle nodes are statements. The numbers inside these two types of nodes map to the basic block numbers from the CFG. The triangle nodes are phi-functions. The pentagons are region nodes.

statement. Statement and predicate nodes contain arbitrary sequential computation. Predicate nodes also contain expressions that are conditioned by a Boolean expression. A region node summarizes a set of control conditions, providing a grouping for a set of nodes executed during a specific control sequence. The entry node is the root node of the PDG. Edges in the PDG represent a dependency. Edges from a region node to predicate and statement nodes indicate that these nodes all execute only when a certain condition is met. Outgoing edges from a predicate node indicate that the execution of the statement or region nodes is control dependent on that predicate. While Ferrante *et al.* [19] did not define data dependencies precisely, they can be represented in a similar manner to DFGs. Figure 4.5 shows the PDG corresponding the ADPCM encoder example.

The PDG is a powerful program representation for hardware synthesis and has been used as the program representation in several academic research synthesis

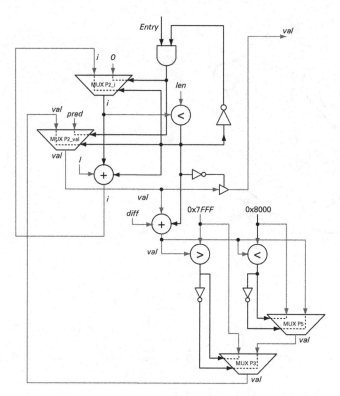

Figure 4.6 The RTL description of the ADPCM encoder node. This is generated based on a one-to-one mapping from the PDG representation.

tools [20–22]. Figure 4.6 shows an RTL description of the ADPCM encoder. This description is based on a one-to-one mapping from the PDG in Figure 4.5 as described in the work by Gong *et al.* [20]. Scheduling, resource allocation, and binding can further optimize the description, as we describe in the following.

4.5   Algorithmic optimization

Algorithmic optimizations use a set of techniques aimed at transforming the program representation in a manner that improves the performance of the application. For the most part, these are traditional optimizations typically used in software compilers. The term "optimization" is somewhat of a misnomer in that these techniques rarely find an optimal solution; rather they are aimed at enhancing some aspect of performance. Optimizations are almost always safe, meaning that they transform the program in a manner that will never change the output of the application, regardless of the inputs.

Muchnick [12] classifies the optimizations into four groups. The first group contains optimizations that work on loops (where most applications spend a majority of their time) and also optimizations that are generally successful across a range of applications. Such optimizations include constant folding, algebraic simplification and reassociation, global value numbering, CSE, loop invariant code motion, strength reduction, dead code elimination, register allocation, software pipelining, loop unrolling, register renaming, and instruction scheduling. The optimizations described in this book lie in this first, most important, group of transformations. Optimizations in the second group contain less impactful loop optimizations (e.g., loop inversion, unnecessary bound checking elimination) and other secondary optimizations applicable to applications without loops (e.g., copy propagation, branch prediction, instruction combining). The third group of optimizations apply to whole procedures or transforms the program in a manner that increases the possibility of applying other optimizations. These include procedure integration, inline expansion, and scalar replacement of aggregates. The fourth and final group of optimizations decrease the size of the code, but typically do not improve performance. Examples include code hoisting and tail merging.

The success of an optimization is highly dependent on the program representation as well as the input application. For example, the abstract syntax tree representation is capable of performing high-level optimizations such as scalar expansion and array renaming, while the CFG is more amenable to low-level optimizations such as CSE and dead code elimination. The input application also plays a large role in the success of the optimizations. For example, looping structures are prevalent in DSP applications; therefore, optimizations targeted towards loops will most likely enhance the performance of such applications substantially. On the other hand, loop optimizations are likely to have limited effect in control applications, where branching program structures dominate. Here, if-conversion[4] and branch optimizations will provide the greatest benefit.

Optimizations specific to a particular type of application are often performed during hardware synthesis. For example, the optimizations discussed in this book are highly specific to polynomial expressions and linear systems. Such optimizations are typically not performed in software compilers (which tend to aim for the common case) since they are only applicable to a small subset of the input applications that the compiler receives. However, as we will show, these application specific optimizations are very powerful since they focus and take advantage of very precise properties and attributes of the program structure.

4.6   Resource allocation

The next step in the synthesis process is resource allocation and scheduling. *Resource allocation* decides the number and types of resources used in a given application implementation. Resource allocation and operation scheduling are

---

[4] If-conversion is a technique that replaces a branch operation and its control dependent paths with a predicated execution. This converts control dependencies to data dependencies and can speed up program execution.

tightly intertwined; one greatly affects the other. As such, they are sometimes performed in different orders. We discuss operation scheduling in Section 4.7.

Before we formally define the problem of resource allocation, we first describe the different types of resources. We break these into three classes: functional units, storage elements, and interconnect logic. Functional units implement arithmetic and logical operations. Storage elements save data specified in the application specification or temporary, intermediate results of computation. Interconnect logic steers the appropriate signals between functional units and storage elements. We now discuss each of these resource classes in detail.

4.6.1   Functional units

Functional units implement data operations, e.g., addition, subtraction, multiplication, division, comparison, trigonometric functions, linear transforms, and polynomial expressions. These can either be purely combinatorial or contain state and internal storage. Therefore, we further categorize functional units into combinatorial and sequential.

A *combinatorial functional unit* is a digital circuit performing an operation that is fully specified by a set of Boolean functions [23]. The value of its output is calculated directly from, and only from, the present inputs. There is no notion of state or memory elements in a combinatorial component. A combinatorial functional unit requires a precise time D to compute, which is the absolute time (delay) from the arrival of the input(s) until the time when the output(s) are available. It is possible that a combinatorial functional unit requires more than one clock cycle, depending on the length of a clock period K. In such cases, the functional unit remains active over several clock cycles, and the input data must remain stable over that entire length of time. The required number of clock cycles for a combinatorial functional unit is the latency $L = \lceil D/K \rceil$. Therefore, we define the timing attributes T of a combinatorial functional unit as $T(D)$.

A *sequential functional unit* is a digital circuit that employs memory elements in addition to combinatorial logic. The value of the output is determined by both the present inputs and the contents of the memory elements, i.e., the current state of the functional unit. A *pipelined sequential functional unit* can start a new computation prior to the completion of the current computation. In other words, it can compute multiple outputs from multiple sets of input data. Pipelining is typically performed by dividing the combinatorial portion of the functional unit into a number of stages, and inserting memory elements between these stages.

The timing attributes of a nonpipelined sequential functional unit are characterized by its latency L, output delay D, and the minimum clock period K. The latency specifies the number of clock cycles required to generate the output after the input is available. The output delay is the length of the critical path, i.e., the delay of the longest path from input(s) to outputs(s) that contains no memory elements. The minimum clock period is the length of the critical path from input to

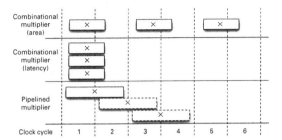

Figure 4.7 Three potential implementations for three independent multiplication operations. The first uses one multiplier, while the second uses three multipliers. The third uses one pipelined multiplier.

output, input to memory element, or memory element to output. The length of the target clock period is normally longer than the minimum clock period. Otherwise, the latency (the number of clock cycles) must be recalculated, and the structure of the functional unit must be augmented with input registers and/or multiplexors in order to insure that the necessary data are available and stored by the minimum clock period. We define the timing attributes of a nonpipelined sequential functional unit as $T(L, D, K)$.

The timing attributes of a pipelined functional unit are defined as $T(I, L, D, K)$ where I is the initiation interval, L is the latency, D is the output delay and K is the minimum clock period [24]. The latency, output delay, and minimum clock period are defined in the same manner as in the nonpipelined functional unit. The initiation interval is the number of clock cycles required to begin a new computation after starting the prior one, or, in other words, the number of clock cycles between one result becoming available and the next result.

Consider a design that contains three independent multiply operations. We are given the choice of using purely combinatorial multipliers or pipelined multipliers. The resource allocation problem determines the number and type of multipliers. Assume that the combinatorial multiplier has area of $335\,000\,\mu m^2$ and delay of 9.28 ns and the pipelined multiplier has a latency of two cycles, a one cycle initial interval, a delay of 5.73 ns, a minimum clock period of 6.84 ns and an area of $360\,000\,\mu m^2$. Also, assume the target clock frequency is 125 MHz, i.e., the length of the clock period is 8 ns. This means that the combinatorial multiplier requires two clock cycles. The pipelined multiplier takes two cycles to compute a result, but can accept a new input every cycle. Figure 4.7 shows the scheduling results for three scenarios:

(1) The first uses one combinatorial multiplier and requires six cycles to complete with a total area of $335\,000\,\mu m^2$.
(2) The second requires three combinatorial multipliers (the total area of $1\,005\,000\,\mu m^2$) and two cycles to compute.
(3) The third uses one pipelined multiplier with an area of $360\,000\,\mu m^2$ and requires four cycles to compute the three multiply operations.

4.6.2   Storage elements

Storage elements save inputs, outputs, and intermediate results required during the computation of the application. Registers and on-chip memory blocks are two common forms of storage elements. Registers typically store scalar variables, small data arrays, and implicit intermediate results. Memory blocks hold bigger pieces of data such as large data arrays.

A *register* is a small amount of storage whose contents can be quickly accessed. Any data that are required across a clock cycle require storage in a register. Registers are described by the number of bits that they store, e.g., 8, 16, 32, and 64, as well as the setup, hold, and ready time which define the timing attributes of a register. The setup time is the minimum amount of time that the data must be available to the register prior to the rising edge of the clock signal. The hold time is a requirement on the stability of the input data after the rising edge of the clock. The ready time is the amount of time required for the data to become stable at the output of a register after the rising edge of the clock signal. A register can save several variables as long as the lifetimes of all of the variables are non-overlapping. This problem of minimizing the number of required registers is called register allocation and is relevant in both software compilation and hardware synthesis. When multiple variables are mapped to a single register, multiplexors are required to route the correct variable to the register at the appropriate time.

On-chip memory blocks typically store large amounts of data, which are often needed by the application as input, output and/or storage for intermediate results. Memory blocks utilize dense memory elements making them more area efficient than registers. However, they have restrictions on the number of elements that can be loaded or stored in any particular cycle. They are described by the number of ports, which are typically limited to a small number, e.g., the two read ports and one write port that are found on on-chip memory blocks in FPGAs [25]. Timing attributes are also described using setup, hold, and ready times. It typically takes one cycle to perform a memory access (read). The setup and hold times are required for both the input data and the address where the data should be stored.

4.6.3   Interconnect logic

As mentioned previously, storage elements and functional units often operate on data stored or produced by different resources. *Interconnect logic*, usually in the form of multiplexors, steers the data to the correct place. Multiplexors are commonly modeled as simple combinatorial components. They have area and timing attributes (delay D) in the same manner as combinatorial functional units. The amount of sharing of a resource roughly determines the size and delay of the interconnect logic that it requires. For example, if a register stores data from four unique locations, then it needs a four-input multiplexor.

4.6.4   Problem definition

We now provide a formal definition of the resource allocation problem. We are given a collection of computing resources, e.g., adders, multipliers, registers, on-chip memory, and multiplexors, in a technology library $R = \{r_1, r_2, \ldots, r_m\}$, i.e., there are m different types of resources. Each resource r_j (A_j, T_j, O) has area A_j, timing attribute T_j, and can execute the operations defined in the set[5] O. The resource allocation problem defines a vector RA of length m, where each element ra_j of the vector denotes the number of resources of type r_j. This requires that $r_j > 0$ and j $(1 < j < m)$.

The target application, architecture, and technology library often impose resource constraints. For example, if an application requires an integer array of input variables and the only available on-chip storage element is a single port memory, then the number of available memory ports will be 1; therefore, only one memory access to this array can be scheduled in any clock cycle. For an example of the architecture specifying a resource constraint, consider FPGAs which include a limited number of integrated on-chip multipliers [25]. In this case, the number of multipliers available for resource allocation must be less than or equal to the number available on the FPGA.

4.7   Operation scheduling

Operation scheduling determines the start time of each operation in the program representation. The objective is to produce a schedule to minimize either the completion time or the computing resources required to meet a given deadline. The program representation can be any of the aforementioned underlying models (see Section 4.4). We focus our discussion on the DFG since it forms the basis for many hardware synthesis program representations and it is the representation that we use predominantly throughout the remainder of the book.

There are two fundamental scheduling types called resource constrained scheduling (RCS) and timing constrained scheduling (TCS). Given a DFG, clock cycle time, resource count, and resource delays, *RCS* finds the minimum number of clock cycles needed to execute the DFG. *TCS* attempts to determine the minimum number of resources needed for a given deadline. In both cases, we only care about the overall time to schedule all of the operations and the number of resources that are required to schedule the operations. However, other multivariate objective functions are also possible. These include power, energy, and area. We focus our discussion on RCS and TCS.

TCS (sometimes called fixed control step scheduling) focuses on determining the minimum resource cost that suits the given latency deadline. Many DSP systems require TCS because the sampling rate dictates the maximum allowable computation time to process each sample. Since the sampling rate is fixed, the main objective is to minimize the cost of the hardware.

---

[5] This will be discussed in more detail in Section 4.7.

RCS is performed when the number and type of resources are known a priori. For instance, during software compilation, the computing resources are fixed depending on the targeted microprocessor. In hardware compilation, the different portions of the application are often modeled and scheduled independently. Therefore, if we wish to maximize resource sharing, each portion should use the same or similar resources.

4.7.1   Problem definition

We now provide a formal definition of operation scheduling. Given a set of operations and a collection of computational units, RCS schedules the operations onto the computing units such that the execution time of these operations is minimized while respecting the capacity limits imposed by the number of computational resources. The operations $O = \{o_1, o_2, \ldots, o_n\}$ can be modeled as a DFG $G(V, E)$, where each node v_i represents an operation o_i, and the edge e_{ij} denotes a dependency between operations v_j and v_i. We assume that "start" is the only entry node in the DFG, i.e., it has no predecessors and "end" is the only exit node, i.e., it has no successors.

Additionally, we have a collection of computing resources, e.g., ALUs, adders, and multipliers, in a technology library denoted by $R = \{r_1, r_2, \ldots, r_m\}$ as described in Section 4.6.4. Each resource $r_j(A_j, T_j, O_{q_j})$ has area A_j, a timing attribute T_j, and can execute the operations O_{q_j}, where $O_{q_j} \subset O$ and $\bigcup_j O_{q_j} = O$. Furthermore, each operation in the DFG must be executable on at least one type of resource. When each of the operations is uniquely associated with one resource type, we call this *homogeneous scheduling*. If an operation can be performed by more than one resource type we call this *heterogeneous scheduling* [26]. An ALU is an example of a resource that can perform many operations (addition, subtraction, and logical operations); hence, it implies heterogeneous scheduling. Moreover, we can assume that the cycle delays for each operation on different types of resources can have a different value, i.e., T_j is a function of the operation i. The start and end vertices have zero delay. Finally, we assume that the execution of the operations is nonpreemptive, i.e., once an operation starts execution, it will finish without being interrupted.

The solution to the scheduling problem is a vector of start times for each of the operations denoted as $S = \{s_1, s_2, \ldots, s_n\}$. For the sake of notational convenience, we also define the finish times of the nodes $F = \{f_1, f_2, \ldots, f_n\}$. Note that the finish time of an operation is equal to the sum of its start time and the delay of the resource q_j to which it is mapped, i.e., $f_i = s_i + T_j$.

The RCS problem is formally defined as minimize s_{end}, which is the start time of the end node, with respect to the following conditions:

(1) An operation can only start when all its predecessors have finished, i.e., $s_i \geq f_j$ if $o_j \prec o_i$.
(2) At any given cycle t, the number of resources needed is less than ra_j for all $1 \leq j \leq |R|$.

TCS is a dual problem of RCS, because in TCS the timing is constrained and the resource usage is optimized, and can be defined using the same terminology presented above. Here, the target is to minimize total resources $\Sigma_j\ ra_j$ or the total cost of the resources (e.g., the hardware area needed), subject to the same dependencies between operations imposed by the DFG and a given deadline D, i.e., $s_{end} < D$.

4.7.2   Operation scheduling algorithms

In this subsection, we describe the several algorithms used to solve the scheduling problem. These include basic algorithms for solving the unconstrained scheduling problem, as well as a few variants of list scheduling. We conclude by briefly discussing some more advanced scheduling algorithms.

4.7.2.1   Unconstrained scheduling algorithms

The unconstrained scheduling problem schedules the operations assuming unlimited resources. The schedule must only follow the operation dependencies. This eases the complexity of the scheduling problem, making it optimally solvable in polynomial time. While this assumption is typically unrealistic, unconstrained scheduling helps to gain insight into the scheduling solution. For example, it can be used to answer questions such as: What is the fastest possible time that the operations can be scheduled? How many resources will this require? Which operations have flexibility in the cycles that they can be scheduled? There are two algorithms for unconstrained scheduling – as soon as possible (ASAP) and as late as possible (ALAP). We describe each in further detail in the following.

The *ASAP* operation scheduling algorithm schedules each operation at the earliest possible clock cycle. This is strictly dictated by the dependencies between the operations. The algorithm is described in Figure 4.8. The vertices of the input DFG are first sorted based on the partial ordering defined by the direct dependencies between the operations (edges). Then the start and end times of the "start" node are set to zero. The algorithm proceeds to go through the sorted list of vertices and assigns a start time to each operation equal to the maximum end time of all of its predecessor operations. The ASAP result provides the lower bound for the start time of each operation.

The *ALAP* operation scheduling algorithm works in a similar manner except here we decide the latest possible time that each operation can be scheduled. The algorithm proceeds by assigning times to the vertices in a reverse partial ordering. The algorithm is formally described in Figure 4.9. It should be noted that ALAP gives the same result as the ASAP algorithm when the directed edges are reversed. The ALAP result provides an upper bound on the start time of each operation with the given target latency.

Both ASAP and ALAP operate on the assumption that there are no resource constraints. Therefore, they are not typically used to solve the general-purpose operation scheduling problem; rather each acts as a method to determine feasible

```
ASAP_Scheduling (DFG G(V,E))
{
  //Sort the vertices by their partial order relationships (≺)
  Sort(G);

  //Set the start and finish time of the "start" node equal to zero
  s_start = f_start = 0;

  for (all v_i in V)
  {
    s_i = 0;
    for (v_j, where v_j ≺ v_i)
      s_i = max(f_j, s_i);
    update f_i;
  }
  return f_end;
}
```

Figure 4.8 The algorithm for ASAP operation scheduling. The start time of each operation is assigned as early as feasible based upon the dependency constraints.

```
ALAP_Scheduling (DFG G(V,E))
{
  //Sort the vertices by their reverse partial order relationships (≻)
  Reverse_Sort(G);

  //Set the start and finish time of the "end" node equal to zero
  s_end = f_end = 0;

  for (all v_i in V)
  {
    f_i = 0;
    for (v_j, where v_j ≻ v_i)
      f_i = min(s_j, f_i);
    update s_i;
  }
  for(all v_i in V)
    s_i = MAX_TIME+s_i;
  return s_end;
}
```

Figure 4.9 The algorithm for ALAP operation scheduling. The start time of each operation is assigned as late as feasible based upon the dependency constraints. MAX-TIME is the latest specified time for the last operation.

time steps where every operation can be scheduled. This is called the mobility of an operation; it describes the total number of time steps that an operation can be scheduled. More formally the *mobility* of operation o_i is defined by the ASAP and ALAP scheduling result $[s_i^S, s_i^L]$. An operation with a small mobility has limited opportunity for scheduling. For example, if an operation has the same start time for both ASAP and ALAP, then it must be scheduled at exactly that time step.

```
List_Scheduling (DFG G(V,E))
{
    Initialize the empty priority list L by adding the virtual start node vₛ
    cycle = 0; s_start = 0; f_start = 0;
    while(v_end is not scheduled)
        for(vᵢ in V and vᵢ is not in L)
            if(vᵢ is not scheduled and ready)
                insert vᵢ in sorted order in L;
        for(vᵢ in L)
            if(an idle resource q exists)
                schedule vᵢ on q at time cycle;
        cycle = cycle + 1;
    return f_end;
}
```

Figure 4.10 The algorithm for list scheduling. The algorithm works in an iterative fashion by scheduling operations one at a time based on their position in a priority list. First the algorithm adds all "ready" vertices into the priority list i.e., all nodes that have each of their predecessors scheduled are added to the priority list. Then, the vertices are selected from the priority list and scheduled at the current cycle if resource constraints allow. The cycle is incremented and the process repeats itself until all nodes are scheduled i.e., the "end" vertex is scheduled.

4.7.3   Constrained operation scheduling algorithms

List scheduling belongs to a class of algorithms that are a simple and effective method of solving an RCS problem [27, 28]. List scheduling algorithms can be viewed as a generalization of ASAP algorithms with the addition of resource constraints. A list scheduling algorithm iteratively constructs a solution using a prioritized ready list. Initially the ready list is empty and the virtual source node is set with a start and an end time of zero. An operation that has every one of its predecessor nodes scheduled is added to the ready list at a position based on a priority function. The priority function defines the type of list scheduling algorithm and this function can be based on the mobility, the number of succeeding operations, the depth (i.e., the minimum number of successor nodes to reach the end node), and so forth. The algorithm then selects the operation with the highest priority and attempts to schedule it. If more than one operation has the same priority, the tie is broken randomly. The algorithm determines if it is possible to schedule the operation in the current cycle based on the available resources. If possible, the operation is scheduled. The algorithm continues through the iteration determining if other operations in the priority list can be scheduled. The iteration ends when all of the operations are checked. Then the ready list is updated due to the fact that the successors of operations that were just scheduled can possibly now be added to the list. The algorithm iterates through this process until all operations are scheduled or, equivalently, the end node is scheduled. The pseudo code for the algorithm is shown in Figure 4.10.

The success of the list scheduling algorithm is highly dependent on the input structure of the DFG and the priority function [1, 29, 30]. A commonly used priority function is the inverse of the mobility, which insures that the scheduling of operations with large mobility is considered only after those operations that have limited flexibility in when they can be scheduled. Many priority functions have been proposed [29, 31–33], and it is commonly agreed that there is no single good heuristic across a range of applications, as the results by Wang *et al.* indicate [34]. It is relatively easy to prove that the list scheduling algorithm always generates a feasible schedule. However, the list scheduling algorithm often produces poor results in pipelined designs due to the lack of look-ahead ability. The simplicity and relatively good results make list scheduling one of the more popular algorithms for operation scheduling.

The *force directed scheduling (FDS)* algorithm [35] is a type of list scheduling that uses a more complicated priority function based on the idea of "forces." A force is the effort required to schedule a particular operation to a specific cycle. The algorithm attempts to find the schedule that requires the minimum effort or force. Therefore, if an operation requires a small force in a certain cycle, it is likely to be scheduled in that cycle. Likewise, if it requires a large force in a certain cycle, it is less likely to be scheduled in that cycle. The primary objective of the algorithm is to distribute operations uniformly across the various resources subject to timing constraints.

The FDS algorithm relies on both the ASAP and the ALAP scheduling algorithms to determine the feasible control steps for every operation o_i i.e., the mobility of o_i is $[s_i^S, s_i^L]$. It assumes that each operation has a uniform probability of being scheduled in any of the cycles within its mobility and zero probability of being scheduled elsewhere. The FDS algorithm tries to minimize the overall concurrency under a fixed latency by scheduling operations one by one. At every time step, the effect of scheduling each unscheduled operation in every possible time step in its frame range is calculated, and the operation and the corresponding time step with the smallest negative effect are selected.

This effect is equated to the force for an unscheduled operation o_i at control step j and comprises two components, namely: (1) the self-force SF_{ij} and (2) the predecessor–successor forces PSF_{ij}. The self-force SF_{ij} represents the direct effect of this scheduling on the overall concurrency. The predecessor and successor forces are calculated by determining the effects that scheduling operation o_i to be in cycle j will have on the mobility of the predecessor or successor operation of o_i. For example, scheduling an operation in a particular cycle often will limit the mobility of a predecessor or successor operation. This will restrict the available options when we eventually schedule these predecessor or successor operations; hence, we should do our best to schedule an operation to be in a cycle that allows the most flexibility in the scheduling of other operations.

Finally, the algorithm compares the total forces obtained for all the unscheduled operations at every possible cycle. The algorithm chooses the operation and the cycle with the best force reduction and increments the partial scheduling result until all operations have been scheduled. The FDS method is constructive because the solution is computed without performing any backtracking. Every decision is made in a greedy manner. FDS does not take into account future assignments of operators to the same cycle. Consequently, it is likely that the resulting solution

Force_Directed_Scheduling (DFG G(V, E))
{
  Perform ASAP and ALAP scheduling;
  Initialize the mobility for each operation o_i;
  Calculate operation probability for each operation o_i;
  while(unscheduled operations remain)
    for(every unscheduled operation o_i)
      for(every time step j within the mobility of o_i)
        Calculate self force SF_{ij};
        Set $F_{ij} = SF_{ij}$;
        for(each predecessor/successor o_l of o_i)
          Calculate PSF_{ijl};
          $F_{ij} = F_{ij} + PSF_{ijl}$;
        Determine smallest force F_{ij};
        Schedule operation o_i at cycle j;
      Update mobility of predecessors/successor of scheduled operation;
}

Figure 4.11 Pseudo code for the FDS algorithm. The algorithm works in an iterative fashion by scheduling operations one at a time based on their forces. The algorithm is initiated by calculating the mobility and operation probabilities which are used to determine the forces. It works in a constructive manner, scheduling the operation with the smallest forces at each iteration. The algorithm terminates when all operations are scheduled.

will not be optimal due to the inability to look ahead and the lack of compromises between early and late decisions. The pseudo code for the FDS scheduling algorithm is given in Figure 4.11.

There are countless other algorithms for operation scheduling; we briefly describe a few of them in the following. Many variants of the operation scheduling problem are NP-hard [36]. Although it is possible to formulate and solve them using integer linear programming (ILP) [37], the feasible solution space quickly becomes intractable for larger problem instances. In order to address this problem, a range of heuristic methods with polynomial runtime complexity has been proposed.

Many TCS algorithms used in high-level synthesis are derivatives of the FDS algorithm [35]. For example, Verhaegh *et al.* [38, 39] provide a theoretical treatment of the original FDS algorithm and report better results by applying gradual time-frame reduction and the use of global spring constants in the force calculation. Due to the lack of a look-ahead scheme, the FDS algorithm is likely to produce a suboptimal solution. One way to address this issue is the iterative method proposed by Park and Kyung [51] based on Kernighan and Lin's heuristic [40] method used for solving the graph-bisection problem. In their approach, each operation is scheduled in an earlier or later step using the move that produces the maximum gain. Then, all operations are unlocked, and the whole procedure is repeated with this new schedule. The quality of the result produced by this algorithm is highly dependent upon the initial solution. More recently, Heijligers and Jess [41] and Sharma and Jain [42] used evolutionary techniques such as genetic algorithms and simulated evolution.

There are a number of algorithms for the RCS problem, including list scheduling [26, 43], FDS [35], a genetic algorithm [33], Tabu search [44], simulated annealing (SA) [30], and graph-theoretic and computational geometry approaches [45, 46]. Among these, list scheduling is the most common due to its simplicity of implementation and capability of generating reasonably good results for small-sized problems.

Wang *et al.* [34] present novel operation scheduling algorithms using the ant colony optimization approach for both the TCS and RCS problems. The algorithms use a unique hybrid approach by combining the MAX–MIN ant system metaheuristic [47] with traditional scheduling heuristics such as list scheduling and FDS. Their algorithms show impressive results compared to a number of algorithms including several variants of list scheduling, FDS and simulated annealing. Furthermore, they present a method of seamlessly switching between solving the TCS and RCS problems in order to perform design space exploration for both the scheduling and resource allocations problem [48].

4.8   Resource binding

Resource binding is the process of assigning each operation to a specific component from the technology library. This differs from resource allocation, which decides the number of instances of each component, by performing an explicit mapping from operation to resource. For example, consider again Figure 4.7. Here we have three independent multiplication operations and we show three different resource allocations. The first case allocates one multiplier and performs the multiplications sequentially. The second allocates three multipliers and executes all of the multiplication operations in parallel. Here we must also decide which multiplier will perform each operation. This is precisely the problem of resource binding. The final case allocates one pipelined multiplier. Note that in the first and final cases the resource binding is trivial since there is only one multiplier; hence each multiply operation is bound to that one multiplier.

It may seem that the binding does not play a large role in the hardware synthesis process. However, the binding affects the amount of steering logic and interconnect. Different bindings can reduce the number and size of the multiplexors required for the final design. Consider the expression $(a+b+c)+(d+e)$. The four operations (labeled o_1 through o_4) are scheduled over three cycles as shown in Figure 4.12. Operations o_1 and o_2 are performed concurrently in the first cycle requiring two adder resources. These two operations must be bound on different adders. However, the remaining two operations (o_3 and o_4) can be executed on either of the adders. Figure 4.13 shows one potential binding. Here operations o_3 and o_4 are bound to the same adder a_1. This results in one two-input multiplexor and one three-input multiplexor. Figure 4.14 displays the implementation when operations o_3 and o_4 are bound to adders a_1 and a_2, respectively. This situation requires four two-input multiplexors, clearly showing that the binding can affect the total number of resources. The effect of binding in larger designs is

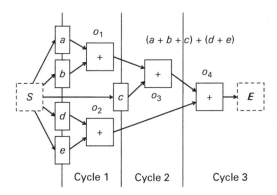

Figure 4.12 The scheduling of the expression $(a+b+c)+(d+e)$ using two adders over three cycles.

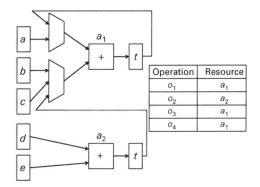

Operation	Resource
o_1	a_1
o_2	a_2
o_3	a_1
o_4	a_1

Figure 4.13 A realization of the data path for the expression $(a+b+c)+(d+e)$ with the resource binding shown in the table. This realization requires two multiplexors – one with two inputs and one with three inputs.

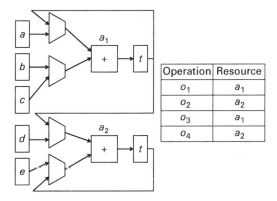

Operation	Resource
o_1	a_1
o_2	a_2
o_3	a_1
o_4	a_2

Figure 4.14 Another realization of the expression $(a+b+c)+(d+e)$ with a different resource binding. In this case, four two-input multiplexors are necessary.

```
void fir_filter (short* input, short coef[64], short* output)
{
  static short regs [64];
  int temp = 0;

  /* Add sample from input and shift old samples */
  loop_shift: for(int i = 63; i >= 0; i--)
    regs[i] = (i==0) ? *input : regs[i-1];

  /* Perform multiply accumulate on input samples and coefficients */
  loop_mac: for(int i = 63; i >= 0; i--)
    temp += regs[i]*coef[i];

  *output = temp>>16;
}
```

Figure 4.15 The C code for a 64-tap FIR filter.

likely to be even more pronounced. Furthermore, the binding also plays a role in power consumption. By changing the binding, we can minimize the switching activity of a functional unit, which in turn lowers the power consumption [49].

4.9   Case study: FIR filter

We illustrate the various steps in hardware synthesis by describing the process of translating a 64-tap FIR filter into a hardware description. FIR filters are common functions in DSP and a prime example of a linear system. Hence, this serves not only as a case study for hardware synthesis techniques, but also provides some insight into the optimization problems that we describe in the following chapters.

Figure 4.15 shows the C code for the 64-tap FIR filter. The fir_filter function has three arguments: (1) input: a pointer to the memory location of the input elements; (2) coeff: a 64-element array that holds the filter coefficient values; and (3) output: a pointer to the memory location to store the output values. The code contains two for loops. The first loop loop_shift moves each value in the regs array by one element and inputs a value from the input memory location. You can assume that each new input to the filter is stored at the location specified by the input pointer. The second loop loop_mac performs the MAC operation on the regs array: it takes each element of the regs array, multiplies it by the corresponding constant coefficient (stored in the coef array) while storing the running sum in the temp variable. Assume that the application specification of the filter requires that one output is produced for every input, a new input arrives every cycle, the latency between inputs and outputs does not matter, the target clock frequency is 300 MHz, and the goal is to design a filter with the smallest possible area.

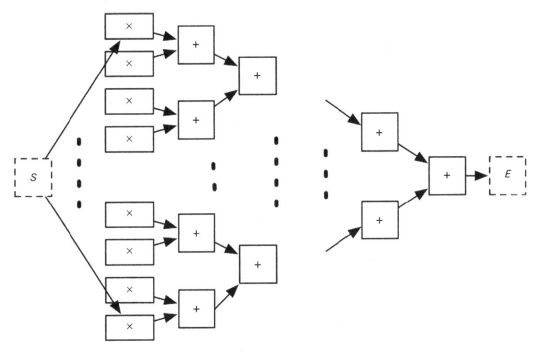

Figure 4.16 The DFG of the unrolled 64-tap filter. The first stage performs the multiplication of the input samples with the constant coefficients. The remaining stages perform the summation to obtain the output value.

The first step in the process translates this C code into a suitable program representation. Assume that we first translate this code into an AST. At this stage we perform a set of algorithmic optimizations, the most prominent of which is loop unrolling. Both loops are fully unrolled because the high throughput required by the specification, i.e., processing one output sample per input sample, dictates such an action. Then, the AST is translated into a DFG – a lower-level program representation. The DFG is shown in Figure 4.16.

Now we should perform resource allocation and scheduling on the DFG. Each operation is assigned to a compatible resource selected from a given technology library. A technology library typically contains a number of different adders that can handle different bitwidths for the input operands and use different micro-architectures (e.g., ripple carry, carry look-ahead) that provide distinctive area and delay characteristics; some are faster but use more area, while others are slower and smaller. There are different multipliers as well. Operations can share the same resource as long as they are executed in different cycles. This sharing can reduce the area, but requires additional interconnect logic that must be balanced with the decrease in the number of resources. A sample technology library is shown in Table 4.1. These numbers are taken from a real industrial technology library. The area results are given in terms of a.u., where a.u. is a variable that

Table 4.1 An example technology library

The first column gives the name of the resource, while the remaining columns describe the delay and area of the resources in three different scenarios: fast, normal and small.

	Fast		Normal		Small	
	D (ns)	Area	D (ns)	Area	D (ns)	Area
Adder (32)	0.51	3974.61	1.17	1565.81	2.62	1219.85
Multiplier (16 × 16)	2.21	9039.54	2.64	6659.56	3.96	5802.82
MUX (1,1,2)	0.08	40.45	0.20	31.48	0.39	23.23
Register (32)		685.72		685.72		685.72

depends on the technology node of the hardware. The size of a.u. is a function of the fabrication process being used; in this case, 1 a.u. is equal to $54 \, \mu m^2$. This is only a small sample of the resources in a technology library.

A scheduling algorithm determines a start time for each operation. After scheduling, resource allocation determines the exact assignment of operations to resources. Then, the connections between the control logic, interconnect logic, and storage elements are described using an RTL hardware description, e.g., Verilog or VHDL.

A substantial portion of the computation in the 64-tap FIR filter comprises an adder tree, which provides the summation of the input samples multiplied with the constant coefficients. In the following, we give the results of a few different scheduling and resource allocation options for an 8-input balanced adder tree. This simple example gives us a flavor of the tradeoffs performed during hardware synthesis. Assume that we use the same application specification for the FIR filter, i.e., we must provide one output every cycle with a target clock frequency of 300 MHz and the goal is to design a filter with the smallest possible area.

A trivial method of satisfying the input constraints is to allocate the fastest resource possible to all operations. Figure 4.17 shows this resource allocation and the scheduling results for the eight-input adder tree. In this case, the scheduling algorithm can schedule all addition operations in one cycle. This is due to the fact that the critical path of the adder tree is equal to three addition operations.[6] In addition, since a fast adder requires 0.51 ns, the critical path is 1.53 ns, which gives a clock frequency of around 650 MHz, well over the desired 300 MHz. This results in a fast overall execution time. This case requires only one register (for the output). However, this solution requires a large area. To

---

[6] Note that it is possible to do this operation faster since the lower bits of the second set of adders can start execution before the higher bits of the first set finish their computation (the same argument is true for the second and third sets of adders). For the sake of simplicity, we assume that each adder has only one delay from inputs to outputs, the longest critical path internal to the add), and not individual bit delays as is required to perform this optimization.

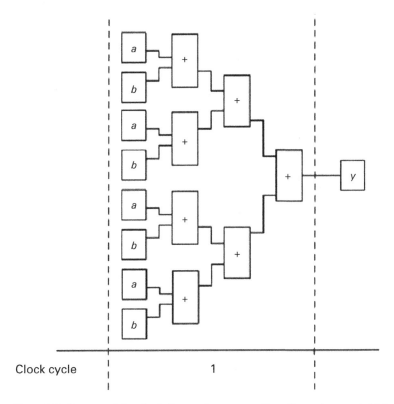

Clock cycle   1

Figure 4.17 One possible scheduling and resource allocation using an eight-input balanced adder tree. Here the output is computed in one cycle using the fast adders. This requires an allocation of eight adders and one register.

be precise, the area is 28 508 a.u. using seven fast 32-bit adders and one 32-bit register.

Another common strategy is to minimize the area of the computational resources, which are only the adders in this simple example. Here we assign all operations to the smallest, and likewise the slowest, resources. The resulting schedule is shown in Figure 4.18. Since the slow adders have a delay of 2.62 ns, it is not possible to schedule two or more dependent addition operations in the same cycle. This would result in a clock frequency that is slower than the 300 MHz target. Therefore, the best latency is three cycles. This also requires seven registers; registers are required for any result that is used in a later clock cycle. There are four operands that must be saved in registers for the results produced in cycle 1 and used in cycle 2, two registers from cycle 2 to cycle 3, and one register for the final result from cycle 3. The overall area here is 13 334 a.u. for seven small adders and seven registers.

Neither of these solutions yields the most area efficient design. The best solution in terms of minimizing area allocates six normal adders and one small adder. This solution is shown in Figure 4.19. As you can see, this case requires three

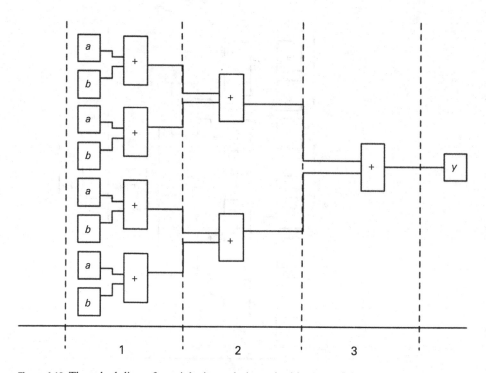

Figure 4.18 The scheduling of an eight-input balanced adder tree when allocating the smallest, therefore slowest, adder to all addition operations. The adder tree requires three cycles to compute the output and seven registers.

registers. The total area is 12 612 a.u. The area reduction is realized through the co-optimization of both the adders and the registers. Since the normal adders have a delay of 1.17 ns, we can chain two adders in one clock cycle while still achieving the 300 MHz target clock frequency. Hence we can perform six addition operations in one cycle and the remaining addition operation using a slow adder in the second cycle.

It is possible to reduce the area further through resource sharing. This means that we reuse resources in different operations. Such sharing can only be done on operations that are executed in different cycles. For example, none of the resources can be shared in the example in Figure 4.17 since they all execute in the same clock cycle. However, in Figure 4.19 we can share the addition operation scheduled in the second clock cycle with any of the adders in the first cycle. The benefit of resource sharing is that we can reduce the overall number of resources when we share them across many operations. However, such sharing comes at a cost; we must add interconnect logic (multiplexors) and associated control logic. Therefore, as we show in the following, increasing the amount of resource sharing does not always lead to a reduction in the area.

In order to investigate the relationship between area and latency, we synthesized a number of different implementations of the 64-tap FIR filter using Catapult® C Synthesis [50] – the state of the art hardware synthesis tool from Mentor Graphics. We synthesized the FIR filter while varying the latency, each time asking the tool

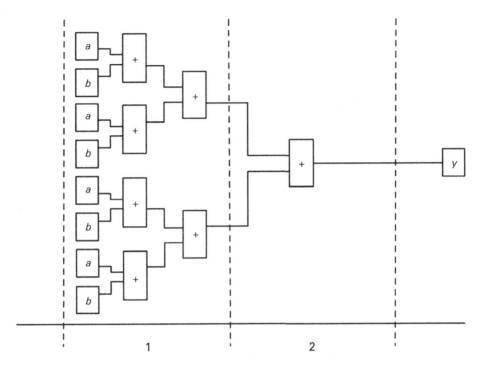

Figure 4.19 The schedule when allocating six normal adders and one slow adder. This requires two cycles and three registers (not including input register) and results in the design with the least possible area, while meeting the specification constraints.

to minimize the area while adhering to the aforementioned application specification constraints. These results are shown in Figure 4.20. The total area contains two portions: one is the area of the functional units, i.e., the adders and multipliers, while the other is the area for the registers and interconnect logic. Three of the graphs ((a), (b) and (c)) vary the initiation interval, while graph (d) shows the results of the adder tree only.

If we only consider the area of the functional units, then the area decreases as the latency increases. This is due to the fact that we increase the opportunity for sharing, and therefore require fewer functional units. However, this typically comes at the expense of an increase in the area of the registers and the interconnect logic. Consider Figure 4.20(a). Here the smallest design, when only considering the area for the functional unit, has a latency of seven clock cycles. The area for its functional units is 389 938 a.u., while its total area is 493 671 a.u. The total area when the latency is six cycles is a little less, 492 812 a.u. A similar trend occurs in the other graphs as well.

4.10   Summary

This chapter gave an overview of the hardware synthesis process. It provided a brief description of the various aspects of the hardware design flow, including the system specification, program representation, algorithmic optimizations,

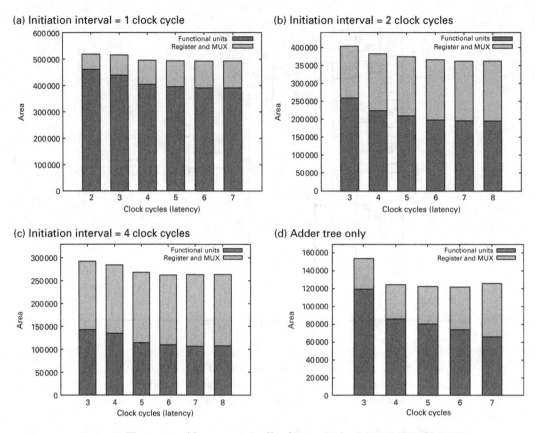

Figure 4.20 The area and latency tradeoffs of a synthesized 64-tap FIR filter. The graphs show the area results, broken down into two components (functional units and register/MUX), while changing the latency. Graphs (a), (b) and (c) vary the initiation interval from one to two to four clock cycles. The final graph (d) shows the results of the adder tree only.

resource allocation, operation scheduling, and resource binding. The chapter concluded with a case study using a 64-tap FIR filter, which offered insight into the issues faced during each step of the hardware synthesis design flow.

References

[1] G. De Micheli, *Synthesis and Optimization of Digital Circuits*. New York, NY: McGraw-Hill, 1994.

[2] M. Sarrafzadeh and C. K. Wong, *An Introduction to VLSI Physical Design*. New York, NY: McGraw Hill, 1996.

[3] D. D. Gajski, J. Zhu, R. Dömer, A. Gerstlauser, and S. Zhoa, *Spec C: Specification Language and Methodology*. Boston, MA: Kluwer Academic Publishers, 2000.

[4] S. Y. Liao, Towards a new standard for system-level design, in *International Workshop on Hardware/Software Codesign San Diego, 2000*, pp. 2–6. New York, NY: ACM, 2000.

[5] I. Page, Constructing hardware-software systems from a single description, *Journal of VLSI Signal Processing*, **12**, 87–107, 1996.

[6] H. Chao, S. Ravi, A. Raghunathan, and N. K. Jha, High-level synthesis of distributed logic-memory architectures, *IEEE/ACM International Conference on Computer Aided Design San Jose, 2002. IEEE/ACM Digest of Technical Papers (Cat. No.02CH37391)*. pp. 564–71. New York, NY: ACM, 2002.

[7] P. Diniz and J. Park, Automatic synthesis of data storage and control structures for FPGA-based computing engines, *IEEE Symposium on Field-Programmable Custom Computing Machines, Napa Valley, 2000*, pp. 91–100. Washington, DC: IEEE Computer Society, 2000.

[8] L. Semeria, K. Sato, and G. De Micheli, Synthesis of hardware models in C with pointers and complex data structures, *IEEE Transactions on Very Large Scale Integration (VLSI) Systems*, **9**, 743–56, 2001.

[9] Mathworks Website, http://www.mathworks.com/

[10] Synplicity Synplify DSP Website, http://www.synplicity.com/products/synplifydsp/

[11] A. V. Aho, S. Ravi, and J. D. Ullman, *Compilers: Principles, Techniques and Tools*. Boston, MA: Addison-Wesley, 1986.

[12] S. S. Muchnick, *Advanced Compiler Design and Implementation*. San Francisco, CA: Morgan Kaufmann Publishers, 1997.

[13] M. S. Hecht, *Flow Analysis of Computer Programs*. New York, NY: Elsevier, 1977.

[14] K. C. Pohlmann, *Principles of Digital Audio*. New York, NY: McGraw-Hill Professional, 2000.

[15] P. Briggs, T. Harvey, and L. Simpson, Static Single Assignment Construction, Technical Report, Rice University, 1995.

[16] R. Cytron, J. Ferrante, B. K. Rosen, M. N. Wegman, and F. K. Zadeck, Efficiently computing static single assignment form and the control dependence graph, *ACM Transactions on Programming Languages and Systems*, **13**, 451–90, 1991.

[17] R. Kastner, W. Gong, X. Hao, *et al.*, Layout driven data communication optimization for high level synthesis, *Design, Automation and Test in Europe, Munich, 2006*, p. 6. Leuven: European Design and Automation Association.

[18] A. Kaplan, P. Brisk, and R. Kastner, Data communication estimation and reduction for reconfigurable systems, in *Design Automation Conference, Anaheim, 2003*, pp. 616–21. New York, NY: ACM, 2003.

[19] J. Ferrante, K. J. Ottenstein, and J. D. Warren, The program dependence graph and its use in optimization, *ACM Transactions on Programming Languages & Systems*, **9**, 319–49, 1987.

[20] W. Gong, G. Wang, and R. Kastner, A high performance intermediate representation for reconfigurable systems, in *International Conference on Engineering of Reconfigurable Systems and Algorithms (ERSA), Las Vegas 2004*. CSREA Press, 2004.

[21] S. A. Edwards, An Esterel compiler for large control-dominated systems, *IEEE Transactions on Computer-Aided Design of Integrated Circuits and Systems*, **21**, 169–83, 2002.

[22] N. Ramasubramanian, R. Subramanian, and S. Pande, Automatic analysis of loops to exploit operator parallelism on reconfigurable systems, in *International Workshop on Languages and Compilers for Parallel Computing, 1998*, pp. 305–22. Springer Verlag, 1998.

[23] M. M. Mano and C. Kime, *Logic and Computer Design Fundamentals*, second edition Englewood Cliffs, NJ: Prentice Hall, 1999.

[24] J. P. Elliott, *Understanding Behavioral Synthesis: A Practical Guide to High-Level Design*. Norwell, MA: Kluwer Academic Publishers, 1999.

[25] *Virtex-II Pro Platform FPGA Data Sheet,* Xilinx Inc. 2003.

[26] H. Topcuoglu, S. Hariri, and W. Min-You, Performance-effective and low-complexity task scheduling for heterogeneous computing, *IEEE Transactions on Parallel and Distributed Systems*, **13**, 260–74, 2002.

[27] J. M. J. Schutten, List Scheduling Revisited, *Operation Research Letters*, **18**, 167–70, 1996.

[28] P. Poplavko, C. A. J. v. Eijk, and T. Basten, Constraint analysis and heuristic scheduling methods, *Workshop on Circuits, Systems and Signal Processing, Veldhoven 2000*, pp. 447–53. Utrecht: STW Technology Foundation, 2000.

[29] R. Kolisch and S. Hartmann, Project scheduling: recent models, algorithms and applications, *Heuristic Algorithms for Solving the Resource-Constrained Project Scheduling Problem*. Amsterdam: Kluwer Academic Publishers, 1999.

[30] P. H. Sweany and S. J. Beaty, Instruction scheduling using simulated annealing, *International Conference on Massively Parallel Computing Systems, Colorado 1998*. Los Amitos, CA: IEEE Computer Society Press, 1998.

[31] T. L. Adam, K. M. Chandy, and J. R. Dickson, A comparison of list schedules for parallel processing systems, *Communications of the ACM*, **17**, 685–90, 1974.

[32] A. Auyeung, I. Gondra, and H. K. Dai, Advances in Soft Computing: Intelligent Systems Design and Applications, *Integrating Random Ordering into Multi-Heuristic List Scheduling Genetic Algorithm*. Berlin: Springer Verlag, 2003.

[33] M. Grajcar, Genetic list scheduling algorithm for scheduling and allocation on a loosely coupled heterogeneous multiprocessor system, *Design Automation Conference, New Orleans* 1999, pp. 280–85. New York, NY: ACM, 1999.

[34] G. Wang, W. Gong, B. DeRenzi, and R. Kastner, Ant colony optimizations for resource- and timing-constrained operation scheduling, *IEEE Transactions on Computer-Aided Design of Integrated Circuits & Systems*, **26**, 1010–29, 2007.

[35] P. G. Paulin and J. P. Knight, Force-directed scheduling for the behavioral synthesis of ASICs, *IEEE Transactions on Computer-Aided Design of Integrated Circuits and Systems*, **8**, 661–79, 1989.

[36] B. David, R. Michael, and G. Izidor, On the complexity of scheduling problems for parallel/pipelined machines, *IEEE Transactions on Computers*, **38**, 1308–13, 1989.

[37] W. Kent, L. Jack, and H. Mark, Optimal instruction scheduling using integer programming, *SIGPLAN Notices*, **35**, 121–33, 2000.

[38] W. F. J. Verhaegh, E. H. L. Aarts, J. H. M. Korst, and P. E. R. Lippens, Improved force-directed scheduling, *Conference on European Design Automation, Amsterdam, 1991*. Los Amitos. Washington, DC: IEEE Computer Society.

[39] W. F. J. Verhaegh, P. E. R. Lippens, E. H. L. Aarts, *et al.*, Efficiency improvements for force-directed scheduling, in *IEEE/ACM International Conference on Computer-Aided Design, Santa Clara, 1992*, pp. 286–291. New York, NY: ACM, 1992.

[40] B. W. Kernighan and S. Lin, An efficient heuristic procedure for partitioning graphs, *The Bell System Technical Journal*, **49**, 291–307, 1970.

[41] M. Heijligers and J. Jess, High-level synthesis scheduling and allocation using genetic algorithms based on constructive topological scheduling techniques, *International Conference on Evolutionary Computation, 1995*, pp. 56–61. Piscataway, NJ: IEEE Press, 1995.

[42] A. Sharma and R. Jain, InSyn: integrated scheduling for DSP applications, *IEEE Transactions on Signal Processing*, **43**, 1966–77, 1995.

[43] T. L. Adam, K. M. Chandy, and J. R. Dickson, A comparison of list schedules for parallel processing systems, *Communications of the ACM*, **17**, 685–90, 1974.

[44] S. J. Beaty, Genetic algorithms versus Tabu search for instruction scheduling, *International Conference on Artificial Neural Nets and Genetic Algorithms, 1993*, pp. 496–501. New York, NY: Springer, 1993.

[45] A. Aleta, J. M. Codina, J. Sanchez, and A. Gonzalez, Graph-partitioning based instruction scheduling for clustered processors, *ACM/IEEE International Symposium on Microarchitecture, Austin, 2001*, pp. 150–59. Washington, DC: IEEE Computer Society, 2001.

[46] S. Ogrenci Memik, E. Bozorgzadeh, R. Kastner, and M. Sarrafzadeh, A super-scheduler for embedded reconfigurable systems, *IEEE/ACM International Conference on Computer Aided Design, San Jose, 2001*, pp. 391–94. Piscataway, NJ: IEEE Press, 2001.

[47] T. Stutzle and H. H. Hoos, MAX-MIN Ant System, *Future Generations Computer Systems*, **16**, 889–914, 2000.

[48] G. Wang, W. Gong, B. Derenzi, and R. Kastner, Exploring time/resource trade-offs by solving dual scheduling problems with the ant colony optimization, *ACM Transactions on Design Automation for Electronic Systems*, **12**, 46, 2007.

[49] E. Musoll and J. Cortadella, "Scheduling and resource binding for low power," *Proceedings of the 8th International Symposium on System Synthesis Cannes, 1995*. New York, NY: ACM, 1995.

[50] Mentor Graphics Catapult C Synthesis Webpage, http://www.mentor.com/products/ esl/ high_level_synthesis/catapult_synthesis/

[51] I.-C. Park and C. M. Kyung, "Fast and near optimal scheduling in automatic datapath synthesis," in *Proceedings of the IEEE/ACM 28th Conference on Design Automation, San Francisco, 1991*, pp. 680–81. New York, NY: 1991.

5 Fundamentals of digital arithmetic

5.1 Chapter overview

This chapter describes some of the basic ideas in digital arithmetic that are necessary to understand the polynomial and linear system optimizations presented in the later chapters. The chapter is divided into five sections. Section 5.2 discusses elementary properties of number systems, focusing on binary number representations including signed digit representations. It provides a high-level overview of both fixed and floating point representations. Section 5.3 gives background material on two-operand addition including ripple carry, carry propagate, and pipelined addition architectures. Then Section 5.4 provides an overview of multiple-operand addition. It gives details on sequential and parallel carry propagate multiple-operand architectures, as well as redundant digit summations using carry save adders and other higher-order counters and compressors. The section ends with a discussion on distributed arithmetic architecture for multiple-operand summations that are typically found in dot product operations. Section 5.5 summarizes the chapter.

5.2 Basic number representation

Number representation plays an important role in the design of algorithms for digital arithmetic. This section provides a brief and concise discussion on number representations that serves as a basis for understanding the topics presented in this book. There are a number of textbooks on digital arithmetic that deal with these topics in great detail [1–3].

5.2.1 Properties of number systems

Before we consider specific number representations, we should discuss fundamental properties that can be used to characterize a number system. At its core, any number system requires a set of digits, a set of values for the digits, and rules for interpreting the digits and values into a number. As an initial example, consider the decimal number system that we all learn as children. A number X is decomposed into a digit vector $X = (X_{n-1}, X_{n-2}, \ldots, X_1, X_0)$. The conventional decimal number system has the set of values $S_i = \{0, 1, 2, \ldots, 9\}$ with a cardinality (i.e., the size of the set) equal to 10. A digit vector of finite size can only represent a finite set of numbers related to the cardinality of the set of values, more specifically

$$\prod_{i=0}^{n-1} |S_i|.$$ (5.1)

For example, a digit vector with five elements can represent up to $100\,000$ unique numbers in the range $\{0, 1, 2, \ldots, 99\,999\}$. The mapping for the decimal number system is described as

$$X = \sum_{i=0}^{n-1} X_i \cdot 10^i.$$ (5.2)

The binary number representation is common in digital circuits as we model circuits using Boolean algebra. A digit in a binary representation has only two possible values in the set $\{0, 1\}$. The mapping is formally described as

$$X = \sum_{i=0}^{n-1} X_i \cdot 2^i.$$ (5.3)

So far we have only discussed representations for natural numbers (the set of integers $\{0, 1, 2, 3, \ldots\}$) or equivalently, unsigned numbers. There are several ways to extend this to represent negative numbers. These include the sign and magnitude representation, which allocates one bit that explicitly encodes the sign: e.g., set that bit (often the most significant bit) to "0" for a positive number, and set it to "1" for a negative number. The remaining bits in the number indicate the magnitude or absolute value. The one's complement form performs a bitwise logical NOT operation on the positive (unsigned) binary number to represent the negative of that number. In the two's complement representation, negative numbers are represented by the bit pattern which is one greater (in an unsigned sense) than the one's complement of the positive value. The two's complement value has only one representation for the number zero, unlike both sign and magnitude and one's complement, which have two representations. Perhaps most importantly, addition in two's complement can be performed just as in the unsigned case due to the fact that two's complement represents numbers in a way that allows end around carry. An n-bit two's complement number can represent the range of numbers $[-2^{n-1}, 2^{n-1} - 1]$. The mapping from digit vector to two's complement is

$$X = -2^{n-1} \cdot X_{n-1} + \sum_{i=0}^{n-2} 2^i \cdot X_i.$$ (5.4)

From the digital hardware perspective, the major advantage of the two's complement representation comes from the fact that any signed number can be added in its original form to give the correct results. In other words, the addition of a negative and a positive number can use the same hardware as the addition of two positive numbers or two negative numbers, i.e., the sign of the number is irrelevant while performing addition (this ignores the need for checking for overflow). The negation operation in two's complement simply requires inverting every bit (bitwise NOT) of the number and adding 1, making it easy to perform addition and subtraction of any signed number. Furthermore, the single unique representation for the number zero removes the arithmetic subtleties of dealing with negative zero. Every negative two's complement number has a "1" as its most significant bit (likewise every positive number has a "0" as its most significant bit), making it easy to check the sign of the number.

The aforementioned integer and binary number representations are both examples of weighted systems, which are the most common type of number system. The mapping is described as

$$X = \sum_{i=0}^{n-1} X_i \cdot W_i, \tag{5.5}$$

where X_i are the elements of the digit vector, as described previously, and W_i are the elements of the weight vector W. Note that Equation (5.5) is a generalized form of Equations (5.2) and (5.3). A radix number system has a weight vector defined as

$$W_0 = 1; \quad W_i = \prod_{j=0}^{i-1} R_j, \tag{5.6}$$

where R_j is the radix for the jth digit. Number systems can be divided into fixed and mixed radix systems. A *fixed radix system* has a constant radix across all digits. For example, the decimal number system and the binary number system have radixes of 10 and 2, respectively as seen in Equations (5.2) and (5.3). *Mixed radix systems* employ at least two different radix values. They are less frequently used for arithmetic and we only employ fixed radix systems throughout this book. A real-life example of a mixed radix system is our method for keeping time. Here the radixes are 60 (for seconds and minutes) and 24 (for hours).

A number system is *nonredundant* if there is exactly one representation for any integer. Equivalently the mapping is a one-to-one relationship. A *redundant number system* has at least one integer that can be represented by more than one digit vector. Many techniques for arithmetic operations implicitly or explicitly use a redundant number system to achieve a faster method for calculation in computer systems. We discuss binary signed digit representations, which are a class of redundant systems, later in this chapter.

We can further characterize number systems into canonical and non-canonical systems. This classification relates to the set of values S_i. A *canonical system* has a set of values defined as $\{0, 1, 2, \ldots, |S_i| - 1\}$, e.g., the integer decimal number system with its set $\{0, 1, 2, \ldots, 9\}$. A *non-canonical system* does not follow this convention. For example, consider a radix 10 number system with the digit set $\{-4, -3, \ldots, 5\}$, where the number $(3, -1, 5)$ is the integer decimal number

$3 \times 10^2 + (-1) \times 10^1 + 5 \times 10^0 = 295$. A noncanonical number system that has a digit set size larger than the radix (i.e., $|S_i| > R_i$) results in a redundant number system. For example, the binary signed digit representation has a digit set $\{-1, 0, 1\}$ with radix of 2; it has two representations for the number five, $(0, 1, 0, 1)$ and $(1, 0, -1, -1)$, making it a redundant number system.

5.2.2   Binary signed digit representations

We focus briefly on the binary signed digit representation due to its use in many low-level software and hardware algorithms to speed up arithmetic operations. *Binary signed digit*, which is sometimes also called ternary balanced notation [4], is a common positional, radix 2 notation with digit set $\{-1, 0, 1\}$. This is a noncanonical number system since it has multiple encodings for the numbers. For example, the number 3 can be represented as bit vector $(0, 1, 1)$ or $(1, -1, 0)$.

The first and perhaps most successful use of binary signed digits was Booth's algorithm for multiplying two numbers [5]. Booth's algorithm performs multiplication of two digits in two's complement representation by recoding one of the digits into a binary signed representation and performing addition, subtraction, and shift operations. Booth's algorithm is typically more efficient in cases where shifting is faster than addition. This was the case for Booth's desk calculator when he invented the algorithm in 1951, and this is also the case for a hardware implementation as shifting involves simple rewiring, and is essentially free.

Before we delve further into the usage and benefits of the binary signed digit format, we first define some basic terminology. Two representations $(X_n, X_{n-1}, \ldots, X_0)$ and $(Y_n, Y_{n-1}, \ldots, Y_0)$ are *equivalent* if they represent the same number, as well as have the same length and Hamming weight. The *Hamming weight* ω is defined as the number of nonzero digits, equivalently the total number of -1 and 1 digits in a binary signed digit representation. The minimal Hamming weight for a binary signed digit is on average equal to $(n + 1)/3$ [6]. A binary signed digit encoding is said to be *canonical* (or *sparse*) if no two adjacent digits are nonzero. This is often also referred to as the *nonadjacent form*.

Reitwiesner developed an optimal algorithm for recoding a number in two's complement representation into a minimal Hamming weight binary signed digit representation [7]. He also proved that this representation is unique under the assumption that the most significant digit is a zero; hence, the reason for calling it a canonical binary signed digit. Reitwiesner's algorithm is outlined in Figure 5.1. The algorithm takes as input a two's complement number $X = (X_{n-1}, \ldots, X_0)$ and outputs the number $Y = (Y_n, Y_{n-1}, \ldots, Y_0)$ in its canonical binary signed digit representation.

At its core, the algorithm is performing the operation $Y = (3X - X) \gg 1$. It performs the subtraction in bit by bit fashion and simply disregards the least significant bit, i.e., performs a right shift by one. The equation can also be written as $Y = (3X - X)/2$, which makes it abundantly clear that $Y = X$, i.e., the input number is the same as the output number, but in the canonical binary signed digit format.

INPUT: $(X_{n-1}, \ldots, X_0)_2$

OUTPUT: $(Y_n, \ldots, Y_0)_{BSD}$

$c_0 = X_{n+1} = X_n = 0$

for $i = 0 \rightarrow n$

$\qquad c_{i+1} = \lfloor (c_i + X_i + X_{i+1})/2 \rfloor$

$\qquad Y_i = c_i + X_i - 2c_{i+1}$

c_i	X_i	X_{i+1}	c_{i+1}	Y_i
0	0	*	0	0
0	0	0	0	1
0	1	1	1	−1
1	0	0	0	1
1	0	1	1	−1
1	1	*	1	0

$$
\begin{aligned}
2X = & \quad (X_{n-1}, X_{n-2}, X_{n-3}, \ldots, X_1, X_0, 0)_2 \\
+ X = & \qquad\quad (X_{n-1}, X_{n-2}, \ldots, X_2, X_1, X_0)_2 \\
\hline
3X = & \ (S_n, S_{n-1}, S_{n-2}, S_{n-3}, \ldots, S_1, S_0, X_0)_2
\end{aligned}
$$

where $3X =$

$$
\begin{aligned}
3X = & \ (S_n, S_{n-1}, S_{n-2}, S_{n-3}, \ldots, S_1, S_0, X_0)_2 \\
- X = & \qquad\quad (X_{n-1}, X_{n-2}, \ldots, X_2, X_1, X_0)_2 \\
\hline
2X = & \ (Y_n, Y_{n-1}, Y_{n-2}, Y_{n-3}, \ldots, Y_1, Y_0, 0)_2
\end{aligned}
$$

Figure 5.1 Reitwiesner's algorithm for canonical signed digit representation with minimal Hamming weight, where * denotes either 0 or 1.

We can write the binary expansion of $3X$ as

$$
X_0 + \sum_{i=0}^{n} S_i \cdot 2^{i+1}. \tag{5.7}
$$

We note that $S_i = (C_i + X_i + X_{i+1})$ modulo 2. C_i is the ith carry in. We can rewrite this expression to eliminate the modulo operation as

$$
S_i = C_i + X_i + X_{i+1} - 2\lfloor (C_i + X_i + X_{i+1})/2 \rfloor, \tag{5.8}
$$

since the carry out C_{i+1} is equal to 1 if and only if there are two or three 1s among C_i, X_i, X_{i+1}, i.e.,

$$
C_{i+1} = \lfloor (C_i + X_i + X_{i+1})/2 \rfloor. \tag{5.9}
$$

Substituting this back into the equation results in

$$
S_i = C_i + X_i + X_{i+1} - 2 \cdot C_{i+1}. \tag{5.10}
$$

Hence, $Y_i = S_i - X_{i+1} = C_i + X_i - 2C_{i+1}$.

Reitwiesner proved that his algorithm produces a canonical signed digit and that the canonical representation has minimal Hamming weight [7]. This is not to say that it is unique. It is possible to produce a non-canonical representation for a number that also has minimal Hamming weight. For example, (0, 1, 0, 1, 1) and (1, 0, −1, 0, −1) are equivalent representations for the number 11 and both have minimal Hamming weight.

Parhami [8] derived a generalized signed digit number system, where the digit set of a radix r number system is defined as $\{-\alpha, \alpha - 1, \ldots, \beta - 1, \beta\}$, where $\alpha \geq 0, \beta \geq 0$

and $\alpha + \beta + 1 \geq r$. The redundancy index ρ for these number systems is defined as $\rho = \alpha + \beta + 1 - r$. As an example, consider the binary-stored carry (BSC) number system [9]. In this number system, $r = 2$, $\alpha = 0$, $\beta = 2$, and $\rho = 1$. The digit set in BSC is $\{0, 1, 2\}$. Since we have a redundancy of 2, we encode the three digits ($\{0, 1, 2\}$) using two binary numbers, e.g., $\{00, 01, 10\}$.

5.2.3   Fixed point representations

It is often useful and necessary to use fixed point representations. This is needed when we require the use of rational numbers; these are the set of numbers expressible as s/t, where s and t are integer numbers and $t \neq 0$. We further constrain this such that $t = 2^i$. Finally, as the name suggests, the binary point in a fixed point number always stays in the same place keeping a prespecified number of integer and fractional bits. The following denotes an unsigned n-bit fixed point binary number consisting of a integer bits and b fractional bits:

$$X = X_{a-1}X_{a-2}\cdots X_1 X_0 \cdot X_{-1}X_{-2}\cdots X_{-b}, \tag{5.11}$$

such that

$$X = \sum_{i=-b}^{a-1} X_i \cdot 2^i. \tag{5.12}$$

This can also be written as

$$X = \left(\frac{1}{2^b}\right) \sum_{i=0}^{a+b-1} 2^i \cdot X_{i-b}. \tag{5.13}$$

We can denote the unsigned fixed point number as $X(a, b)$, where a and b, respectively, indicate the number of integer bits and the number of fractional bits of the representation. Note that the unsigned integer representation is a special case of the unsigned fixed point representation where $b = 0$. In this case, Equation (5.13) reduces to Equation (5.3).

Choosing the number of integer and fractional bits requires a tradeoff between resolution, range, and accuracy. *Resolution* is defined as the smallest nonzero magnitude. This is directly related to the number of fractional bits, i.e., the resolution of a binary fixed point number is $1/2^b$. The *range* is the difference between the most negative number and the most positive number, i.e., $2^a - 2^{-b}$, which is largely dependent on the number of integer bits; the range increases as a grows larger. *Accuracy* is the magnitude of the maximum difference between a real value and its representation, i.e., the accuracy is equal to $1/2^{b+1}$. The accuracy is related to the resolution by the following: accuracy(x) = resolution(x)/2. For example, consider a fixed point representation with one fractional bit. A worst-case scenario for a fixed point representation would be the number 1/4 since it is exactly 1/4 away from both the representable numbers 0 and 1/2. Therefore, fixed point numbers are computationally efficient for arithmetic operations, yet may suffer from limited resolution, range, and accuracy.

We can also use the two's complement representation when dealing with fixed point numbers. The value of an n-bit rational number is interpreted as

$$X = \left(\frac{1}{2^b}\right)\left[-2^{n-1} \cdot X_{n-1} + \sum_{i=0}^{n-2} 2_i \cdot X_i\right]. \tag{5.14}$$

An n-bit number X lies in the range

$$-2^{n-1-b} \leq X \leq 2^{n-1-b} - \frac{1}{2^b}. \tag{5.15}$$

DSP applications often use a normalized, fractional representation where the numbers reside in the range $(-1, 1)$. This bounds the growth of the number representation during multiplication. An n-bit representation is defined as

$$X = -X_0 + \sum_{b=1}^{n-1} X_b \cdot 2^{-b}. \tag{5.16}$$

Here the sign bit is denoted as $-X_0$ and X_b are binary variables as in the previous equations; X_{n-1} is the least significant bit.

5.2.4   Floating point representations

In floating point numbers the resolution and range issues are ameliorated by allocating part of the representation to an exponent. Contrast this with fixed point notation where the exponent is implicit. By explicitly stating the exponent, we increase the range of representable numbers. This allows us to encode extremely large and very small numbers. As such, a floating point representation is used as a characterization of a real-number system. However, since we are still dealing with a finite number of bits, we obviously can only represent a fixed set of numbers. As is the case with any fixed point system, the number of encodings of an n-bit number is 2^n.

The representation of a floating point number contains two components: the significand (or mantissa) M_x and the exponent E_x. A floating point number is derived as follows:

$$X = M_x \cdot 2^{E_x}. \tag{5.17}$$

This assumes a base of 2, which is most common, e.g., it is used in the IEEE 754 floating point number standard [10]. Of course, other bases could be used; these simply correspond to changing the "2" in Equation (5.17) to your chosen base. The IEEE 754 standard has a number of subtleties including exponent biasing and representations for positive and negative infinity and invalid numbers (denoted NaN – "not a number"). This book focuses almost exclusively on fixed point number systems, and we will therefore not discuss the finer details of floating point numbers and the IEEE 754 standard.

The main advantage of the floating point representation is the increase in range as compared to a fixed point notation. The range of an n-bit two's complement fixed point number is $2^n - 1$. The range of the floating point representation is

$$(2^m - 1) \cdot 2^{2^{n-m-1}}, \tag{5.18}$$

where n is the total number of bits and m is the number of bits of the significand. To give a more concrete example of a floating point range, consider the case of a single precision 32-bit IEEE 754 floating point number. Here we have 32 bits ($n = 32$) with 23 bits for the significand ($m = 23$). Therefore, the dynamic range is

$$(2^{23} - 1) \cdot 2^{2^{32-23}-1} \approx 1.4 \times 10^{45}. \tag{5.19}$$

Compare this to the dynamic range of a 32-bit fixed point number which is $2^{32} - 1$ $\approx 4.3 \times 10^9$.

One major disadvantage of a floating point representation is its accuracy. Since we must encode the exponent and possibly a sign bit,[1] we have fewer bits to represent the significand. This means that, in the general case, the accuracy is reduced. However, it should be noted that the accuracy of numbers that are close to "0" is very high. This is due to the largest representable negative exponent. Since small numbers are often used extensively in the real-number system, the IEEE 754 standard employs a method called subnormal numbers that increases the accuracy of the numbers around zero. Another disadvantage is that floating point arithmetic can introduce round off errors, which can make analysis of floating point computation difficult.

Perhaps the most significant disadvantage of floating point numbers is their computational complexity. Addition of two floating point numbers requires normalizing the two numbers, adding the numbers, properly rounding the result, renormalization, and handling numerous exceptions. A typical floating point addition takes five cycles – a five-fold increase over fixed point addition; multiplication and division take even longer, in some cases as many as 24 and 157 cycles, respectively [11]. As a result, many embedded architectures (e.g., microcontrollers) do not have hardware floating point units and DSP applications shy away from the use of floating point representation due to significant slowdown in computation time compared with fixed point representation.

5.3 Two-operand addition

We start our discussion on arithmetic operations with perhaps the most basic and commonly occurring operation – the addition of two positive fixed point radix-2 (binary) numbers. Moreover, we begin by looking at the simplest case – the addition of two one-bit numbers.

---

[1] As is the case in the IEEE 754 standard.

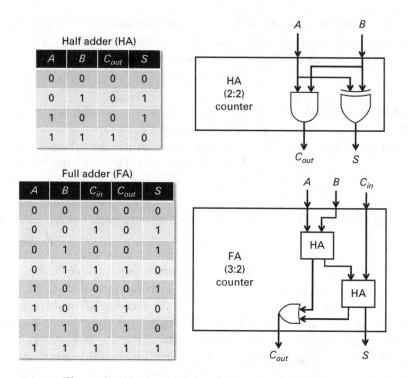

Half adder (HA)			
A	B	C_{out}	S
0	0	0	0
0	1	0	1
1	0	0	1
1	1	1	0

Full adder (FA)				
A	B	C_{in}	C_{out}	S
0	0	0	0	0
0	0	1	0	1
0	1	0	0	1
0	1	1	1	0
1	0	0	0	1
1	0	1	1	0
1	1	0	1	0
1	1	1	1	1

Figure 5.2 The truth tables and implementations for a half adder or equivalently a (2:2) counter and a full adder i.e., (3:2) counter.

The addition of two one-bit numbers gives a result in the range [0, 2]. This creates a truth table as described in Figure 5.2. Therefore, it requires two outputs – a sum (S) and a carry out (C_{out}). The resulting half adder is often called a [2:2] counter because it takes two one-bit numbers and encodes them into a two-bit number. The carry out causes most of the headaches for developing fast multi-bit adders; we will discuss this in more detail shortly. Due to the carry, we require a full adder, or equivalently a [3:2] counter to compute multi-bit operands. Figure 5.2 also shows the truth table and a possible implementation of a full adder.

Half and full adders act as building blocks for a binary n-bit two-operand addition. Before we discuss implementation details for two-operand adders, we should provide a formal definition. An unsigned n-bit binary adder has two operands A and B, each representing a number in the range [0, $2^n - 1$]. It has a third input carry in, $C_{in} \in \{0, 1\}$. There are two outputs – the sum S in the range [0, $2^n - 1$] and carry out $C_{out} \in \{0, 1\}$. The operation is described succinctly as

$$A + B + C_{in} = 2^n \cdot C_{out} + S. \qquad (5.20)$$

Note that when n = 1, this reduces into a full adder.

There are a large number of different implementations for two-operand addition. We primarily focus on the basic implementations that should be familiar to most readers. Therefore, we do not provide a large amount of detail and refer readers to arithmetic textbooks for more details [1–3]. However, we do feel that it is important to at least mention these basic implementations as they provide much insight into the essential challenges that the optimizations in this book confront.

5.3.1 Ripple carry adder (RCA)

The RCA is perhaps the simplest implementation of two-operand addition (see Figure 5.3). It is a cascaded array of full adders where each full adder calculates a sum bit (S_i) from the corresponding input bits (A_i, B_i) along with the carry out bit from the previous input bits (A_{i-1}, B_{i-1}). The worst case delay of a ripple carry adder corresponds to the path starting at the $A\emptyset$ or $B\emptyset$ and propagating through each full adder in the chain reaching either C_{out} or S_{n-1}. The determination of whether C_{out} or S_{n-1} is computed last depends on the implementation of the full adder. In the implementation of the full adder given in Figure 5.2, C_{out} will be determined after S_{n-1}, therefore, the delay of the ripple carry adder is roughly equal to the delay of the carry chain, which is linear to the size of the operands, i.e., $O(n)$. The area of the ripple carry adders is $n \times$ area(FA); hence, both the area and the delay of a ripple carry adder are $O(n)$.

The calculation of the carries limits the speed of two-operand addition. There are a number of ways to reduce the delay of addition including reducing the carry delay, changing the linear delay to something smaller (e.g., $O(n)$ to $O(\log n)$), adding a completion signal such that always waiting for the worst case delay is not necessary, and finally employing a different number representation.

We first consider a switched ripple carry adder, which is often called a Manchester adder. The switched ripple carry adder relies on the fact that a carry out is not always a function of the carry in of that stage. To see this more clearly, consider the case where the two operand bits A_i and B_i are both equal to "0." It is clear that the carry out from this ith stage will be "0." A similar situation occurs when A_i and B_i are both equal to "1." Here the carry out will be "1" regardless of the value of the carry in. These two cases are denoted "kill" and "generate." When one of A_i and B_i is "0" and the other is "1," then the carry out is equal to the value of the carry in to that stage. This case is called "propagate." Figure 5.4 gives the truth table for all of these cases.

The cases, kill, generate, propagate are computed with a NOR, AND, and XOR, respectively, making the KGP unit as shown in Figure 5.4. We can then use this KGP unit along with a set of switches to quickly generate all of the carries. Note that the kill, generate, and propagate values of each stage are ready at the same time – the delay time of the KGP unit. Therefore, the switches are all set at the same time. In the worst case, the carry propagates from C_{in} to C_{out}, just as in the ripple carry adder. However, here the carry propagation only has to go through one switch at each stage. The delay is still $O(n)$; however, if the switch delay is small, then this scheme is effective. Note that the calculation of an individual C_{out} in the ripple carry adder is equal to the delay through two half adders and one OR gate if you use the implementation shown in Figure 5.2.

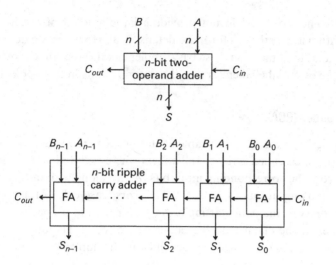

Figure 5.3 The interface for an n-bit adder and the implementation details of an n-bit ripple carry adder.

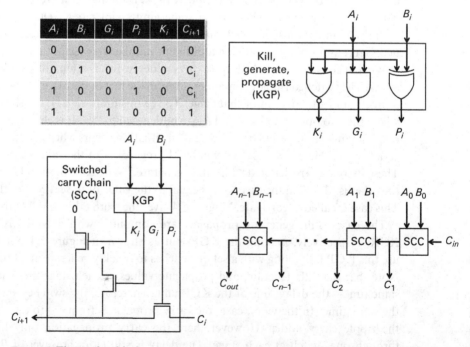

Figure 5.4 The truth table for generate (G_i), propagate (P_i) and kill (K_i) along with their implementation. The KGP unit is used to create a switched carry chain unit. In turn these are connected in series to quickly produce the set of carries needed to compute two-operand n-bit addition. This is called switched ripple carry or Manchester addition.

5.3.2   Carry look-ahead adder (CLA)

The next implementation that we consider for addition is the CLA. The basic premise here is to compute the carry bits in parallel. In the extreme case, we can compute all the carries simultaneously. This can become prohibitively expensive as the size of the adder increases (i.e., the number of bits of the operands increases). Therefore, we generally restrict the total number of carries that we compute in parallel. Furthermore, we can compute the carries in a hierarchical fashion, which provides a delay reduction from $O(n)$ to $O(\log n)$.

For the sake of simplicity and to aid understanding, let us first consider a fully parallel implementation for a four-bit CLA adder. Once again, we will use the ideas of generating and propagating carries in order to calculate the carries. Referring again to Figure 5.4, we note that the ith carry out is a function of the generate and propagate of the ith input bits (A_i and B_i). More specifically we can write this function recursively as

$$C_{i+1} = G_i + C_i \cdot P_i. \tag{5.21}$$

This equation states there is a carry out from the current bit (note that $Carryout_i = C_{i+1}$) if the current input bits (A_i and B_i) generate a carry or if there is a carry in, and the current input bits propagate it. Using this function recursively allows us to calculate each C_i based solely on generate and propagate functions of the current and previous input bits (G_0 through G_i and P_0 through P_i, respectively). To demonstrate this more concretely, consider the calculation of C_2. Based on Equation (5.21), we calculate C_1 as

$$C_1 = G_0 + C_0 \cdot P_0. \tag{5.22}$$

We can then substitute this into Equation (5.21) again to calculate the value of C_2:

$$C_2 = G_1 + (G_0 + C_0 \cdot P_0) \cdot P_1. \tag{5.23}$$

A two-bit CLA implementation is shown in Figure 5.5. The sum bits S_i can be generated as $P_i \oplus C_i$. This is due to the fact that when the propagate signal is "true," exactly one of the inputs is "1." In this case, we will get a "1" in S_i if C_i is "0." If C_i is "1," then the result of addition is 10_2 meaning the S_i is "0." If both C_i and P_i are "0," then S_i is also "0."

It is clear that if we create a larger CLA adder, the hardware required to calculate the carries of the higher-order bits will become too large to be practical. However, it is possible to apply the CLA concept recursively. As we shall see, this will allow us to reduce the delay of the carry chain to $O(\log n)$.

To make larger CLAs, we must first compute the generate and propagate functions for the two-bit CLA. These functions are shown in Figure 5.5. The generate function G^1 describes the cases in which these two bits will create a carry. This is true when the most significant bits invoke a carry or the least significant bits invoke a carry and that carry is propagated through the most significant bits, i.e.,

$$G_1^0 + G_0^0 \cdot P_1^0. \tag{5.24}$$

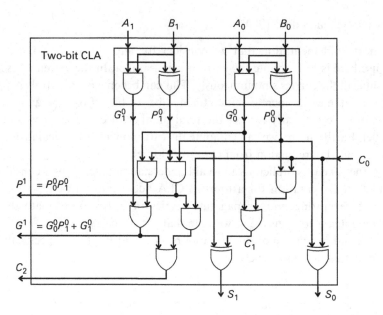

Figure 5.5 The logical depiction of a two-bit CLA. The circuit generates the carry as well as the propagate and generate values for the two input bits ($A_{0,1}$ and $B_{0,1}$).

A carry in to these two bits will propagate through if, and only if, both bit pairs propagate it, i.e.,

$$P_0^0 \cdot P_1^0. \tag{5.25}$$

We can generalize these statements for the case of an m-bit CLA adder as

$$P = \underset{i=0}{\overset{m-1}{\mathrm{AND}}} P_i, \tag{5.26}$$

$$G = \underset{j=0}{\overset{m-1}{\mathrm{OR}}} \left(\underset{i=j+1}{\overset{m-1}{\mathrm{AND}}} P_i \right) \cdot G_j. \tag{5.27}$$

Figure 5.6 shows a four-bit CLA formed by using two two-bit CLAs along with a two-bit carry look-ahead generator (CLG). The carry look-ahead generator computes the generate and propagate signals for this four-bit CLA, which can be used recursively once again to create a three-level CLA. The propagate and generate signals for this level are equivalent to those from the two-bit CLA that we just described.

Figure 5.7 extends the CLA to another (third) level. Here we simply replicate the two-bit CLG. This third-level CLG creates the carry for the eight sets of input bits. We can see the power of the CLA for reducing the delay of the carries. The critical path of the carry for the fourth set of bits (C_4) goes through one two-bit CLA and one two-bit CLG. Note that C_4 for a ripple carry adder must pass through four full adders. The delay saving is even more evident when we consider C_8.

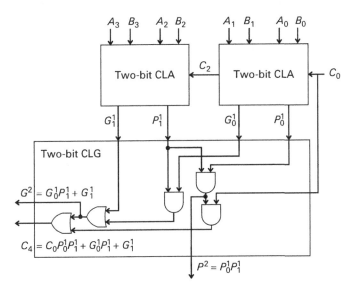

Figure 5.6 The schematic for a four-bit CLA. It includes two two-bit CLAs as well as a two-bit CLG. The CLG produces generate and propagate signals for four inputs (A_{0-3}, B_{0-3}) using the generate and propagate signals computed in the two two-bit CLAs. The CLG also generates C_4.

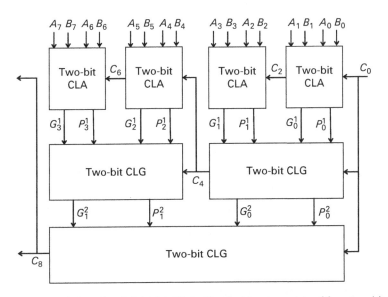

Figure 5.7 A three-level eight-bit CLA. The first level consists of four two-bit CLAs. The next two levels are composed using two-bit CLG circuits. A CLA reduces the carry chain by recursively calculating higher-order carry bits. For example, the delay for C_6 is equal to the delay through a two-bit CLA, a two-bit CLG, and another two-bit CLA. Contrast this with a ripple carry adder where the delay of C_6 must pass through six full adders.

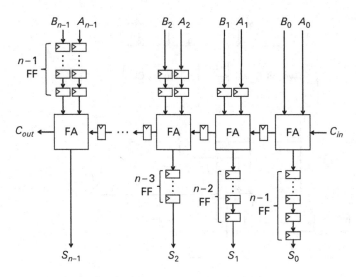

Figure 5.8 A pipelined n-bit ripple carry adder. (FA – full adder.)

The delay of C_8 for a ripple carry adder is equivalent to the delay of eight full adders. On the other hand, the delay of C_8 in the CLA goes through one CLA and two CLGs. This is a saving of approximately eight full adders to three CLA levels. As we project this to even more levels, the benefits become even more pronounced. More formally, the delay of an n-bit CLA using groups of two bits is equal to the summation of the delay through one two-bit CLA, $(\log_2 N - 1)$ CLGs to compute the P and G as well as an additional $(\log_2 N - 1)$ CLGs to compute carries of the bits, and finally an XOR gate for each of the sum bits (as shown in Figure 5.5).

5.3.3 Pipelined adder

Many DSP applications are driven by throughput rather than strictly delay requirements. It is possible to increase the throughput of an adder by pipelining. One does this by introducing flip flops (FFs) into the design. The FFs are generally used to shorten the length of the critical path, which, in the case of addition, primarily deals with the carry chain. Figure 5.8 shows a pipelined n-bit ripple carry adder. The adder is pipelined at every bit, which allows it to handle n addition operations at any instance. You can see that an FF is added to the carry chain between every full adder. We must also add FFs to the inputs and outputs to insure the data is properly synchronized.

5.4 Multiple-operand addition

The summation of multiple operands plays a major role in many arithmetic algorithms. For example, multiplication requires the addition of shifted versions of the multiplicand. Filters and other linear systems perform a summation of the input samples multiplied by a set of constants. Polynomial equations require the addition of a number of variables along with multiplications that again require additional summations.

In this section, we describe some of the basic tenets of multiple-operand addition. We start by formalizing the problem. Then we discuss the addition of multiple operands using carry propagate adders, e.g., any of the two-operand adders described in the previous section. After that, we show how redundant digit representations can be employed to reduce the time required to calculate multiple-operand summations. We start with carry save adders (CSAs), and then expand these ideas to higher-order counters and compressors. Finally, we describe the distributed arithmetic method for multiple-operand addition.

5.4.1   Definitions

The fundamental problem that we are tackling is the summation of m operands. In order to simplify the notation and discussion, we assume that each operand has n bits. The formulation and algorithms can be extended to handle operands with varying bit widths though we do not discuss such cases in this section. The problem is succinctly stated as:

$$S = \sum_{i=1}^{m} O_i[n] \tag{5.28}$$

Figure 5.9 gives a graphical depiction of Equation (5.28). Here we have m operands $(O_1, O_2, O_3, \ldots, O_m)$, where each operand has n bits. The resulting value S requires

$$n + \lceil \log_2 m \rceil \tag{5.29}$$

bits in order to correctly maintain the range of summed operands. We can view this as the summation of an $n \times m$ rectangle of bits.

The summation of unsigned operands is straightforward. Signed operands require a bit of housekeeping. In the simplest case, each two's complement operand is sign extended such that it is $n + \lceil \log_2 m \rceil$ bits wide. This requires additional hardware and/or time to sum the extended bits. It is possible to simplify this procedure so that it does not require extraneous range for the input operands though we will not provide the details in this book. For a detailed discussion on how this is done, please see [1].

5.4.2   Sequential carry propagation summation

We start our discussion of multiple-operand addition with the most basic case: the sequential summation of the multiple operands using any of the two-operand adders described in Section 5.3. The two-operand adders from Section 5.3 are often described as carry propagate adders (CPAs) because they produce a result in a conventional fixed radix number representation, e.g., two's complement. To do this, they must handle the propagation of results from one bit to the next

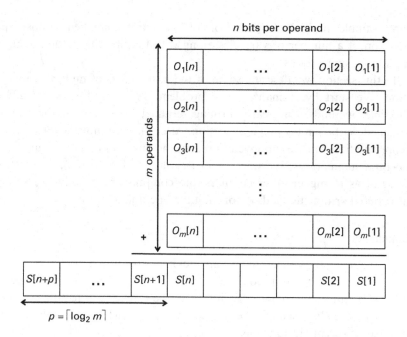

Figure 5.9 The summation of m operands each with n bits into the number S; S requires $n + \lceil \log m \rceil$ bits in order to maintain the range of the summed operands.

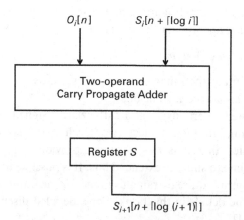

Figure 5.10 Sequential summation of i numbers using CPAs. O_i are the n-bit input operands and S_i is the summation of the first i input operands. The summation requires $O(\log i)$ additional bits as it progresses to handle the range extension required to add multiple operands.

internally. As we discussed earlier, CPAs are primarily classified by the way they compute the propagation of values from lower to higher bits.

Figure 5.10 depicts a sequential summation of multiple operands using a CPA. The m operands ($O_1[n]$ through $O_m[n]$) are fed to the adder one at a time. $S_i[n + \lceil \log i \rceil]$ holds the running summation of the operands. $S_1[n]$ is initially set to 0. Note that the number of bits increases by a factor of $O(\log i)$ as we sum through the ith input operand. Therefore, for summing m operands, we require an $O(n + \log m)$-bit CPA.

This type of multiple-operand addition is simple and area efficient; however, its delay depends on both n (the number of bits of the operands) and m. The dependence on n is a function of the delay of the specific CPA that is utilized. For example, a ripple carry adder has a delay of $O(n)$, while a CLA has a delay of $O(\log n)$, as described in the previous section. Therefore, the total delay of an $m \times n$ summation is $O(mn)$ using a ripple carry adder and $O(m \log n)$ using a CLA.

5.4.3 Parallel carry propagation summation

We can tradeoff area for time by performing many additions in parallel. Once again consider the summation of m operands. These operands can be summed using a tree as shown in Figure 5.11. The tree has depth of $O(\log m)$. The delay of the summation depends on the type of CPA that is employed. If we use ripple carry adders, the delay is $O(n \log m)$ and if we use CLAs it is $O(\log mn)$. This reduces the delay compared with the delay of the serial carry propagation summation. Of course, the reduction in delay does not come without a cost. The area of this parallel carry propagation summation architecture is $O(m)$ CPAs. This compares to $O(1)$ CPAs needed in the serial carry propagation summation architecture.

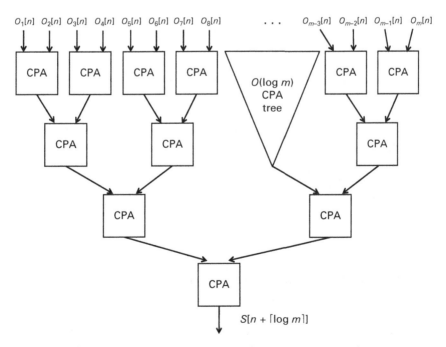

Figure 5.11 Parallel summation of m numbers using a tree of CPAs. O_i are the n-bit input operands and S is the summation of the m input operands. The summation requires $O(n + \log m)$.

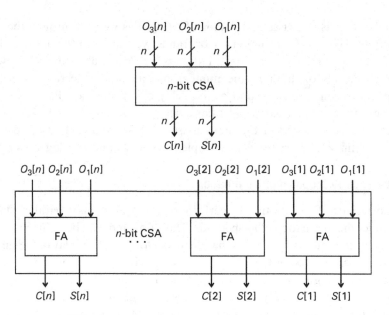

Figure 5.12 CSA: three operands O_1, O_2, and O_3 are summed into a two-bit encoded output denoted by C and S, where C is the carry bit and S is the sum bit. (FA = full adder.)

5.4.4   Redundant digit summation

It is possible to reduce this delay further by employing redundant digit representations during the summation of the operands. The redundant digit representation allows us to reduce the delay by largely eliminating carry propagate calculation. While the use of a redundant digit representation can decrease the time to compute a multiple-operand addition, it does have some drawbacks. First, the output is in a redundant representation, which may not be suitable for the given application. Transforming the redundant number into a more conventional form, e.g., two's complement, can combat this. This is often done using a CPA. Also, redundant number systems require additional bits for encoding which depends on the amount of redundancy in the representation. The final drawback is that some operations, e.g., comparison and sign detection, are not trivial especially when compared to a fixed radix system.

5.4.5   Carry save adder (CSA)

Perhaps the most fundamental use of redundant numbers is summation using CSAs. An n-bit CSA is built using n full adders. It takes as input three n-bit numbers and outputs two encoded n-bit numbers commonly called the sum (S) and carry (C). The architecture of a CSA is shown in Figure 5.12. This representation is redundant since the $S[i]$ bit has the same weight as the $C[i-1]$ bit.

If we wish to find the nonredundant number we must sum $S[i]$ with $C[i]$ left shifted by one bit. This requires a CPA. Figure 5.13 shows this transformation

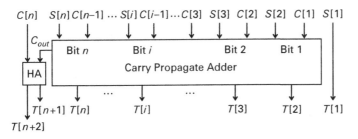

Figure 5.13 The transformation of the redundant numbers $C[n]$ and $S[n]$ into the non-redundant number $T[n+2]$. A carry propagate adders is used to compute $T[n+2] = S[n] + C[n] \ll 1$. (HA – half adder.)

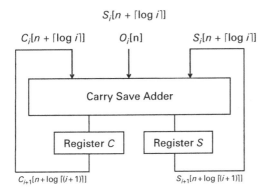

Figure 5.14 Sequential summation of i numbers using a CSA. O_i are the n-bit input operands and S_i is the summation of the first i input operands. The summation requires $O(\log i)$ additional bits as it progresses to handle the range extension required to add multiple operands. The resultant number is left in redundant form (C, S).

from redundant number to nonredundant number (e.g., two's complement) $T = S + C \ll 1$. The least significant bit of T (i.e., $T[1]$) is solely determined by $S[1]$. The resultant number T requires $n + 2$ bits. The most significant bit of T is determined by the carry out of the CPA added with $C[n]$.

Figure 5.14 shows a sequential architecture for summing i n-bit operands using a CSA. In each cycle one new operand is fed into the CSA. $C_1[n]$ and $S_1[n]$ are both initially set to 0. The runtime of this architecture is $O(m)$ since the CSA performs its calculation in $O(1)$. Note that the final representation is left in a redundant number system (in terms of C and S). This can be converted to a nonredundant form by using a CPA, as described previously and shown in Figure 5.13. With this conversion (assuming a fast $O(\log n)$ CPA), the total runtime of this sequential CSA architecture is $O(m + \log n)$. The area of this architecture is $O(m + \log n)$. Compare this to the runtime and the area of the sequential CPA architecture which are $O(m \log n)$ and $O(m + \log n)$, respectively, assuming we use a fast CPA. As you can see, the use of redundant numbers allows us to eliminate the

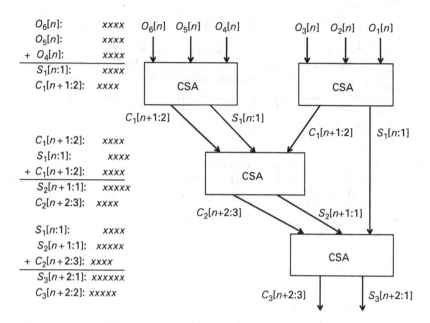

The following summation tables appear alongside the figure:

$O_6[n]$: $xxxx$
$O_5[n]$: $xxxx$
$+ O_4[n]$: $xxxx$
$S_1[n{:}1]$: $xxxx$
$C_1[n+1{:}2]$: $xxxx$

$C_1[n+1{:}2]$: $xxxx$
$S_1[n{:}1]$: $xxxx$
$+ C_1[n+1{:}2]$: $xxxx$
$S_2[n+1{:}1]$: $xxxxx$
$C_2[n+2{:}3]$: $xxxx$

$S_1[n{:}1]$: $xxxx$
$S_2[n+1{:}1]$: $xxxxx$
$+ C_2[n+2{:}3]$: $xxxx$
$S_3[n+2{:}1]$: $xxxxxx$
$C_3[n+2{:}2]$: $xxxxx$

Figure 5.15 A parallel summation of six operands using CSAs. The carry outputs (C_i) are left shifted by one bit. This situation must be taken care of when summing input numbers. For example, the final CSA has inputs with different ranges in different bit positions. The final result is left in redundant representation.

dependence on the number of bits in the operands. We do still have a $O(\log n)$ dependence; however, this is due to the fact that we are using a CPA to transform out of the redundant number system. If we had left the number in redundant representation, the runtime of the summation would be independent of n.

It is possible to perform a parallel summation of operands in a similar manner to the parallel implementation using CPAs (see Section 5.4.3 and Figure 5.11). The major differences lie in the fact that we are using CSAs, which have three inputs and two outputs. The result of the carry output is left shifted by one bit; we must be cognizant of this fact during the summation. Figure 5.15 shows the summation of six operands. Here we assume that each of the operands has four bits (i.e., $n = 4$). The two CSAs at the top level reduce operands $O_1 - O_6$ to four operands. Note that the carry outputs $C_1[n + 1{:}2]$ are shifted by one bit as they are fed into the second level CSA. This CSA computes the results from C_1 as well as the S_1. The output of the CSA is a sum S_2, which is a five-bit number ([$n + 1{:}1$]), while the carry out C_2 is a four-bit number, but left shifted by two bits ([$n + 2{:}3$]). The final CSA reduces the six operands into the sum and carry outputs. This sum is a six-bit number [$n + 2{:}1$] and the carry is a five-bit number shifted left by one bit [$n + 2{:}3$]. These two redundant numbers can be transformed into a two's complement number system in a similar manner to that shown in Figure 5.13 though they must be shifted correspondingly.

5.4.6   Counters and compressors

The full adders used in the CSAs described in the previous subsection are also called [3:2] counters since they compute the sum of three one-bit numbers into a two-bit encoded number. We can extend this idea beyond three numbers and it is often quite beneficial to do this when we must sum a large number of operands. The next logical counter takes four inputs. Since these four inputs will create an output between zero and four, we need three outputs – a [4:3] counter. This idea can be extended even further, e.g., to a [7:3] counter, a [15:4] counter and so on.

A compressor is similar to a counter in that it takes a number of one-bit inputs and outputs their sum as an encoded number with fewer bits. In addition, the compressor takes as input some carry in signals and produces the same number of carry out signals. As an example, consider the [4:2] compressor shown in Figure 5.16. The figure shows two consecutive bits of an adder that internally utilizes [3:2] counters. One of the carry outputs from the $(i-1)$th bit is fed into the [4:2] compressor for the ith bit. This bit is summed along with the sum output of the first full adder and one of the inputs (here it is operand $O_1[i]$). Note that the critical path of this structure is two full adders. Therefore, even though there is a carry, it is limited, unlike the carry chain in a CPA. Hence the delay of this adder is $O(1)$.

Figure 5.17 shows the functional depiction of an n-bit [4:2] compressor adder. There are four n-bit operands that are summed into two redundant n-bit outputs. The figure is quite similar to a CSA with the obvious difference that there are four input operands as opposed to three input operands in the CSA. The [4:2] compressor adder has $O(1)$ delay where the constant is the delay through two full adders and has an area of $O(n)$.

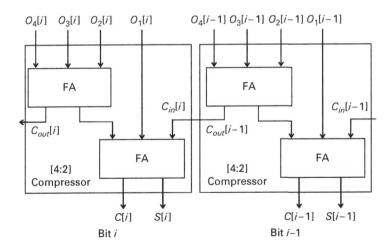

Figure 5.16 The ith and $(i-1)$th bits of an adder bit implemented using [4:2] compressors. The four input operands are transformed into a redundant number system that utilizes two bits per output. The compressors have a limited carry chain that only requires a delay through the next higher compressor bit. Therefore, this adder still has $O(1)$ delay.

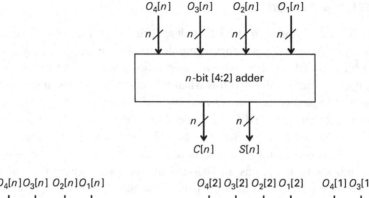

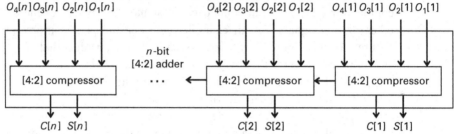

Figure 5.17 A [4:2] compressor adder tree. Four n-bit operands are compressed into a redundant number system where each of the n bits is encoded in two bits.

We can extend this further to a [5:2] compressor adder. Once again, as with the [4:2] compressor, five inputs output a value in the range 0–5, hence, requiring three bits. The [5:2] compressor adder uses three full adders. The carry out of the full adders is fed into the next higher bits in a similar manner as was done with the [4:2] compressor tree. Figure 5.18 shows two bit slices of the [5:2] compressor adder. Much like the other redundant adders, the [5:2] adder has $O(1)$ delay where the constant is the propagation through three full adders and it has an area of $O(n)$.

5.4.7   Distributed arithmetic

The term "distributed arithmetic" is derived from the fact that the arithmetic operations are not easily apparent and are often "distributed" in an unfamiliar manner. The most common form of distributed arithmetic computes the sum of a product computation, or equivalently a vector dot product operation; these are frequently found in filtering and frequency transformation functions. It performs constant multiplication in a bit serial manner using lookup tables.

The method itself is rather old and was developed in the late 1960s independently by Croiser *et al.* [12] and Zohar [13]. It languished in obscurity for several decades but has seen a resurgence since the 1990s due to the increased use of FPGAs in DSP applications. Since an FPGA is essentially an array of small LUTs, distributed arithmetic maps extremely well to their architecture.

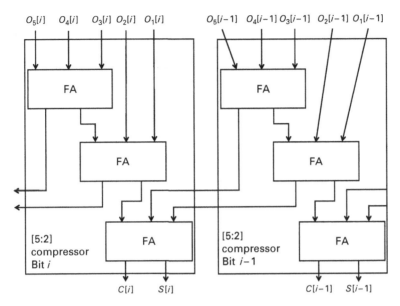

Figure 5.18 The ith and $(i-1)$th bits of an adder bit using [5:2] compressors. The five input operands are transformed into a redundant number system that utilizes two bits per output. The compressors have a limited carry chain that only requires a delay through the next higher compressor bit. Therefore, this adder still has $O(1)$ delay.

For an example of distributed arithmetic, consider the evaluation of an inner product:

$$Y = \sum_{k=1}^{K} A_k \cdot X_k, \tag{5.30}$$

where A_k are a set of constant coefficients and X_k are the input data. This operation is equivalent to an FIR filter or a one-dimensional linear system. Substituting Equation (5.16) into Equation (5.30) for each X_k results in the following:

$$Y = \sum_{k=1}^{K} A_k \left[-X_{k0} + \sum_{b=1}^{B-1} X_{kb} \cdot 2^{-b} \right]. \tag{5.31}$$

Now, by exchanging the order of the summations we get the following:

$$Y = \sum_{b=1}^{B-1} \left[\sum_{k=1}^{K} A_k \cdot X_{kb} \right] \cdot 2^{-b} + \sum_{k=1}^{K} A_k \cdot (-X_{k0}). \tag{5.32}$$

This is the distributed arithmetic form of the sum of products. The key insight in this computation is that the term

$$\sum_{k=1}^{K} A_k \cdot X_{kb} \tag{5.33}$$

consists of binary constants A_k, which means that it will only have 2^K possible values. This allows us to precompute all these values, store them in a lookup table,

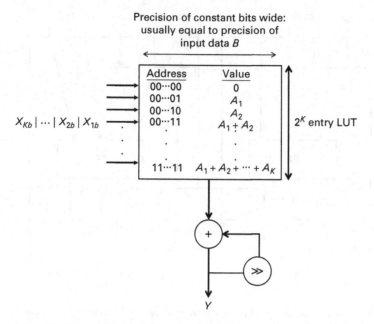

Figure 5.19 Distributed arithmetic architecture for inner product computation. The bits are fed serially into the lookup table, which is used in lieu of a multiplier. The result is summed and shifted with the previous partial products.

and use the individual inputs X_{kb} as an address in the lookup table. This is done in a bit serial manner allowing each input value to be accumulated and shifted.

This process is perhaps made clearer by expanding the terms in Equation (5.31):

$$Y = A_1 \cdot \left(-X_{10} + X_{11} \cdot 2^{-1} + X_{12} \cdot 2^{-2} + \cdots + X_{1(B-1)} \cdot 2^{-(B-1)}\right)$$
$$+ A_2 \cdot \left(-X_{20} + X_{21} \cdot 2^{-1} + X_{22} \cdot 2^{-2} + \cdots + X_{2(B-1)} \cdot 2^{-(B-1)}\right) + \cdots$$
$$+ A_K \cdot \left(-X_{K0} + X_{K1} \cdot 2^{-1} + X_{K2} \cdot 2^{-2} + \cdots + X_{K(B-1)} \cdot 2^{-(B-1)}\right). \quad (5.34)$$

In this case, each summation involves all bits from one variable. Each line is computing the product of one of the constants multiplied by one of the input variables and then summing each of these results. Therefore, there are K summation lines – one for each of the constants A_k.

Now, consider the same inner product calculation by using the expansion from Equation (5.32):

$$Y = [A_1 \cdot X_{11} + A_2 \cdot X_{21} + A_3 \cdot X_{31} + \cdots + A_K \cdot X_{K1}] \cdot 2^{-1}$$
$$+ [A_1 \cdot X_{12} + A_2 \cdot X_{22} + A_3 \cdot X_{32} + \cdots + A_K \cdot X_{K2}] \cdot 2^{-2} + \cdots$$
$$+ [A_1 \cdot X_{1(B-1)} + A_2 \cdot X_{2(B-1)} + A_3 \cdot X_{3(B-1)} + \cdots + A_K \cdot X_{K(B-1)}] \cdot 2^{-(B-1)}$$
$$+ A_1 \cdot (-X_{10}) + A_2 \cdot (-X_{20}) + A_3 \cdot (-X_{30}) + \cdots + A_K \cdot (-X_{K0}). \quad (5.35)$$

Here, each line is calculating the final product by using one bit (of the same significance) from all input values. The first summation line calculates the value of the output resulting when $b = 1$, or the most significant bit; the second line when $b = 2$, and so on. The last corresponds to the sign bit. This effectively replaces the constant multiplication with a lookup table. Since each X value is Boolean, we can hold all possible values of the constants A in the lookup table with 2^K entries. Then the computation corresponding to each line of Equation (5.35) is performed by addressing the lookup table with the appropriate values as dictated by the individual X variables. Each line is computed serially and the outputs are shifted by the appropriate amounts. The result of the final computation (Y) is available after B cycles. This is usually, but not always, equal to the width of the input data. The last line of Equation (5.35), which corresponds to the sign bit, must be handled in a special manner due to the negation of the X variables. This can be handled by storing 2^K additional entries in the lookup table corresponding to the negative values stored, or by adding additional control logic that subtracts this result instead of adding it. Figure 5.19 presents a visual depiction of the distributed arithmetic version of inner product computation.

5.5   Summary

This chapter presented material on some fundamental ideas and properties of digital arithmetic that are required to understand the polynomial expressions and linear systems optimizations found in later chapters. The chapter started with a discussion of the basic properties of number systems, including definitions of integer, binary, signed digits representations, as well as an overview of fixed and floating point numbers. The following section described several methods for two-operand addition, which included ripple carry and carry look-ahead adders. Section 5.4 focused on multiple-operand addition using methods such as sequential and parallel carry propagation, more complex summation using redundant digit representations, and distributed arithmetic.

References

[1] M. D. Ercegovac and T. Lang, *Digital Arithmetic*. San Francisco, CA: Morgan Kaufmann Publishers, 2004.

[2] B. Parhami, *Computer Arithmetic: Algorithms and Hardware Designs*. New York, NY: Oxford University Press, 2000.

[3] K. Hwang, *Computer Arithmetic: Principle, Architecture and Design*. New York, NY: Wiley, 1979.

[4] D. E. Knuth, *The Art of Computer Programming/Seminumerical Algorithms*, **2**, second edition. Boston, MA: Addison-Wesley, 1981.

[5] A. D. Booth, A signed binary multiplication technique, *The Quarterly Journal of Mechanics and Applied Mathematics*, **4**, 235–40, 1951.

[6] S. Arno and F. S. Wheeler, Signed digit representations of minimal Hamming weight, *IEEE Transactions on Computers*, **C-42**, 1007–10, 1993.

[7] G. W. Reitwiesner, Binary arithmetic, *Advances in Computers*, **1**, 231–308, 1960.

[8] B. Parhami, Generalized signed-digit number systems: a unifying framework for redundant number representations, *IEEE Transactions on Computers*, **39**, 89–98, 1990.

[9] D. Etiemble and K. Navi, Algorithms and multi-valued circuits for the multioperand addition in the binary stored-carry number system, *International Symposium on Computer Arithmetic, Ontario 1993*. Ascafaway, AJ: IEEE, 1993.

[10] IEEE, IEEE 754: Standard for Binary Floating-Point Arithmetic.

[11] M. J. Schulte, N. Lindberg, and A. Laxminarain, Performance evaluation of decimal floating-point arithmetic, *Proceedings of the 6th IBM Austin Center for Advanced Studies Conference, 2005*. IBM, 2005.

[12] A. Croisier, D. J. Esteban, M. E. Levilion, and V. Rizo, Digital filter for PCM encoded signals. United States Patent 3777 130, December 3, 1973.

[13] S. Zohar, The counting recursive digital filter, *IEEE Transactions on Computers*, **C22**, 328–38, 1973.

6 Polynomial expressions

6.1 Chapter overview

This chapter presents some of the issues in the optimization of polynomial expressions. The chapter starts with an introduction to polynomial expressions and their possible optimizations, with illustrative examples. Then, the details of some techniques for manipulating polynomial expressions are presented. This is followed by a description of algebraic techniques used for the optimization of multiple-variable polynomial expressions. The usefulness of these techniques is demonstrated through experimental results. Finally, the chapter presents an ILP-based approach to obtain the optimal solution to the problem.

6.2 Polynomial expressions

A polynomial is an expression constructed from one or more variables and constants using the operations addition, subtraction, multiplication, and raising to the power of nonnegative integer numbers. Examples of polynomial functions are: $x^3 - 6x^2 + 10$ and $x^3y^2 + 15x^2y^2 - 6zx^4$. The first is a univariate polynomial, while the second is a multivariate polynomial. Univariate polynomials consist of at most one distinct variable, whereas multivariate polynomials can contain any number of variables.

A polynomial function can be thought as a summation of terms (both positive and negative). The degree of a term is the sum of the powers of each variable of the term. The degree of the term with the highest degree is the polynomial's degree. For example, the degree of the first aforementioned polynomial is 3, while the degree of the second polynomial is 5.

Polynomial functions are used to encode a number of problems in basic sciences such as chemistry and physics. Furthermore, polynomial functions appear in many computing problems such as computer graphics and DSP.

In computer graphics applications, a curve or a surface is often defined by interactively specifying a set of control points. Given the coordinates of the control points, polynomials are used to specify parametric equations for the curves and the surfaces. Bezier and spline formulations [1] are some of the techniques used for displaying curves and surfaces which are defined with control points.

The Bezier formulation takes the set of control points as input and generates an approximation curve by adding a sequence of polynomial functions formed from the coordinates of those points [2]. The Bezier formulation was devised by the French engineer Bezier for the design of the Renault automobile engine. Suppose that $n + 1$ control points are designated by $p_k = (x_k, y_k, z_k)$, where $0 \leq k \leq n$; the Bezier parametric vector function $P(u)$ is given as

$$P(u) = \sum_{k=0}^{n} p_k B_{k,n}(u), \qquad B_{k,n}(u) = C(n,k)u^k(1-u)^{n-k}. \tag{6.1}$$

$C(n, k)$ is the binomial coefficient. The Bezier vector equation can be written in explicit form for individual curve coordinates as:

$$x(u) = \sum_{k=0}^{n} x_k B_{k,n}(u),$$

$$y(u) = \sum_{k=0}^{n} y_k B_{k,n}(u), \tag{6.2}$$

$$z(u) = \sum_{k=0}^{n} z_k B_{k,n}(u).$$

These polynomials approximate the curve or surface to the set of control points. These functions have to be computed for every point of the curve or surface which is being generated. Since they are computationally very expensive, efficient methods are necessary to compute these functions without compromising the desired accuracy.

6.3   Problem formulation

Polynomial expressions are compute intensive as they contain a number of additions and multiplications which are expensive operations. These calculations take many clock cycles to compute on a processor. When implemented in an ASIC, they occupy a large area and consume a lot of power in addition to increasing clock periods. It is, therefore, imperative to reduce the number of operations in polynomial expressions as much as possible. These reductions can be achieved by factoring these expressions and finding common subexpressions among multiple-polynomial expressions. Unfortunately, not many tools are available to perform this, especially for multiple-variable expressions.

The problem of optimization of polynomial expressions can be stated as follows: given a set of polynomial expressions of any degree and consisting of any number of variables, find an implementation that has the least number of operations (additions, subtractions, and multiplications).

6.4   Related optimization techniques

The Horner method is the most popular one for evaluating polynomial expressions. (The Horner form was explained in detail in Section 3.3.7.)

The Horner method is the default method of evaluating Taylor series approximations to trigonometric functions in many libraries such as the GNU C Library [3]. For example, consider the following expression for sin (x) which has been approximated to four terms:

$$\sin(x) = x - \frac{x^3}{3!} + \frac{x^5}{5!} - \frac{x^7}{7!}. \tag{6.3}$$

The Horner form of this expression can be written as:

$$\sin(x) = x\left(1 + x^2\left(-\frac{1}{3!} + x^2\left(\frac{1}{5!} - \frac{x^2}{7!}\right)\right)\right). \tag{6.4}$$

Most libraries hand-optimize the resulting Horner form to remove the redundant computations of x^2. The expression is then rewritten as:

$$X = x^2$$
$$\sin(x) = x\left(1 + X\left(-\frac{1}{3!} + X\left(\frac{1}{5!} - \frac{X}{7!}\right)\right)\right). \tag{6.5}$$

The Horner form is a good representation for polynomials with single variables, but does not provide good results for multivariate polynomials. Furthermore, it cannot find common subexpressions automatically to further reduce the number of operations.

Traditional compiler optimization methods have been designed for general-purpose applications and do not do a good job of optimizing polynomial expressions. Some of the early work in code generation for arithmetic expressions [4, 5] proposed algorithms to minimize the number of program steps and the number of storage references given a fixed number of registers. In [6] these techniques were extended to handle expressions with common subexpressions. Some work was done to optimize code having arithmetic expressions using factorization techniques [7]. The technique presented in [7] was very limited in that it could only optimize expressions which contained one type of associative and/or commutative operator at a time. As a result it could not optimize general polynomial expressions which have multiplication, addition, and subtraction operations.

In Section 2.3, an example is shown where the Horner form is used to optimize a quartic polynomial used in computer graphics. This example is repeated in Figure 6.1. Figure 6.1(a) shows the original polynomial, which has 23 multiplications. Applying the iterative two-term CSE algorithm on a DFG representation of the polynomial results in an implementation with 16 multiplications as shown in Figure 6.1(b). Applying the Horner transform to this polynomial results in an implementation with 17 multiplications. But applying the algebraic techniques discussed in this chapter results in an implementation with only 13 multiplications. The limitation of the CSE technique is that it cannot perform factorization of polynomial expressions. Furthermore, its effectiveness depends on the order in which the operations occur in the DFG of the expression. For example, it cannot

(a)
$$P = zu^4 + 4avu^3 + 6bu^2v^2 + 4uv^3w + qv^4$$

(b)
$$d_1 = u^2$$
$$d_2 = v^2$$
$$d_3 = uv$$
$$P = d_1^2z + 4ad_1d_3 + 6bd_1d_2 + 4wd_2d_3 + qd_2^2$$

(c)
$$P = zu^4 + (4au^3 + (6bu^2 + (4uw + qv)v)v)v$$

(d)
$$d_1 = v^2$$
$$d_2 = 4v$$
$$P = u^3(uz + ad_2) + d_1(qd_1 + u(wd_2 + 6bu))$$

Figure 6.1 Optimization of the quartic spline polynomial: (a) unoptimized polynomial; (b) optimization using CSE; (c) optimization using the Horner transform; (d) optimization using the algebraic technique.

detect that the expressions $F_1 = (a \times b) \times c$ and $F_2 = (a \times c) \times b$ are equivalent. The limitation of the Horner transform is that it does not do a good job with multivariate polynomials such as the one shown in the figure. Furthermore, it does not detect common subexpressions automatically to further reduce the number of operations.

Symbolic algebra techniques are commonly used for the symbolic manipulation of polynomials. Using the concept of Gröbner bases [8], the Buchberger algorithm [8] can be used to decompose a polynomial expression into a set of library polynomials. This procedure is called *simplification modulo set of polynomials*. For example, consider the following multivariate polynomial: $P = x + x^2 + x^3 + y + xy + x^2y$. Assuming, there are library polynomials, $L = \{(x + y), (1 + x + x^2)\}$, using simplification modulo set of polynomials, P can be optimized as $P = (x + y) \times (1 + x + x^2)$.

This technique has been used for both high-level synthesis [9, 10, 11] and low-power embedded software optimization [12]. It has been applied in high-level datapath synthesis for producing a minimum component and minimum latency implementations of polynomials. The quality of results from these techniques depends heavily on the set of library elements. For example, the decomposition of the polynomial expression $(a^2 - b^2)$ into $(a + b) \times (a - b)$ is possible only if there is a library element $(a + b)$ or $(a - b)$. It should be noted that just having an adder in the library will not suffice for this decomposition. There should be an addition expression $(a + b)$ or $(a - b)$ in the library for the decomposition to happen. Therefore, if there are a large number of variables $a, b, c, d, e, f, g, \ldots$ in the expression, we will need to have adder expressions involving every combination of variables such as $(a + b), (c + d), (a + c), (a + g), (f + g), \ldots$, just to cover a decomposition involving one addition. Though this problem can be addressed by having a large number of library elements, the runtime of the algorithm can become excessively large. While this method is useful for arithmetic decomposition of a datapath into library elements, it cannot simplify a set of polynomials by factoring and eliminating common subexpressions.

Algebraic methods have been successfully applied to the problem of multi-level logic synthesis for minimizing the number of literals in a set of Boolean expressions [13, 14, 15]. These techniques are typically applied to a set of Boolean expressions consisting of thousands of literals and hundreds of variables. The optimization is achieved by decomposition and factorization of the Boolean expressions. Rectangle covering methods have been used to perform this optimization [16], but due to the high algorithmic complexity, faster heuristics such as *fast-extract* (FX) have also been developed [15]. There are two main algorithms used in the rectangle covering method: *distill* and *condense*. The distill algorithm is preceded by a *kernelling* algorithm, where a subset of algebraic divisors are generated. Using these divisors, distill performs multiple cube decomposition and factorization. This is followed by the condense algorithm, which performs single cube decomposition. For example, consider the set of Boolean expressions

$$\begin{aligned} F_1 &= abc + abd, \\ F_2 &= pab + pde. \end{aligned} \tag{6.6}$$

The *distill* algorithm factorizes the expressions as:

$$\begin{aligned} F_1 &= ab(c + d), \\ F_2 &= p(ab + de). \end{aligned} \tag{6.7}$$

The *condense* algorithm extracts the common term "*ab*" from the set of equations and rewrites them as

$$\begin{aligned} t_1 &= ab, \\ F_1 &= t_1(c + d), \\ F_2 &= p(t_1 + de). \end{aligned} \tag{6.8}$$

These algebraic properties are based only on the commutative, associative, and distributive properties of the Boolean operators AND and OR. These properties are also shared by the arithmetic ADD and MULTIPLY operators. The SUBTRACT operation shares the properties of associativity and distributivity. By modifying the methods described in [13, 14, 15], it is possible to optimize polynomial expressions of any order and consisting of any number of variables.

6.5   Algebraic optimization of arithmetic expressions

There are two different algebraic techniques which can be used for optimizing arithmetic expressions. These methods are greedy heuristics which attempt to find an implementation of a polynomial with the minimum weighted number of operations (ADD, MULTIPLY, and SUB). Both these techniques are described in detail in this section.

6.5.1   Optimization using rectangle covering methods

In this method, multiple-term common subexpressions and single-term common subexpressions are found by computing intersections among a set of subexpressions. Factorization is done by finding a subset of algebraic factors using a technique called *kernelling*. Both these intersections and factorization opportunities are represented in a matrix in the form of *rectangles*.

An optimal covering of the matrix with rectangles corresponds to an implementation with the least number of arithmetic operations.

In this subsection, the canonical representation used to represent the polynomial expressions is described first. This is followed by a description of the terminology used in this technique. Finally the algorithm is explained in detail with an illustrative example.

6.5.1.1   Canonical representation of arithmetic expressions using the ordered matrix

The arithmetic operators $+$ and $\times$ have the properties of associativity and commutativity, which makes it possible for the same arithmetic expressions to be written in different ways. In order to make the optimizations independent of the initial order of terms and variables, it is necessary to represent the expressions in a canonical form on which the optimizations are performed. To represent polynomials in a canonical form, all variables and the absolute values of all distinct constants used in the expressions are ordered first and the expressions are then written in a matrix. There is one matrix for each expression, but the number of columns for all expressions is the same and is equal to the number of distinct variables and constants in the set of expressions. There is one row for each term in the expression. Each row has a field to indicate a positive $(+)$ or a negative $(-)$ sign. Each element (i, j) in the matrix represents the exponent of the variable j in the term i.

For example, consider the degree 5 polynomial shown in Figure 6.2(a). Assume that the variables are ordered as $\{x, y, z, 15, 6\}$. Note that for the algebraic techniques discussed in this chapter, each distinct constant in the expression is treated as a separate variable. The matrix representation of this polynomial is shown in Figure 6.2(b). The first term of the polynomial is x^3y^2. All variables in the expression can be included in this term by writing as $x^3y^2z^015^06^0$. Therefore, the first row of the matrix is $+3\ 2\ 0\ 0\ 0$. Since the term is positive, a "$+$" sign is associated with this row in the matrix.

The algebraic techniques for factoring and CSE work independently of the order in which the terms of the polynomial are written and hence the ordering of the rows of the matrix is not important. Furthermore, the algorithms work independently of the order of the variables that appear in the polynomials, and

(a)

$$P = x^3y^2 + 15x^2y^2 - 6zx^4$$

(b)

±	x	y	z	15	6
+	3	2	0	0	0
+	2	2	0	1	0
−	4	0	1	0	1

Figure 6.2 (a) Example polynomial expression; (b) matrix representation of the polynomial expression.

hence the ordering of the columns is also not important once a fixed ordering of the literals is decided.

6.5.1.2 Terminology used to explain the algebraic technique

The algebraic techniques discussed in this chapter borrow many concepts used in the optimization of Boolean functions [13, 14, 15]. This chapter retains some of the terminology used in those techniques to explain the optimization for arithmetic functions. These terms are explained as follows:

(1) **Literal**: a literal is used to represent a variable or a constant. For example, in the polynomial of Figure 6.2(a), x, y, z, 15 and 6 are all literals.

(2) **Cube**: a cube is essentially a term in a polynomial expression. It is defined as the product of literals each of which is raised to a constant, nonnegative integer power. Each cube also has a positive or a negative sign associated with it. For the example polynomial of Figure 6.2(a), the cubes are $+x^3y^2$, $+15x^2y^2$ and $-6zx^4$.

(3) **Sum of products (SOP)**: an SOP representation of a polynomial is the sum of the cubes of the polynomial. The algebraic technique presented in this chapter assumes that all polynomials are initially represented in their SOP form.

(4) **Cube-free expression**: a cube-free polynomial expression in the SOP form is an expression, in which no cube can divide all cubes of the expression. The example polynomial of Figure 6.2(a) is not cube-free, because the cube "x^2" can divide all cubes of the expression. Dividing the polynomial by x^2 yields the polynomial $P' = xy^2 + 15y^2 - 6zx^2$. This is a cube-free expression.

(5) **Kernel**: a kernel is a cube-free subexpression that is obtained (by division) from a polynomial expression. As discussed above, the subexpression P' is a kernel of the example polynomial in Figure 6.2(a).

(6) **Co-kernel**: a co-kernel is a cube that is used to divide a polynomial to obtain a kernel. As discussed above, the cube x^2 is used to divide the polynomial P to obtain the kernel $P' = xy^2 + 15y^2 - 6zx^2$. Hence x^2 is a co-kernel.

6.5.1.3 Rectangle covering algorithm

The rectangle covering algorithm comprises two main procedures. The first procedure finds multiple-term common subexpressions and factorizations and is called the distill algorithm. The second procedure finds single-term common subexpressions and is called the condense algorithm. The distill algorithm makes use of kernels to perform its optimizations.

6.5.1.4   Generating kernels of polynomial expressions

The set of kernels of the expressions can be used to find the minimal algebraic factorizations as well as to find all multiple-term common subexpressions in the set of expressions. This is illustrated by the following two theorems.

THEOREM 1 *All minimal algebraic factorizations of a polynomial expression can be obtained from the set of kernels and co-kernels of the expression.*

Proof Consider the minimal algebraic factorization of $P = C \times F_1 + F_2$. By definition, the subexpression F_1 is cube-free since the only cube that evenly divides all the terms of F_1 is "1." Otherwise, the factorization is not minimal. It has to be proved that F_1 is a part of a kernel expression with the corresponding co-kernel C. Let $\{t_i\}$ be the set of the original terms of the expression P that cover the terms in F_1. Since F_1 is obtained from $\{t_i\}$ by dividing it by C ($F_1 = \{t_i\}/C$), the common cube of the terms $\{t_i\}$ is C. Let $\{t_j\}$ be the set of the original terms of P that also have C as the common cube among them and do not overlap with any of the terms in $\{t_i\}$. Now consider the expression $K_1 = (\{t_i\} + \{t_j\})/C = \{t_i\}/C + \{t_j\}/C = F_1 + \{t'_j\}$, where $\{t'_j\} = \{t_j\}/C$. The expression K_1 is cube-free since F_1 is cube-free. K_1 covers all terms of the original expression P that contain cube C. Therefore, by definition, K_1 is a kernel of the expression P with the cube C as the corresponding co-kernel. Since the kernel generation procedure generates all kernels and co-kernels of the polynomial expressions, the kernel $K_1 = F_1 + \{t'_j\}$ will be generated with the corresponding co-kernel C. Since F_1 is a part of this kernel expression, the theorem is proved. *QED*

THEOREM 2 *There is a multiple-term common subexpression in the set of polynomial expressions iff there is a multiple-term intersection among the set of kernels belonging to the expressions.*

Explanation Multiple-term common subexpressions involve intersections between kernel expressions yielding two or more terms (cubes). For example, the intersection between the kernels $K_1 = a + b \times c + d$ and $K_2 = b \times c + d + f$, is the multiple-term subexpression ($b \times c + d$).

Proof The *if* case is trivial. Let K_1 be the multiple-term intersection. It means there are multiple instances of the subexpression K_1 among the set of expressions. For the *only if* case, assume that f is a multiple-term common subexpression among the set of expressions. If the expression f is cube-free, then f is a part of some kernel expressions as proved in Theorem 1. Each instance of expression f will, therefore, be a part of some kernel expression and an intersection among the set of kernels will detect the common subexpression f. If f is not a cube-free expression, then let C be the largest cube that divides all terms of f and let $f' = f/C$. The expression f' is now a cube-free expression, and reasoning as above, each instance of f' will be detected by an intersection among the set of kernels. *QED*

FindKernels({P$_i$}, {L$_i$})

{

    {P$_i$}: Set of polynomial expressions;

    {L$_i$}: Set of literals;

    {D$_i$}: Set of kernels and co-kernels = ϕ;

    for (all expressions P$_i$ in {P$_i$}) {

        {D$_i$} = {D$_i$} $\cup$ **{Kernels**(0, P$_i$, 1)} $\cup$ {P$_i$,1};

    }

    return {D$_i$};

}

Kernels(i, P, d)

{

    i: Literal number ;

    P: Expression in SOP;

    d: Cube;

    D = ϕ; // D is the set of divisors

    for(j = i; j < |{L$_i$}|; j++)

    {

        If(L$_j$ appears in more than one row)

        {

            F$_t$ = **Divide** (P, L$_j$);

            C = Largest cube dividing all cubes of F$_t$;

            if((L$_k$ $\notin$ C) for all (k < j))

            {

                F$_1$ = Divide(F$_t$, C); // kernel

                D$_1$ = Merge(d, C, L$_j$);// co-kernel

                D = D $\cup$ D$_1$ $\cup$ F$_1$;

                D = D $\cup$ Kernels (j, F$_1$, D$_1$);

            }

        }

    }

    return D;

}

Divide(P,d)

{

    P: Expression;

    d: Cube;

    Q: Set of rows of P that contain cube d;

    for(all rows R$_i$ of Q) {

        for (all columns j in the row R$_i$) {

            R$_i$[j] = R$_i$[j] − d[j];

        }

    }

    return Q;

}

Merge(C$_1$, C$_2$, C$_3$)

{

    C$_1$, C$_2$, C$_3$: cubes;

    Cube M;

    for(i = 0; i < |{L$_i$}|; i++)

        M[i] = C$_1$[i] + C$_2$[i] + C$_3$[i];

    return M;

}

Figure 6.3 Kernel generation algorithm.

6.5.1.5   Kernel generation algorithm

The algorithm for extracting all kernels and co-kernels of a set of polynomial expressions is shown in Figure 6.3. The main algorithm Kernels is recursive. It extracts kernels by dividing the polynomial expressions by each of the literals. After generating a kernel, the Kernels algorithm is called again with the generated kernel now as the polynomial expression. The arguments of this function are the polynomial P, the literal index i, and the co-kernel d, which is the co-kernel that has been generated before the call to the Kernels function. For the first call to the

Kernels function, the polynomial passed is the original polynomial expression. The variable index is 0, and the co-kernel is initialized to 1 or empty set. During kernel generation, the polynomial expression is divided by every literal L_j that appears in more than one row of the expression to obtain the temporary polynomial F_t. After this, the biggest cube C that divides all cubes of F_t has to be determined. This cube C is used to obtain the kernel. The biggest cube is the one that has the greatest literal count $\Sigma\, C[i]$ among all cubes and is contained in each cube of the expression. $C[i]$ is the integer power of the ith literal of cube C. For example, each row of the matrix in Figure 6.2(b) represents a cube. Dividing F_t by the cube C gives the kernel. The corresponding co-kernel is the cube that is used to divide the polynomial expression to obtain this kernel expression. This co-kernel is obtained by multiplying the literal L_j with the cube C and the cube d, which is the co-kernel that was present before the current call to the Kernels function. Before dividing F_t by the cube C, a check is made to see if the cube C contains any variable that was processed before the current variable (appears before the literal L_j in the literal ordering). The kernel is extracted and subsequent recursive call is done only if there is no such literal in the cube C. This is done so that there is no repetition of the kernel that was already generated. In addition to the kernels generated from the recursive algorithm, the original expression is also added as a kernel with co-kernel "1". This helps to detect whether one polynomial is a kernel of another polynomial.

The function **Divide** is used to divide the SOP polynomial expression by a cube d. The quotient of the division is formed only from those rows that completely contain the cube d. A row R of an SOP expression is said to contain a cube d if for each element of the row $R[i] \geq d[i]$. Division is performed by subtracting the cube d from each of these rows. In the Kernels routine, the biggest cube C dividing all cubes of the SOP expression has to be determined. This cube C is used to obtain the kernel. The biggest cube is the one with the greatest literal count $\Sigma C[i]$ contained in each cube of the expression.

The function **Merge** is used to find the product of the cubes d, C, and L_j, which is done by summing the corresponding elements of the cubes.

Figure 6.4 illustrates the working of the Kernels algorithm for the example polynomial shown in Figure 6.2(a). The literal set for this polynomial is $\{x, y, z, 15, 6\}$. For ease of explanation, this is also assumed to be the ordering of the literals. In the first step, the polynomial P is divided by the variable x to obtain the expression $F_t = x^2y^2 + 15xy^2 - 6zx^3$. The biggest cube dividing all cubes of this expression is x. Dividing F_t by x gives the kernel $xy^2 + 15y^2 - 6zx^2$. The corresponding co-kernel is x^2. The Kernels routine is called recursively with this kernel expression as the polynomial and the co-kernel as x^2. Dividing first by literal x gives the kernel $y^2 - 6zx$. The corresponding co-kernel is x^3. Since this kernel does not contain any literal that appears in all its cubes, the call to the Kernels function will not obtain any kernels, therefore, that call is not shown in this figure. Division of the polynomial by y gives the kernel $x + 15$, with the corresponding co-kernel x^2y^2. After this, there are no more literals that appear in multiple cubes of the

Polynomial $P = x^3y^2 + 15x^2y^2 - 6zx^4$
Literal set $L = \{x, y, z, 15, 6\}$
Initial co-kernel $= d = 1$
Call Kernels$(P, 0, d)$

1. $i = 0; L_i = x$.

    x appears in more than one cube of P.
    Divide P by x.
    $F_t = P/x = x^2y^2 + 15xy^2 - 6zx^3$.
    Biggest cube dividing all cubes of F_t is $C = x$.
    $F_1 = F_t/C = xy^2 + 15y^2 - 6zx^2$ (Kernel)
    $D_1 = L_i \times C \times d = x^2$ (Co-kernel)
    Call Kernels$(F_1, 0, D_1)$

2. $P = xy^2 + 15y^2 - 6zx^2; i = 0; d = x^2$.
    $L_i = x$,
    $F_t = P/L_i = y^2 - 6zx$.
    $C = 1$.
    $F_1 = F_t/C = y^2 - 6zx$ (Kernel).
    $D_1 = L_i \times C \times d = x^3$ (Co-kernel).

3. $P = xy^2 + 15y^2 - 6zx^2; i = 1; d = x^2$,
    $L_i = y$,
    $F_t = P/L_i = xy + 15y$,
    $C = y$.
    $F_1 = F_t/C = x + 15$ (Kernel).
    $D_1 = L_i \times C \times d = x^2y^2$ (Co-kernel).

4. $P - x^3y^2 + 15x^2y^2 - 6zx^4; i = 1; d = 1$.
    $L_i = y$
    $F_t = P/L_i = x^3y + 15x^2y$
    $C = x^2y$
    Here $L_0 = x \in C$.
    Therefore, kernelling is not done as it would give the same kernel
    $(x + 15)$.

Figure 6.4 Example of performing kernelling on a polynomial.

polynomial and the algorithm does not produce any more kernels. The algorithm then returns to the original stack. Here the original polynomial is divided by the next literal, y, to obtain $F_t = x^3y + 15x^2y$. The biggest cube dividing F_t is x^2y. Since this cube contains the literal x, which has already been processed, dividing by this cube gives a kernel $(x + 15)$ that has already been generated. Therefore, this iteration is skipped. No more kernels are generated in subsequent iterations. The final set of kernels and their corresponding co-kernels for the example polynomial in Figure 6.2(a) are:

$$[x^2](xy^2 + 15y^2 - 6zx^2), \qquad [x^3](y^2 - 6zx), \quad \text{and} \ [x^2y^2](x + 15).$$

6.5.1.6 Finding intersections and performing factorizations using kernels and co-kernels

After generating the set of kernels for the polynomial expressions, multiple-term common subexpressions can be found by performing intersections among the kernels. According to Theorems 1 and 2, all multiple-term common factors can be detected by performing intersections among the set of kernels. Furthermore, each kernel and co-kernel pair represents a possible factorization opportunity for a polynomial. All multiple-term common subexpressions and factorizations can be detected by arranging the kernels and co-kernels in a matrix called the kernel-cube matrix (KCM) [14–16]. This matrix has one row for each kernel generated using the algorithm in Figure 6.3 and one column for each distinct cube of a kernel.

The polynomials in Figure 6.5 are used to explain the technique. In this figure, the subscript numbers show the term numbers, which will be used in the explanation of the technique. Figure 6.6 shows the kernels and the co-kernels that are extracted for these polynomials. In Figure 6.7, these kernels and co-kernels are arranged in a KCM. In this matrix, there are five rows for the five kernels that are extracted. Since there are five distinct kernel cubes, the matrix has five columns. The kernels corresponding to the original expressions (with co-kernel "1") are not shown to simplify the representation.

$$P_1 = a^3b_{(1)} + a^2b^2c_{(2)}$$
$$P_2 = 8a_{(3)} + 8bc_{(4)} - abc_{(5)}$$
$$P_3 = 8ab_{(6)} - a^2b_{(7)}$$

Figure 6.5 Example of performing kernelling of polynomial.

P_1: $[a + bc](a^2b)$, $[a^3b + a^2b^2c](1)$
P_2: $[8 - a](bc)$, $[8 - bc](a)$, $[a + bc](8)$, $[8a + 8bc - abc](1)$
P_3: $[8 - a](ab)$, $[8ab - a^2b](1)$

Figure 6.6 Kernels and co-kernels for the example polynomials in Figure 6.5.

		Kernel cubes				
		a	bc	8	$-bc$	$-a$
C o - k e r n e l s	8	$1_{(3)}$	$1_{(4)}$	0	0	0
	a^2b	$1_{(1)}$	$1_{(2)}$	0	0	0
	a	0	0	$1_{(3)}$	$1_{(5)}$	0
	ab	0	0	$1_{(6)}$	0	$1_{(7)}$
	bc	0	0	$1_{(4)}$	0	$1_{(5)}$

Figure 6.7 KCM for the example polynomials in Figure 6.5.

The original terms in the set of expressions can be found in the KCM. An element (i, j) in the matrix is "1" if the product of the co-kernel represented by row "i" and the kernel cube represented by the column "j" is an original term in the set of expressions. Otherwise, the element is "0." This can be seen in the KCM of Figure 6.7. For the elements marked with a "1," there is a subscript number that represents the term number in the polynomials. Since all kernels and co-kernels are represented in the KCM, all terms are covered in the matrix. As some terms may be covered by more than one kernel, there may be more than one element (i, j) of the matrix covering the same term. In Figure 6.7, it can be observed that the term numbers 3, 4, and 5 are covered twice in the matrix.

In the KCM, **rectangles** are used to detect multiple-term common subexpressions and algebraic factorization opportunities. A rectangle is defined as a set of rows and a set of columns such that all elements contained in the rectangle are "1." Another requirement for a rectangle is that no term is covered more than once by the rectangles. A multiple-term common subexpression corresponds to a rectangle with more than one row and more than one column. An algebraic factorization opportunity appears as a rectangle with a single row and more than one column. The columns and the rows that make up a rectangle need not be adjacent. As one can see in Figure 6.7, the elements corresponding to the last two rows and the columns "8" and "$-a$" form a rectangle even though the columns are nonadjacent. This rectangle represents the common factor "8 – a." The rectangle comprising the row "a" and the columns "8" and "$-bc$" shows a possible factorization opportunity.

Since finding the best set of rectangles that will cover the matrix is an NP-hard problem [17], heuristic algorithms have to be used to achieve acceptable performance. One greedy approach is to enumerate all prime rectangles in the matrix and choose the one that gives the best value. A prime rectangle is defined as a rectangle that is not completely contained in another rectangle (i.e., the set of rows and columns covering the prime rectangle is not a subset of a larger rectangle). Each rectangle has a value associated with it, which represents improvement in some parameters caused by selecting that rectangle and rewriting the set of polynomial expressions using the subexpression represented by the rectangle. The value of the rectangle can be decided in a number of ways depending on the desired implementation. One obvious way is to value a rectangle based on the savings in the number of additions and subtractions resulting from the selection of the rectangle. Once all useful (positive value) prime rectangles are selected from the matrix, the set of polynomial expressions are rewritten by substituting the subexpressions corresponding to the selected rectangles. After rewriting the polynomials, the process of generating kernels, constructing the KCM, and finding rectangles is repeated in the next iteration. The iterations stop when one iteration produces no useful rectangle. This greedy algorithm is illustrated in Figure 6.8.

In Figure 6.9, all prime rectangles of the KCM are highlighted with dashed lines. As one can see in the figure, there are three prime rectangles. The first rectangle covers the columns "a" and "bc" and the rows "8" and "a^2b." The

```
FindKernelIntersections ({P_i}, {L_i})
{
    while(1)
    {
        D = FindKernels ({P_i}, {L_i});
        KCM = Form Kernel Cube Matrix (D);
        {R} = Set of new kernel intersections = φ;
        {V} = Set of new variables = φ;
        if (no favorable rectangle) return;
        while(favorable rectangles exist)
        {
            {R} = {R} ∪ Best Prime Rectangle;
            {V} = {V} ∪ New Literal;
            Update KCM;
        }
        Rewrite {P_i} using{R};
        {P_i} = {P_i} ∪ {R};
        {L_i} = {L_i} ∪ {V};
    }
}
```

Figure 6.8 Algorithm to find kernel intersections.

		Kernel cubes				
		a	bc	8	$-bc$	$-a$
C o- k e r n e l s	8	$1_{(3)}$	$1_{(4)}$	0	0	0
	a^2b	$1_{(1)}$	$1_{(2)}$	0	0	0
	a	0	0	$1_{(3)}$	$1_{(5)}$	0
	ab	0	0	$1_{(6)}$	0	$1_{(7)}$
	bc	0	0	$1_{(4)}$	0	$1_{(5)}$

Figure 6.9 Prime rectangles in the KCM.

second covers the columns "8" and "$-bc$" and row "a." The third covers columns "8" and "$-a$" and rows "ab" and "bc." Since the columns of this rectangle are not contiguous, they are joined by a dashed line as shown. The rectangle comprising of the rows "8" and "a^2b" and the columns "a" and "bc" corresponds to the common subexpression "$a + bc$." By extracting and eliminating this common subexpression the number of multiplications and additions will be reduced by 5 and 1, respectively. This is the most useful rectangle of all prime rectangles in the KCM. After this rectangle is selected, the terms that are covered by this rectangle have to be removed from the matrix. Therefore, the 1s in the matrix that cover the terms 1, 2, 3, and 4 are removed from the matrix (i.e., changed to 0s).

The modified matrix is shown in Figure 6.10. This matrix has only one rectangle comprising of the row "ab" and the columns "8" and "$-a$." This rectangle

		\multicolumn{5}{c}{Kernel cubes}			
		a	bc	8	$-bc$	$-a$
C o- k e r n e l s	8	0	0	0	0	0
	a^2b	0	0	0	0	0
	a	0	0	0	$1_{(5)}$	0
	ab	0	0	$1_{(6)}$	0	$1_{(7)}$
	bc	0	0	0	0	$1_{(5)}$

Figure 6.10 Prime rectangles in the KCM.

$$P_1 = a^2bd_1 \qquad d_1 = a + bc$$
$$P_2 = 8d_1 - abc \qquad d_2 = 8 - a$$
$$P_3 = abd_2$$

Figure 6.11 Expressions after kernel extraction.

represents the algebraic factorization $ab(8-a)$. This factorization saves two multiplications. Further iterations of the algorithm produce no more useful rectangles. The optimized set of rectangles is shown in Figure 6.11. In this figure, the variables d_1 and d_2 represent the subexpressions corresponding to the two rectangles that were extracted.

6.5.1.7 Finding single-term common subexpressions using rectangle covering

The algorithm for finding multiple-term common subexpressions and factorizations cannot find single-term common factors such as "abc" or "$4def$." We now describe an algorithm for finding single-term common factors. First, all terms of the polynomial expressions are written in a matrix form as shown in Figure 6.2(b), with a predefined variable ordering. Then, the rectangle covering technique is used to extract single-term common subexpressions. Each rectangle should then consist of at least two rows and two columns. The matrix is called the cube intersection matrix (CIM) since it is used to find intersections among cubes. Each element (i, j) in this matrix represents the integer exponent of the variable j in the term i. Therefore, there can be elements in this matrix that are greater than 1. This is different from the KCM, where each element is either "1" or "0." The value of a rectangle in this matrix is equal to the number of multiplications saved by rewriting the expressions by extracting and substituting the single-term common subexpression corresponding to the rectangle. For the set of optimized expressions in Figure 6.11, the CIM is shown in Figure 6.12.

A greedy iterative heuristic can be used to cover the CIM with the best prime rectangles. In each iteration of the algorithm, the best prime rectangle is selected. The CIM is then rewritten by subtracting the cube from the rows covered by the rectangle. The pseudo code for this algorithm is shown in Figure 6.13.

	Term	+/-	a	b	c	8	d_1	d_2
C u b e s	1	+	2	1	0	0	1	0
	2	+	0	0	0	1	1	0
	3	−	1	1	1	0	0	0
	4	+	1	1	0	0	0	1
	5	+	1	0	0	0	0	0
	6	+	0	1	1	0	0	0
	7	+	0	0	0	1	0	0
	8	−	1	0	0	0	0	0

(Top header over columns a, b, c, 8, d_1, d_2: **Literals**)

Figure 6.12 CIM containing prime rectangles.

Find Cube Intersections ({P_i}, {L_i})
{
    while(1)
    {
        M = Cube Literal incidence matrix
        {V} = Set of new variables = ∅;
        {C} = Set of new cube intersections = ∅;

        if(no favorable rectangle present) return;

        while(favorable rectangles exist)
        {
            Find B=Best Prime Rectangle;
            {C} = {C} ∪ Cube corresponding to B;
            {V} = {V} ∪ New Literal;
            Collapse(M,B);
        }
        M = M ∪ {C};
        {L_i} = {L_i} ∪ {V};
    }
}
Collapse(M,B)
{
    for(all rows i of M that contain cube B)
        for(all columns j of B)
            M[i][j] = M[i][j] − B[j];
}

Figure 6.13 Algorithm to extract single-term common subexpressions (the Condense algorithm).

For the matrix shown in Figure 6.12, there are two prime rectangles with a value greater than 0. One of the rectangles corresponds to the term "*ab*" and spans the rows 1, 3, and 4, and the columns "*a*" and "*b*". By extracting the common subexpression "*ab*" and substituting it in the set of expressions, a total of two multiplications is saved. The cube corresponding to this common subexpression is

	Term	+/−	a	b	c	8	d_1	d_2	d_3
							Literals		
	1	+	1	0	0	0	1	0	1
	2	+	0	0	0	1	1	0	0
	3	−	0	0	1	0	0	0	1
C u b e s	4	+	0	0	0	0	0	1	1
	5	+	1	0	0	0	0	0	0
	6	+	0	1	1	0	0	0	0
	7	+	0	0	0	1	0	0	0
	8	−	1	0	0	0	0	0	0
	9	+	1	1	0	0	0	0	0

Figure 6.14 CIM after extracting the common cube "ab."

$$P_1 = ad_1d_3 \qquad d_1 = a + bc$$
$$P_2 = 8d_1 - d_3c \qquad d_2 = 8 - a$$
$$P_3 = d_2d_3 \qquad d_3 = ab$$

Figure 6.15 Polynomials in Figure 6.5 after optimization (kernel extraction and single-term common subexpression elimination).

obtained from the minimum number from each column in the rectangle. In this example, the cube corresponding to the common subexpression "ab" is "110000." To substitute this cube into the set of cubes, the cube is subtracted from rows 1, 3, and 4. The cube corresponding to the extracted common subexpression $d_3 = ab$ is then inserted as a new row in the matrix. This matrix is shown in Figure 6.14. The final set of expressions after extracting multiple-term common subexpressions and factorizations (the Distill algorithm) and after extracting single-term common subexpressions (the Condense algorithm) is shown in Figure 6.15.

6.5.2 Optimization using divisor extraction methods

The rectangle covering method has worst-case exponential complexity. Another approach to optimizing arithmetic expressions is using divisor extraction. Like rectangle covering, divisor extraction is also a greedy iterative algorithm, but its runtime is polynomial in the number of terms in the expressions. In each iteration of the algorithm all possible subexpressions of a certain length (minimum 2) are listed. These subexpressions are called **divisors**. Then, the best divisor in the list i.e., the one that saves the most operations, is selected. After that the set of expressions is rewritten using the extracted divisor.

The advantage of this algorithm is that it can be used for different implementation schemes. The method can be used to optimize pipelined multiplier blocks in FIR filters and fast arithmetic circuits using carry save addition trees for example. More details about the application of this algorithm are given in Chapter 7.

(a) Divisors formed from a single term
    for(all single terms $\Pi\,x_i$ in the set of expressions)
    {
        for(every pair of literals x_i and x_j $(i \neq j)$) {
            Divisor $d = x_i * x_j$;
        }
    }

(b) Diviors formed from two terms
    for(all expressions P_i in the set of expressions)
    {
        for(every pair of terms T_j and T_k $(j \neq k)$ of expression P_i) {
            C = Largest cube dividing both terms T_{ij} and T_{jk};
            Divisor $d = (T_j + T_k)/C$;
        }
    }

Figure 6.16 Extracting divisors for polynomial expressions: (a) divisors formed from a single term; (b) divisors formed from two terms.

The method of finding all divisors varies depending on the type of arithmetic expression and the length of the divisor. For polynomial expressions, there are two types of divisors. The first type contains only a single term (e.g., $a \times b$ or $a \times b \times c$). The second type contains multiple terms (e.g., $a \times b + c \times d + e$). The length of a divisor of the first type is defined as the number of literals that are contained in the divisor. The length of a divisor of the second type is defined as the number of terms that are contained in the divisor. In the most common case, the divisor length is chosen as 2 (i.e., two-literal single-term divisors and two-term divisors are used), though in some cases a divisor length of 3 is also useful, e.g., for high-speed arithmetic circuits (more details can be found in Chapter 7).

Figure 6.16 illustrates the algorithms for generating divisors for polynomial expressions. Figure 6.16(a) shows the algorithm for generating two-literal single-term divisors. Figure 6.16(b) shows the algorithm for generating two-term divisors. For example, consider the term x^2y^2z. There are ten divisors for this term; they are $x \times x, x \times y, x \times y, x \times z, x \times y, x \times y, x \times z, y \times y, y \times z, y \times z$. Note there are multiple repeated divisors, corresponding to each repeated literal, e.g., x^2 has two district literals. Consider the pair of terms $\{+x^3y, +x^2y^2z\}$. The largest cube that divides both these terms is $C = x^2y$. Dividing these terms by C gives the divisor $(x + y \times z)$. Each distinct divisor has a value associated with it that represents the number of operations that are saved by extracting the divisor and substituting it into the set of expressions. The set of distinct divisors for the polynomial expressions in Figure 6.5 is shown in Figure 6.17. The value associated with each divisor (i.e., savings in the number of additions and multiplications) is also shown in the figure.

The algorithm for iteratively extracting divisors is called concurrent arithmetic extraction (CAX) and is shown in Figure 6.18. Using this algorithm for the set of expressions, the divisor $d_1 = (a + b \times c)$ is selected. Then, the divisor $d_2 = a \times b$ is extracted. Finally, the divisor $d_3 = (8 - a)$ is selected. For this example, the CAX algorithm achieves the same result as the rectangle covering algorithm.

Divisor	Number of operations saved	
	Additions	Multiplications
$a \times a$	0	2
$b \times c$	0	2
$a \times b$	0	4
$8 \times a$	0	1
$a \times c$	0	1
$8 \times b$	0	1
$8 \times c$	0	0
$a + b \times c$	1	5
$8 - b \times c$	0	1
$8 - a$	1	4

Figure 6.17 Divisors extracted for example polynomials.

```
Concurrent_Arithmetic_Extraction
{
    P = Set of polynomial expressions;
    change = TRUE;

    while(change)
    {
        change = FALSE;
        D = find_divisors_and_compute_values(P);
        d = find_best_divisor with value > 0;
        if(d) {
            change = TRUE;
            substitute_divisor(d, P);
        }
    }
}
```

Figure 6.18 Algorithm for CAX.

6.6 Experimental results

The algebraic techniques for optimizing polynomial expressions presented in this chapter were validated on a set of real-life examples. The experiments were done for both software and hardware implementations. The software experiments demonstrated the improvement in performance and energy consumption for the examples optimized by these algebraic techniques over conventional techniques. The hardware experiments took the same examples and showed the improvement in area, latency, and energy consumption for the synthesized netlists.

The examples were taken from signal processing and computer graphics applications. Table 6.1 compares the number of additions (A) and multiplications (M) for

Table 6.1 Comparing the number of additions and multiplications used in polynomials optimized by different techniques

Application	Function	Unoptimized +/×	CSE +/×	Horner +/×	Kernel extraction +/×
Fast convolution	FFT	7/56	7/20	7/30	7/10
Gaussian noise filter	FIR	6/34	6/23	6/20	6/13
Graphics	Quartic spline	4/23	4/16	4/17	4/13
Graphics	Quintic spline	5/34	5/22	5/23	5/16
Graphics	Chebyshev	8/32	8/18	8/18	8/11
Graphics	Cosine wavelet	17/43	17/23	17/20	17/17
Average		7.8/37	7.8/20.3	7.8/21.3	7.8/13.3

Table 6.2 Improvement in latency and energy consumption for execution on StrongARM™ SA1100 for polynomials optimized using algebraic methods over those optimized using CSE and the Horner form

Application	Function	Reduction in latency and energy consumption			
		Over CSE Latency (%)	Over Horner Energy (%)	Over CSE Latency (%)	Over Horner Energy (%)
Fast convolution	FFT	26.8	26.1	44.0	42.3
Gaussian noise filter	FIR	30.5	26.4	16.5	16.1
Graphics	Quartic spline	7.0	10.7	35.5	35.1
Graphics	Quintic spline	23.4	24.8	23.3	26.2
Graphics	Chebyshev	33.4	31.3	27.5	25.4
Graphics	Cosine wavelet	39.1	39.0	9.7	12.8
Average		26.7	26.4	26.1	26.3

the different applications produced by the different methods, CSE, the Horner transformation, and the algebraic kernel intersection method, discussed in this chapter. The first two applications are from signal processing [18] and the next four examples are from three-dimensional computer graphics [2]. From the table it can be seen that these polynomials have a large number of multiplications. The number of multiplications is significantly reduced by all the optimization techniques, but the algebraic kernelling techniques are the most effective, since they perform efficient factorizations of multivariate polynomials, which the other techniques do not.

The Jouletrack simulator [19] was used to estimate the reduction in latency and energy consumption for computing the polynomials on the StrongARM™ SA1100 microprocessor. The same set of randomly generated inputs was used for simulating the different programs. Table 6.2 shows the results of these experiments; it demonstrates the reduction in the latency and energy consumption for the polynomials optimized using algebraic techniques compared to those

Table 6.3 Synthesis results with minimum hardware constraints (only 1 *A*, 1 *M*)

Application	Function	Area saving over (%)		Energy saving over (%)		Energy-delay saving over (%)	
		CSE	Horner	CSE	Horner	CSE	Horner
Fast convolution	FFT	18.6	6.5	33.5	69.9	58.4	90.8
Gaussian noise filter	FIR	7.5	0.1	13.6	25.6	20.4	39.4
Graphics	Quartic spline	0.3	−4.2	21.6	29.3	39.0	48.8
Graphics	Quintic spline	−7.5	−24.2	29.4	10.4	47.6	25.9
Graphics	Chebyshev	5.6	2.5	37.0	28.7	57.1	46.1
Graphics	Cosine wavelet	3.7	2.0	44.8	36.8	62.8	54.8
Average		4.7	−2.8	30.0	33.4	47.5	50.9

optimized using the CSE and Horner methods. The latency was measured in terms of the number of clock cycles to execute the examples. The energy consumption was the total energy consumption in joules that the processor core consumed for computing the polynomials. On an average, the latency was reduced by 26.7% compared with CSE technique and by 26.3% compared with the Horner form of the polynomials. The energy consumption was reduced by 26.4% compared with the CSE technique and 26.3% compared with the Horner form.

The polynomials were synthesized using the RTL synthesis tools Synopsys Behavioral Compiler™ and Synopsys Design Compiler™, to get an estimate for the area, latency, and energy consumption if these polynomials were to be completely implemented on an ASIC. The input to the synthesis tools was an RTL description of the polynomials implemented using the three different techniques. The hardware experiments were performed in two different modes: with minimum hardware constraints and with medium hardware constraints. With minimum hardware constraints, the polynomial is executed with the least hardware resources. Typically the hardware includes just an adder, a multiplier, multiplexors, and registers. The reduction in area, energy, and energy-delay product of the polynomials optimized using the algebraic technique was measured and compared with the polynomials optimized using CSE (C) and Horner transform (H). These results are shown in Table 6.3. The results show that there is not much difference in area for the different implementations, but there is a significant reduction in total energy consumption (averages of 30% over CSE and 33.4% over Horner), and energy-delay product (averages of 47.5% over CSE and 50.9% over Horner). Since the latency of the polynomials is reduced, it is possible to reduce energy consumption by scaling down the voltage. Since the energy consumption varies with the square of the voltage, this is a very effective method of reducing the energy consumption. This method is called voltage scaling. Potential energy savings were calculated for this technique for the same set of examples. The results are also illustrated in Table 6.3.

Table 6.4(a) Synthesis results with medium hardware constraints

Application	Function	Area saving over (%)		Energy saving over (%)		Energy delay saving over (%)	
		CSE	Horner	CSE	Horner	CSE	Horner
Fast convolution	FFT	44.0	48.0	9.8	63.9	−12.7	81.0
Gaussian noise filter	FIR	30.5	3.9	16.1	39.2	9.7	44.1
Graphics	Quartic spline	14.8	1.0	9.7	29.6	20.3	58.7
Graphics	Quintic spline	8.3	3.7	42.5	29.1	44.9	37.0
Graphics	Chebyshev	8.9	9.0	28.2	29.5	39.5	40.6
Graphics	Cosine wavelet	8.0	6.6	41.4	40.8	58.4	59.7
Average		19.0	12.0	24.6	38.7	26.7	53.5

Table 6.4(b) Multipliers (M) and Adders (A) allocated with medium hardware constraints

Application	Function	CSE		Horner		Algebraic technique	
		M	A	M	A	M	A
Fast convolution	FFT	4	2	4	1	2	1
Gaussian noise filter	FIR	3	1	2	1	2	1
Graphics	Quartic spline	4	1	4	1	4	1
Graphics	Quintic spline	3	1	3	2	3	2
Graphics	Chebyshev	4	1	4	2	4	2
Graphics	Cosine wavelet	3	1	3	1	3	2

The scaled down voltage for the new latency was obtained with library parameters and the reduction in latency of the polynomial optimized using the algebraic technique compared to the other two techniques (CSE and Horner form). The results (Table 6.3, column 4) show an energy reduction of 30.0% compared with CSE (C) and 33.4% reduction compared with Horner (H) with voltage scaling.

Medium hardware constraints perform a tradeoff between area and energy efficiency. By performing certain operations in parallel, the schedule length can be reduced and also the energy consumption compared to that produced with minimum hardware constraints. In the experiments with medium hardware constraints, the maximum number of multipliers was limited to four. The scheduler in the synthesis tool allocates fewer than four multipliers, if the same latency can be achieved with fewer multipliers. Table 6.4(a) shows the results with medium hardware constraints. Table 6.4(b) shows the number of additions (A) and multiplications (M) that are allocated by the scheduler for the different techniques.

The results show a significant reduction in total energy consumption (averages of 24.6% compared with CSE (C) and 38.7% compared with the Horner (H) scheme), as well as energy-delay product (averages of 26.7% compared with CSE and 53.5% compared with Horner). Reduction in energy-delay product was achieved for every example except the first one, which actually showed an increase of 12.7% compared to that produced by the CSE transform. This is due to the fact that when four multipliers are used the latency of the CSE optimized expression is much less than the one optimized using the algebraic method (which uses two multipliers). The delay for the Horner scheme is much worse than for both CSE and the algebraic technique because the nested additions and multiplications of the Horner scheme typically result in a longer critical path.

6.7 Optimal solutions for reducing the number of operations in arithmetic expressions

The algebraic techniques for finding common subexpressions which were discussed in Section 6.5 were all based on heuristic greedy algorithms. In general the problem of finding the optimal solution to CSE is NP hard [17]. All research efforts in applying CSE for general purpose applications [20], for polynomial expressions [21, 22], for constant multiplications [23–25], and for integer exponentiation [26, 27] use greedy algorithms where the best common subexpression was extracted in every step of the algorithm. Finding minimal representations using integer linear programming (ILP) has been explored in [23] for the case of constant multiplications. This section illustrates the use of ILP for finding the exact solution of a general class of CSE problem.

6.7.1 Modeling CSE as an ILP problem

The CSE problem can be cast as an ILP problem thereby giving scope for finding the optimum solution. In [28] the authors developed a circuit model for representing all solutions corresponding to all possible common subexpressions. Finding the representation of the expression which has the minimum number of operations is then equivalent to activating a minimal number of gates in the circuit such that the output of the circuit is 1. The gate minimization problem can be modeled as an ILP problem. In [28], this methodology was applied to find the optimum representation for the constant multiplications in the transposed form of FIR filters. In this configuration, the set of constants can be seen as multiplying a single variable.

The method first enumerates a set of ways in which each constant multiplication can be implemented (this enumeration could include only binary representation, only minimal signed digit representation, etc). For example, some ways of implementing $7 \times X$ are $(8-1) \times X$, $(3+4) \times X$, $(2+5) \times X$, and $(1+6) \times X$. All these alternatives are then represented using an AND–OR circuit where each AND gate represents an addition or a subtraction and each OR gate collects the different ways of computing a particular value (i.e., partial product). Figure 6.19 illustrates such an AND–OR circuit for computing $7 \times X$. Four ways are considered for decomposing 7: $(8-1)$, $(6+1)$, $(5+2)$, and $(3+4)$. These four ways are summed

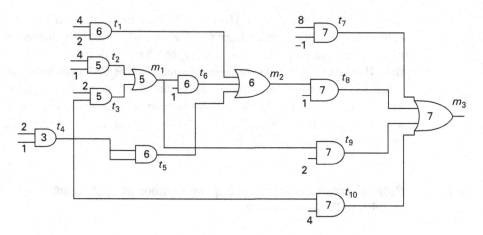

Figure 6.19 AND–OR circuit showing the partial sums that can be used to obtain the constant 7.

by the final OR gate. Each partial sum which is not a power of 2 is also explored for different ways in which it can be implemented. For example, the partial sum 6 can be implemented as $(4 + 2)$, $(5 + 1)$, and $(3 + 3)$. The optimization problem can be considered as a minimization of the total number of AND gates (which represent the additions and subtractions) such that the outputs of the OR gates corresponding to required sums are set to 1. This can easily be translated into an ILP problem by writing Boolean clauses in conjunctive normal form (CNF) for each gate and then converting each Boolean clause into one integer linear constraint.

6.7.1.1   From CNF form to ILP clauses

The CNF of a gate is a valid, satisfiable Boolean equation in conjunctive form representing the functionality of the gate. For example, the CNF of a two-input AND gate can be written as

$$F = (y' + a)(y' + b)(y + a' + b'),$$

where "a" and "b" are the inputs and "y" is the output of the AND gate.

This equation will always evaluate to 1 for all valid assignments of values to a, b, and y. This implies that each clause in the CNF must evaluate to 1. Each clause in the CNF can be converted into an ILP clause by representing a signal a' as $1 - a$ and constraining the clause to be greater than or equal to 1. Therefore, for the above AND gate, the ILP clauses are obtained as shown in Figure 6.20.

For the AND–OR circuit shown in Figure 6.19, the optimization function to the ILP solver can be set as

$$\text{Minimize } G = t_1 + t_2 + t_3 + t_4 + t_5 + t_6 + t_7 + t_8 + t_9 + t_{10},$$

such that $m_3 = 1$ and subject to circuit constraints.

$a-y\geq0$
$b-y\geq0$
$y-a-b\geq-1$

Figure 6.20 ILP clauses for a two-input AND gate with inputs a and b and output y.

To model circuit constraints, the constraints of each AND gate in the circuit are listed as shown in Figure 6.20. In this example, the minimum of G, such that m_3 is equal to 1, can be achieved by selecting only the gate output t_7. By using only one AND gate (corresponding to one addition), the multiplication $7 \times X$ can be achieved. Thus, $7 \times X$ can be calculated using one left shift and one addition as $X \ll 3 - X$.

6.7.2 Generalizing the ILP model for solving a larger class of redundancy elimination problems

The ILP model developed in [28] and illustrated in Subsection 6.7.1 can be applied to a more general class of redundancy elimination problem. Optimal solutions using ILP can be formulated for the problems of optimizing polynomial expressions, multi-variable constant multiplications and the integer exponentiation. This subsection shows how the ILP model can be extended to these cases.

First the case of polynomial expressions is considered. A method of generating all different factorizations of each polynomial is required. These different factorizations constitute the different ways of implementing the polynomials. Generating all possible algebraic factorizations can be extremely expensive and unnecessary. The factorizations using kernels and co-kernels introduced in Subsection 6.5.1 are minimal in the sense that they produce the minimal number of operations (additions and multiplications). Furthermore, generating all kernels guarantees the detection of common subexpressions between polynomials. This subsection presents an algorithm for generating the AND–OR circuit representing all "good algebraic factorizations." The ILP optimization functions and the constraints can be directly derived from this circuit as shown in Subsection 6.7.1.

The algorithm for generating the AND–OR circuit (GenCkt) is described using pseudo code in Figure 6.21. This algorithm is called for each polynomial in the set of polynomial expressions. The algorithm recursively finds solutions for different subexpressions in the polynomial. The different subexpressions are essentially all possible partitions of the polynomial expression. Only bipartitions are considered as we assume that additions and multiplications are two-operand operations. For each partition, the algorithm GenCkt is recursively called to obtain the circuit for the subexpression corresponding to the partition. The algorithm keeps track of the subexpressions computed by means of a hash table. The hash table is designed such that it is able to take into account the commutativity and associativity of addition and multiplication operations. Therefore, the same key is generated for both the subexpressions $a + b + c$ and $c + a + b$.

```
Node GenCkt( {T_i} )
{
     // {T_i}: Set of terms representing the polynomial expression
     // This function returns a node representing the gate output that computes the
     polynomial

     result = HASH({T_i});
     If (result != ∅) {
       return result; // This polynomial has already been computed
     }

     If(|{T_i}| > 1)   {                    // If the polynomial has more than 1 term
         Term CK = CoKernel({T_i});         // Returns the co-kernel of this polynomial
         {T_i} = {T_i}/(CK);                // Dividing the polynomial by the co-kernel

         result = HASH({T_i});
         If(result != ∅) {          // Check to see if the kernel has been generated already
           CKNode = GenCkt(CK);                     // generating a node for the co-kernel
           result = CombineAND(result, CKNode, x)   // combining the kernel with the co-kernel
           return result;
         }
     }
     ORGate = new Node;

     // Generate all possible partitions of the subexpression {T_i}
     {{T_i}^A, {T_i}^B} = GenAllPartitions({T_i});

     for(all partitions {T_i}_j^A and {T_i}_j^B)
     {   Node N_1 = GenCkt( {T_i}_j^A);           // Creating the circuits for each combination
         Node N_2 = GenCkt( {T_i}_j^B);
         Node ANDi;
         If(|T_i| == 1) // If the polynomial has only 1 term
             ANDi = CombineAND(N_1, N_2, x);
         else
             ANDi = CombineAND(N_1, N_2, +);
         ORGate->Insert(ANDi);                 // insert ANDi as one of the inputs of ORGate
     }

     If(CK != '1')
     {
         CKNode = GenCkt(CK);
         result = CombineAND(ORGate, CKNode, x);
     }
     else
         result = ORGate;

     HashTable->Insert(result);                 // Insert the result in the Hash Table
     return result;
}
```

Figure 6.21 Algorithm GenCkt used to generate an AND–OR circuit for a polynomial.

The algorithm has a set of terms representing the polynomial as input. The co-kernel (CK in the algorithm) of the polynomial is equal to a term that can divide all terms of the polynomial. The polynomial is then divided by this co-kernel to get the kernel. This kernel is then hashed to see if it has already been computed. If it has already been computed, a node representing the computed subexpression is returned by the hash table. This node is then combined with the node representing the co-kernel using the CombineAND operation and the resultant node is returned. The function CombineAND returns a node that represents an AND gate combining the two nodes. The AND gate may represent either a multiplication or an addition, and is passed as an argument to the CombineAND function. An OR gate (ORGate in the algorithm) is created to collect all different ways of computing the polynomial.

The function GenAllPartitions takes as input a set of terms and generates all possible bi-partitions of the $\{T_i\}$ terms. The number of partitions for N terms is $C(N)$, where

$$C(N) = \binom{N}{1} + \binom{N}{2} + \cdots + \binom{N}{\lfloor N/2 \rfloor} = o(2^{N-1}).$$

If the number of terms of the polynomial is only one ($|\{T_i\}| = 1$), then the function returns all possible binary partitions of the literals in the term. If the term has N literals, then the number of combinations is given by the above equation $C(N)$.

The function GenCkt is recursively called for each subexpression of the partition and the two subexpressions are then combined using the CombineAND function. The resultant node ANDi is then inserted into the OR gate as one of the ways of computing the polynomial. After combining all pairs, the co-kernel node (CKNode) is then combined with the OR gate to obtain the resultant polynomial node. This node is then inserted into the hash table.

Figure 6.22 illustrates the working of the algorithm for a polynomial expression. For this polynomial, the co-kernel a^2b is first extracted. After dividing the original polynomial by this co-kernel, the polynomial $(ab + ac + bc)$ is obtained. There are three possible partitions of this kernel: $\{(ab), (ac + bc)\}$, $\{(ab + ac), (bc)\}$, and $\{(ab + bc), (ac)\}$. The three alternatives are summed in the final OR gate as shown in the Figure 6.23. The co-kernel a^2b is also explored by generating different partitions. The optimization function for this circuit can be written as:

$$\text{Minimize} \sum_{i=1}^{i=16} t_i$$

$$\text{such that: } t_{16} = 1.$$

The constraints for each gate in the circuit can be generated as described in Subsection 6.7.1. Intuitively, one can see the solution for this problem can be obtained by setting $\{t_1, t_2, t_3, t_4, t_{15}, t_{16}\} = 1$, which corresponds to the solution:

$$t_1 = a \times b$$

$$F = a \times t_1 \times (c \times (a + b) + t_1).$$

$F = a^3b^2 + a^3bc + a^2b^2c$　　// The original polynomial

$CK = a^2b$
$F = F/CK = (ab + ac + bc)$

All possible combinations $\{\{T_i\}^A, \{T_i\}^B\}$ are
$\{\{(ab) + (ac + bc)\}, \{(ac) + (ab + bc)\}, \{(bc) + (ab + ac)\}\}$

⇓　　　　　⇓　　　　　⇓

$\{\{(ab), c*(a + b)\}, \{(ac), b*(a + c)\}, \{(bc), a*(b + c)\}$

Evaluating $CK = a^2b$

All possible combinations $\{\{T_i\}^A, \{T_i\}^B\}$ are
$\{\{(a*a) *(b)\}, \{a*b) *(a)\}\}$

Figure 6.22 Example showing the steps in generating the AND–OR circuit.

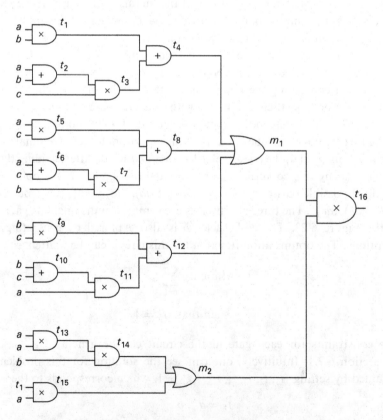

Figure 6.23 AND–OR circuit for the example polynomial generated by algorithm GenCkt.

This solution has four multiplications and two additions, and is the implementation with the least cost.

The method described in this section can be easily extended to the case of linear arithmetic expressions. The kernel generation method can be applied as described in Chapter 7, to remove the common arithmetic shift. The only differences with the method for polynomials are that the implementation for co-kernels does not have to be explored if the expressions will be implemented in hardware (shift operations can be performed in hardware for free). Furthermore, only addition and subtraction operations are used; there is no need for multiplications. The optimality of the result is restricted to the chosen representation of the constants. If the constants are encoded using canonical signed digits (CSD), then the final result is optimal only for the CSD representations. Considering other representations along with CSD is possible, but it substantially increases the complexity of the algorithm.

6.8   Summary

This chapter presented some of the existing techniques for optimizing polynomials, such as the Horner transform and the symbolic algebra technique, and discussed their shortcomings. Then, it presented two algebraic techniques: kernel extraction in conjunction with rectangle covering and concurrent arithmetic extraction (CAX). Experimental results showed the superiority of these techniques over the existing ones. Finally, the chapter discussed some ideas on finding optimal solutions to the polynomial optimization problem using integer linear programming. In the next chapter, some of the presented algorithms will be used for optimizing linear systems.

References

[1] R. H. Bartels, J. C. Beatty, and B. A. Barsky, *An Introduction to Splines for Use in Computer Graphics and Geometric Modeling*. San Francisco, CA: Morgan Kaufmann Publishers, Inc., 1987.
[2] D. Hearn and M. P. Baker, *Computer Graphics*, 2nd edition. Upper Saddle River, NJ: Prentice-Hall Inc.
[3] GNU C Library, http://www.gnu.org/software/libc
[4] A. V. Aho and S. C. Johnson, Optimal code generation for expression trees, *Journal of the ACM*, **23** 488–501, 1976.
[5] R. Sethi and J. D. Ullman, The generation of optimal code for arithmetic expressions, *Journal of the ACM*, **17**, 715–28, 1970.
[6] A. V. Aho, S. C. Johnson, and J. D. Ullman, Code generation for expressions with common subexpressions, *Journal of the ACM*, **24**, 146–60, 1977.
[7] M. A. Breuer, Generation of optimal code for expressions via factorization, *Communication of the ACM*, **12**, 333–40, 1969.

[8] T. Becker and V. Weispfenning. *Grobner Bases*. New York. NY: Springer-Verlag, 1993.

[9] G. D. Micheli, *Synthesis and Optimization of Digital Circuits*: New York, NY: McGraw-Hill, Inc, 1994.

[10] H. De Man, J. Rabaey, J. Vanhoof, *et al.*, CATHEDRAL-II-a computer-aided synthesis system for digital signal processing VLSI systems, *Computer-Aided Engineering Journal*, **5**, 55–66, 1988.

[11] A. Peymandoust and G. D. Micheli, Using symbolic algebra in algorithmic level DSP synthesis, *Design Automation Conference, Las Vegas, 2001*. New York, NY: ACM, 2001.

[12] A. Peymandoust, T. Simunic, and G. D. Michell, Low power embedded software optimization using sumbolic algebra, *Design Automation and Test in Europe, Paris, 2002*, pp. 1052–1058. Washington DC: IEEE Computer Society, 2002.

[13] A. S. Vincentelli, A. Wang, R. K. Brayton, and R. Rudell, MIS: multiple level logic optimization system, *IEEE Transactions on Computer Aided Design of Integrated Circuits and Systems*, **6**, 1062–81, 1987.

[14] R. K. Brayton and C. T. McMullen, The decomposition and factorization of Boolean expressions, *International Symposium on Circuits and Systems, 1982*. Washington, DC: IEEE Computer Society, 1982.

[15] J. Rajski and J. Vasudevamurthy, The testability-preserving concurrent decomposition and factorization of Boolean expressions, *IEEE Transactions on Computer-Aided Design of Intergrated Circuits and Systems*, **11**, 778–793, 1992.

[16] R. K. Brayton, R. Rudell, A. S. Vincentelli, and A. Wang, Multi-level logic optimization and the rectangular covering problem, *International Conference on Compute Aided Design, 1987, Los Amitos, CA*: IEEE Computer Society Press, 1987.

[17] R. Rudell, Logic synthesis for VLSI design, Ph.D. Thesis, University of California, Berkeley, 1989.

[18] P. M. Embree, *C Algorithms for Real-Time DSP*. Upper Saddle River, NJ: Prentice Hall, 1995.

[19] A. Sinha and A. P. Chandrakasan, Jouletrack-a Web based tool for software energy profiling, *Proceedings of the annual ACM IEEE Design Automation Conference, Las Vegas, June 2001*. pp. 220–225. New York, NY: ACM, 2001.

[20] S. S. Muchnick, *Advanced Compiler Design and Implementation*. San Francisco, CA. Morgan Kaufmann Publishers, 1997.

[21] A. Hosangadi, F. Fallah, and R. Kastner, Factoring and eliminating common subexpressions, polynomial expressions, *International Conference on Computer Aided Design [ICCAD], San Jose, 2004*, pp. 169–174. Washington, DC: IEEE Computer Society, 2004.

[22] A. Hosangadi, F. Fallah, and R. Kastner, Energy efficient hardware synthesis in polynomial expressions, *International Conference on VLSI Design, Kolkata, India, 2005*. pp. 653–58. Washington, DC: IEEE Computer Society.

[23] M. Potkonjak, M. B. Srivastava, and A. P. Chandrakasan, Multiple constant multiplactions: efficient and versatile framework and algorithms for exploring common subexpression elimination, *IEEE Transactions on Computer Aided Design of Intergrated Circuits* and Systems, **15**(2), 151–65, 1996.

[24] A. Hosangadi, F. Fallah, and R. Kastner, Common subexpression involving multiple variables for linear DSP synthesis, *IEEE International Conference on Application*

Specific Architectures and Processors (ASAP), Galveston, 2004. Washington, DC: IEEE Computer Society, 2004.

[25] A. Hosangadi, F. Fallah, and R. Kastner, Reducing hardware compleity of linear DSP systems by interatively eliminating two term common subexpressions, *Asia South Pacific Design Automation Conference, Shanghai, 2005.* New York, NY: ACM, 2005.

[26] P. Downey, B. Leong, and R. Sethi, Computing sequences with addition chains, *SIAM Journal of Computing,* **10**, 638–46, 1981.

[27] K. Koyama, and T. Tsuruoka, Speeding up elliptic cryptosystems by using a signed binary window method, *Proceedings of the 12th Annual International Cryptography Conference on Advances in Cryptography, Santa Barbara, August, 1992*, pp. 345–47. London: Springer Verlag, 1992.

[28] P. F. Flores, J. C. Monteiro, and E. C. Costa, An exact algorithm for the maximal sharing of partial terms in multiple constant multiplications, *International Conference on Computer Aided Design (ICCAD), San Jose, 2005.* Washington, DC: IEEE Computer Society, 2005.

7 Linear systems

7.1 Chapter overview

This chapter provides a thorough discussion of the issues surrounding the optimization of linear systems. Section 7.2 describes fundamental properties, and presents a list of common linear transforms. Then, Section 7.3 formalizes the problem. Sections 7.4 and 7.5 introduce two important cases of linear system optimization, namely single- and multiple-constant multiplication. While the algorithms to solve these problems are important, they do not fully take advantage of the solution space; thus, they may lead to inferior results. Section 7.6 describes the relationship of these two problems to the linear system optimization problem and provides an overview of techniques used to optimize linear systems. Section 7.7 presents a transformation from a linear system into a set of polynomial expressions. The algorithms presented later in the chapter use this transformation during optimization. Section 7.8 describes an algorithm for optimizing expressions for synthesis using two-operand adders. The results in Section 7.9 describe the synthesis of high-speed FIR filters using this two-operand optimization along with other common techniques for FIR filter synthesis. Then, Section 7.10 focuses on more complex architectures, in particular, those using three-operand adders, and shows how CSAs can speed up the calculation of linear systems. Section 7.11 discusses how to consider timing constraints by modifying the previously presented optimization techniques. Specifically, the section describes ideas for performing delay aware optimization. The majority of the optimizations in this chapter focus on hardware implementations; however, Section 7.12 describes how to apply these same techniques to speed up software implementations of linear systems. Finally, Section 7.13 provides concluding remarks.

7.2 Linear system basics

A linear system is a mathematical model based on linear operations. Linear operations adhere to two properties, namely additivity and homogeneity. Given two vectors x and y, and a scalar a, these properties are formally described as:

$$\text{additivity: } f(x + y) = f(x) + f(y), \tag{7.1}$$

$$\text{homogeneity: } f(a \cdot x) = a \cdot f(x). \tag{7.2}$$

Another way to state this is that for vectors x_n and scalars a_n the following equality holds:

$$f(a_1x_1 + a_2x_2 + \cdots + a_nx_n) = a_1f(x_1) + a_2f(x_2) + \cdots + a_nf(x_n). \quad (7.3)$$

A linear system is a common computation model and can be found in many application domains. A prominent example is computer graphics where geometric manipulations including translation, rotation, and scaling of two-dimensional or three-dimensional objects are performed using a transformation matrix [1]. A transformation matrix describes a set of linear mappings between two vector spaces. Take, for example, the scaling (enlargement or contraction) of a two-dimensional object. This is done by multiplying every point (x, y) of the object by a constant value a, i.e., $x' = a \cdot x$ and $y' = a \cdot y$. The following transformation matrix represents the scaling operation:

$$\begin{bmatrix} x' \\ y' \end{bmatrix} = \begin{bmatrix} a & 0 \\ 0 & a \end{bmatrix} \begin{bmatrix} x \\ y \end{bmatrix}. \quad (7.4)$$

Other transformation matrices include rotation of an object by some angle θ:

$$\begin{bmatrix} x' \\ y' \end{bmatrix} = \begin{bmatrix} \cos\theta & -\sin\theta \\ \sin\theta & \cos\theta \end{bmatrix} \begin{bmatrix} x \\ y \end{bmatrix}, \quad (7.5)$$

and shearing, which is visually similar to slanting [1]. The transformation matrices for shearing by the constant k parallel to the x and y axes, respectively, are:

$$\begin{bmatrix} x' \\ y' \end{bmatrix} = \begin{bmatrix} 1 & k \\ 0 & 1 \end{bmatrix} \begin{bmatrix} x \\ y \end{bmatrix}, \quad (7.6)$$

$$\begin{bmatrix} x' \\ y' \end{bmatrix} = \begin{bmatrix} 1 & 0 \\ k & 1 \end{bmatrix} \begin{bmatrix} x \\ y \end{bmatrix}. \quad (7.7)$$

More formally, the following defines a transformation matrix: if V and W are vectors with finite dimensions, every linear transform from V to W can be represented as a matrix. The linear transform $f(x) = A \cdot x$ describes a linear transform $R^n \rightarrow R^m$, where n and m are two nonnegative integers.

Linear systems also have roles as mathematical abstractions or models of computation in other applications besides graphics, including automatic control theory, signal processing, and telecommunications. The primary focus of this chapter is on signal processing; however, the techniques are applicable across any application that computes linear systems.

Some of the more familiar and important linear transforms include the following:

- discrete Fourier transform (DFT) [2],

$$DFT_n = [\omega_n^{kl}]_{0=k,\, l<n}, \quad \omega_n = e^{-2\pi j/n}. \quad (7.8)$$

- Walsh–Hadamard transform (WHT) [3],

$$WHT_n = \begin{bmatrix} WHT_{n/2} & WHT_{n/2} \\ WHT_{n/2} & -WHT_{n/2} \end{bmatrix}. \quad (7.9)$$

- real discrete Fourier transform (RDFT), also known as real-valued DFT [4],

$$RDFT_n = \left[\begin{bmatrix} I''_n \\ \cos\dfrac{2\pi kl}{n} \\ -\sin\dfrac{2\pi kl}{n} \end{bmatrix} \right]; \tag{7.10}$$

$$RDFT2_n = \left[\begin{bmatrix} I''_k \\ \cos\dfrac{\pi k(2l+1)}{n} \\ -\sin\dfrac{\pi k(2l+1)}{n} \end{bmatrix} \right]; \tag{7.11}$$

$$RDFT3_n = \left[\begin{matrix} \cos\dfrac{\pi(2k+1)l}{n} \\ -\sin\dfrac{\pi(2k+1)l}{n} \end{matrix} \right]. \tag{7.12}$$

- discrete Hartley transform (DHT)[1] [5],

$$DHT_n = \left[\begin{bmatrix} I''_n \\ \cos\dfrac{2\pi kl}{n} \\ \cos\dfrac{2\pi kl}{n} \end{bmatrix} \right]; \tag{7.13}$$

$$DHT2_n = \left[\begin{bmatrix} I''_n \\ \cos\dfrac{\pi k(2l+1)}{n} \\ \cos\dfrac{\pi k(2l+1)}{n} \end{bmatrix} \right]; \tag{7.14}$$

$$DHT3_n = \left[\left[\begin{matrix} \cos\dfrac{\pi(2k+1)l}{n} \\ \cos\dfrac{2\pi(2k+1)l}{n} \end{matrix} \right] \right]. \tag{7.15}$$

- discrete cosine transform (DCT) and its inverse (IDCT) [6]

$$DCT1_n = \left[\cos\dfrac{kl\pi}{n-1} \right]; \tag{7.16}$$

$$DCT2_n = \left[\cos\dfrac{k(2l+1)\pi}{2n} \right]; \tag{7.17}$$

---

[1] $\mathrm{cas}(x) = \cos(x) + \sin(x)$.
$\mathrm{cms}(x) = \cos(x) - \sin(x)$.

$$DCT3_n = \left[\cos\frac{(2k+1)l\pi}{2n}\right];$$ (7.18)

$$DCT4_n = \left[\cos\frac{(2k+1)(2l+1)\pi}{4n}\right];$$ (7.19)

$$DCT3_N(r) = \left[\cos\frac{r_k l\pi}{n}\right].$$ (7.20)

- discrete sine transform (DST) [7],

$$DST1_N = \left[\sin\frac{(k+1)(l+1)\pi}{n+1}\right];$$ (7.21)

$$DST2_N = \left[\sin\frac{(k+1)(2l+1)\pi}{2n}\right];$$ (7.22)

$$DST3_N = \left[\sin\frac{(2k+1)(l+1)\pi}{2n}\right];$$ (7.23)

$$DST4_n = \left[\sin\frac{(2k+1)(2l+1)\pi}{4n}\right];$$ (7.24)

$$DST3_N(r) = \left[\sin\frac{r_k(l+1)\pi}{n}\right].$$ (7.25)

- modified discrete cosine transform (MDCT) and its inverse (IMDCT) [8],
- finite impulse response (FIR) filter [9], and
- downsampled FIR filter (as part of the wavelet transform) [10].

7.3   Problem formulation

A linear system can be formalized using the notion described in the previous section. If X and Y are input and output vectors, respectively, and A is the transformation matrix, the linear system can be written as

$$\begin{bmatrix} Y_1 \\ Y_2 \\ \vdots \\ Y_m \end{bmatrix} = \begin{bmatrix} A_{1,1} & A_{1,2} & \cdots & A_{1,n} \\ A_{2,1} & A_{2,2} & \cdots & A_{2,n} \\ \vdots & \vdots & \vdots & \vdots \\ A_{m,1} & A_{m,2} & \cdots & A_{m,n} \end{bmatrix} \begin{bmatrix} X_1 \\ X_2 \\ \vdots \\ X_n \end{bmatrix}.$$ (7.26)

The transformation matrix A is an $m \times n$ matrix, where $A_{i,j}$ represents the (i,j)th element. An output signal Y_i is the product of the ith row of the transformation matrix A and the n input samples of X:

$$Y_j = \sum_{j=1}^{N} A_{i,j} \cdot X_j.$$ (7.27)

As a specific example, consider a four-point DCT, which is a common linear system used for compression in many signal processing systems, e.g., JPEG [11] and MPEG compression [12]. The DCT expresses a datum as a sum of sinusoids, in a similar manner to a Fourier transform, but uses only real numbers corresponding to the cosine value of a complex exponential. DCT has a strong energy compaction that is ideal for compression of image and video data, where most of the signal information is found in the lower-frequency components. The examples throughout this section refer to the following four-point DCT:

$$
\begin{bmatrix} Y_1 \\ Y_2 \\ Y_3 \\ Y_4 \end{bmatrix} = \begin{bmatrix} \cos(0) & \cos(0) & \cos(0) & \cos(0) \\ \cos(\pi/8) & \cos(3\pi/8) & \cos(5\pi/8) & \cos(7\pi/8) \\ \cos(\pi/4) & \cos(3\pi/4) & \cos(5\pi/4) & \cos(7\pi/4) \\ \cos(3\pi/8) & \cos(7\pi/8) & \cos(\pi/8) & \cos(5\pi/8) \end{bmatrix} \begin{bmatrix} X_1 \\ X_2 \\ X_3 \\ X_4 \end{bmatrix}. \tag{7.28}
$$

Expanding this matrix–vector product yields four equations (one for each of the outputs Y_1, Y_2, Y_3, and Y_4), each with a summation of four terms consisting of a constant multiplication of the four input variables (X_1, X_2, X_3, and X_4) as shown below:

$$
\begin{aligned}
Y_1 &= \cos(0) \cdot X_1 + \cos(0) \cdot X_2 + \cos(0) \cdot X_3 + \cos(0) \cdot X_4 \\
Y_2 &= \cos(\pi/8) \cdot X_1 + \cos(3\pi/8) \cdot X_2 + \cos(5\pi/8) \cdot X_3 + \cos(7\pi/8) \cdot X_4 \\
Y_3 &= \cos(\pi/4) \cdot X_1 + \cos(3\pi/4) \cdot X_2 + \cos(5\pi/4) \cdot X_3 + \cos(7\pi/4) \cdot X_4 \\
Y_4 &= \cos(3\pi/8) \cdot X_1 + \cos(7\pi/8) \cdot X_2 + \cos(\pi/8) \cdot X_3 + \cos(5\pi/8) \cdot X_4
\end{aligned} \tag{7.29}
$$

Two points arise regarding the DCT:

(1) Although it is an example of a two-dimensional linear system, it can be viewed as a set of one-dimensional filters. However, additional optimizations can be performed if optimizations are considered across linear equations (Y_1, Y_2, Y_3, and Y_4).

(2) Similar constants appear in the transformation matrix. It is often advantageous to convert constant multiplications into a corresponding set of shifts and additions. Careful decomposition into shifts and additions, while optimizing the resulting equations, leads to tremendous benefits with respect to execution time, area, throughput, and power/energy.

Section 7.4 describes a simplified version of the linear system optimization problem: the multiplication of a single variable by a constant number. Section 7.5 tackles the problem of multiple constant multiplication by considering some simple examples to give a basic understanding of the issues, which are faced later in the chapter.

7.4   Single-constant multiplication (SCM)

The multiplication of a variable x by a known integer of fixed point constant c can be decomposed into a set of additions, subtractions, and binary shift operations. In *single-constant multiplication*, the decomposition with the minimum number of operations is found. This problem is NP-complete [13]. The problem has some similarity with the addition chain problem [14], but the addition chain problem only considers add operations, while the ability to use subtraction and shift in single-constant multiplication fundamentally alters the problem.

The most straightforward method for single-constant multiplication transforms the constant c into its binary representation, converts the 1s into shifts based on their positions, and sums the shifted values. As an example, consider $c = 45$,

$$45 \cdot x = 101101_2 \cdot x = x \ll 5 + x \ll 3 + x \ll 2 + x. \tag{7.30}$$

This requires three additions and three shift operations. A shift operation is "free" in a hardware implementation (it only involves rewiring), therefore, only the number of additions is important, i.e., the number of "1" entries in the constant representation. The number of additions using the binary representation is one less than the number of "1" instances.

Another method uses shifts and subtractions by translating the "0" values into shift operations while subtracting them from the constant of the same length consisting of only 1s. The constant 45 requires six bits and the corresponding six-bit constant of all 1s (111111) is 63. This gives the following:

$$45 \cdot x = (63 - 18) \cdot x = (111111_2 - 010010_2) \cdot x = (x \ll 6 - x) - x \ll 4 - x \ll 1. \tag{7.31}$$

The term $(x \ll 6 - x)$ represents the number 63 and the following two terms, $(x \ll 4)$ and $(x \ll 1)$, represent the terms $16x$ and $2x$, respectively.

The CSD representation encodes a constant number using the minimal number of nonzero digits. Therefore, when transforming a constant multiplication into a sequence of shifts and additions, the CSD representation yields the minimum number of additions. Using CSD in the previous example gives the following:

$$45 \cdot x = 10\bar{1}0\bar{1}01 \cdot x = x \ll 6 - x \ll 4 - x \ll 2 + x. \tag{7.32}$$

In this case, CSD does not provide any benefit; however, on average CSD is better than using a binary representation. The average case cost for CSD is $b/3 + O(1)$ while the worst-case cost for CSD remains $b/2 + O(1)$ where b is the number of bits of the constant [15]. The vast majority of linear system optimizations use the CSD representation for constant encoding.

Figure 7.1 shows the CSD value and area results for a constant multiplication using Synopsys Design Compiler Ultra™ [16] for a TSMC 90 nm library [17]. It plots the scaled area for constant multiplication in the range [1,100]. The results are obtained simply by synthesizing the constant value multiplied by an eight-bit variable. Both results are scaled to the largest value; hence, all data points lie in the range [0,1].

The results show that the area and the number of nonzero digits in CSD encoding are highly correlated. There is some variation in the area results, but, generally speaking, the area of the constant multiplier mirrors the number of nonzero values in the CSD representation. The delay values also follow a similar trend, though for the sake of clarity and brevity, these are not shown.

Despite the fact that CSD minimizes the number of nonzero elements for the constant representation, it is not optimal. It is possible to decompose the result to

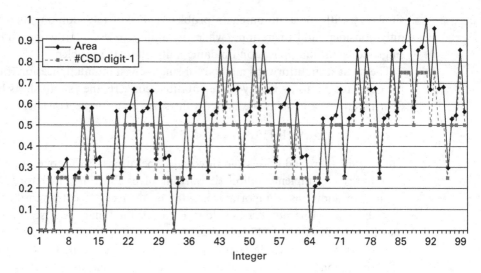

Figure 7.1 Scaled comparison of the area of a constant multiplier for numbers 1–100 vs. the corresponding number of nonzero digits in the CSD representation of the number.

further reduce the number of operations. Consider again multiplication by the constant 45.

Extracting the common subexpression $8x + x$ means that the constant multiplication requires only two add/subtract operations as opposed to three operations needed in previous methods. This is the optimal case as shown in Figure 7.2. Dempster and Macleod [18] developed an exhaustive method to find the optimal decomposition for constants up to 12 bits; their work was extended by Gustafsson *et al.* [19] to handle constants up to 19 bits. In fact, for multiplications with constant positive integers, 45 is the smallest number for which the CSD representation does not create the optimal number of operations. The asymptotic worst-case cost (number of additions/subtractions required) for the optimal representation is an open question at the time of writing this book. However, it appears that the optimal case is better than $O(b)$, where b is the bitwidth of the number [20].

We now return to our running example and continue the transformation of the four-point DCT. The constants of the transformation matrix A are scaled to convert them into integers using nine bits. For example, $\cos(0) = 1$, and therefore 256, the largest representable nine-bit integer number. Similarly $\cos(\pi/8) \approx 0.924$, which when transformed to a nine-bit scaled integer is 237 ($237/256 \approx 0.926$). Transforming the remainder of the numbers yields the constant matrix:

$$A = \begin{bmatrix} 256 & 256 & 256 & 256 \\ 237 & 98 & -98 & -237 \\ 181 & -182 & -182 & 181 \\ 98 & -237 & 237 & -98 \end{bmatrix}. \tag{7.33}$$

In the previous sections of this chapter several techniques were presented for converting a constant multiplication with a single variable into a set of shift and add

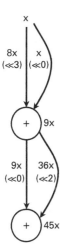

Figure 7.2 The minimal number of shift and add operations to multiply the variable x by the constant 45. The reduction in additions comes from the sharing of the term 9x. The arrows indicate a shift operation, while the nodes denote addition. The total number of operations is two additions and four shift operations.

operations; most of them revolve around the use of signed digit representation [21] for the constant value. Encoding each of these constants using CSD results in

$$A_{CSD} = \begin{bmatrix} 100000000 & 100000000 & 100000000 & 100000000 \\ 100010011 & 010100010 & 010100010 & 100010011 \\ 011001011 & 011001010 & 011001010 & 011001011 \\ 010100010 & 100010011 & 100010011 & 010100010 \end{bmatrix}. \tag{7.34}$$

The number -98 at position $A_{4,4}$ is represented as $0\bar{1}010\bar{0}0\bar{1}0$. Therefore,

$$\begin{aligned} A_{4,4} \cdot X_4 &= -98 \cdot X_4 \\ &= 0\bar{1}010\bar{0}0\bar{1}0 \cdot X_4 \\ &= -128 \cdot X_4 + 32 \cdot X_4 - 2 \cdot X_4 \\ &= -X_4 \ll 7 + X_4 \ll 5 - X_4 \ll 1. \end{aligned} \tag{7.35}$$

7.5 Multiple-constant multiplication (MCM)

MCM is an extension of single-constant multiplication where a single variable is multiplied by a set of constants $c_1, c_2, \ldots, c_n$. This operation is useful in many linear transforms; the most obvious is the transposed form of FIR filters. Figure 7.3 shows an MCM block and its usage in a transposed FIR filter. This block can also be used as a building block for other linear system transforms, e.g., DFT and other trigonometric transforms that involve 2×2 rotations, i.e., the simultaneous multiplication by two constants.

The MCM problem is at least as hard as the single-constant multiplication problem since the latter is a subset of the MCM problem; since the single-constant

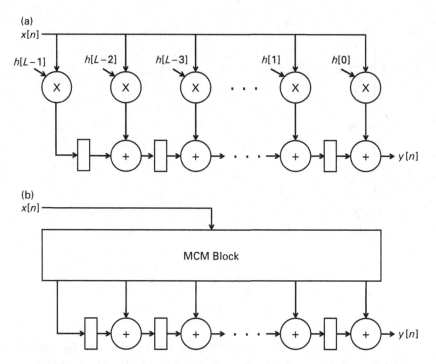

(a)

(b)

Figure 7.3 (a) The transposed form of an FIR filter. (b) The multiplications are replaced by an MCM block.

multiplication problem is NP-complete, the MCM problem is also NP-complete. One potential solution to the MCM problem is simply to optimize each single-constant multiplication independently. However, in general, by sharing the intermediate computations required by each constant, MCM can be decomposed into fewer operations than the total number of SCM operations that would be needed.

Consider the example in Figure 7.4, which shows the multiplication of two constants, 81 and 23. Figures 7.4(a) and (b) depict the best optimization for each variable individually. The nodes denote addition, while the edges show the required amount of shifting. For example, the "80×" node in Figure 7.4(a) takes the original variable x, shifts it four and six bits, which is equivalent to multiplication of x by 16 and 64, respectively. Both Figure 7.4(a) and (b) require two additions, resulting in four additions to perform both multiplications. Figure 7.4(c) shows the simultaneous optimization of the two variables. The variables can share a common multiplication 9×, hence, the overall number of additions for both variables is reduced by one (i.e., total of three additions).

Solutions of the MCM problem can be divided into four general classes:

- digit-based recoding algorithms,
- CSE algorithms,
- graph-based algorithms, and
- hybrid algorithms.

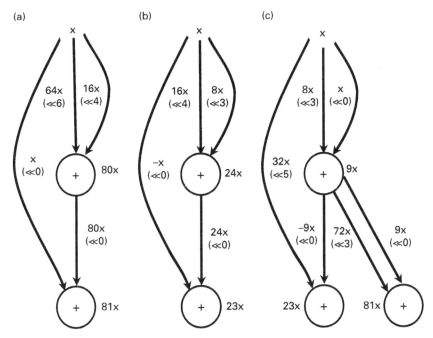

Figure 7.4 Multiplication of the constants 81 and 23. (a), (b) The optimization of each variable independently; this requires two additions per constant for a total of four additions. (c) The simultaneous optimization of both variables. The variables can share one addition resulting in three additions for the multiplication of both constants.

Digit-based recoding algorithms directly create the constant multiplication based upon a specific encoding of the constant. These methods typically use a CSD representation since they have the least number of nonzero digits and therefore create a solution with a small number of additions/subtractions for a single constant. It is possible to use a mix of number systems to achieve substantially better results [22]. The digit-based recoding class of algorithms are the easiest to implement but typically achieve the worst results.

The second class of algorithms uses *CSE* to find recurring subpatterns that occur across various constants. In the MCM problem, the common subexpressions are sets of additions, subtractions, and shift operations, but CSE is a well-known compiler optimization used to find and extract commonly occurring sequences of operations [23]. Compiler literature typically considers CSE algorithms based on value numbering [24] and Sethi–Ullman numbering [25] using a peephole optimization framework [26, 27]. CSE can be performed both locally (on a set of operations in a basic block, i.e., those without control flow operations) and globally (across control blocks, function calls, files, etc.). CSE is a powerful optimization, yet typically it does not take advantage of associative, commutative, and distributive properties. Fisher and LeBlanc [28] provide a simple yet very effective method to exploit commutativity and associativity during CSE. There are many other variants of CSE, targeting different control structures and situations. For example, Briggs and Cooper [29] show how to take advantage of associativity and distributivity while targeting loop invariant operations. Intuitively, CSE techniques explicitly targeting multiple constants perform better than general techniques or those aimed at other situations. The interested reader is referred to Aho *et al.* [30] for a survey of common subexpressions. This section focuses solely on CSE techniques for solving the MCM problem.

Potkonjak *et al.* [31] use an iterative bipartite matching algorithm in an attempt to minimize the number of operations in the constant multiplication. Each iteration extracts the two best matching constants. The algorithm performs a preprocessing scaling of the input constants to increase the solution space. The scaling is effective in reducing the number of operations, yet expands the search space exponentially. The major drawback of this algorithm is that it cannot find common subexpressions among shifted forms of the constants. For example, the algorithm cannot detect the common subexpression "101" in the constants "0101" and "1010."

Mehendale *et al.* [32] specifically target area reduction for FIR filters. Their algorithm identifies and eliminates two nonzero bit patterns (or equivalently subexpressions). Their technique works on both the direct and the transposed form of the FIR filter. They employ an iterative CSE algorithm that searches for the pattern with the highest frequency of occurrence over all constants. They extract this pattern, update the statistics of the other patterns, and search for any additional patterns caused by this pattern being selected. Their algorithm can recognize shifted patterns (e.g., it will find the pattern "101" in the constants "0101" and "1010"). Hartley [33] also uses an algorithm to look for two-bit patterns, while also considering the latch-count, which introduces issues related to timing.

Pasko *et al.* [34] propose an extension of the technique from Mehendale *et al.* [32] to handle patterns of arbitrary size. They also cast the problem as a set of matrix optimizations. However, they use an exhaustive bit pattern enumeration algorithm to extract all common digit sequences, which in practice limits the size of the patterns that they can optimize. The size of the pattern grows as

$$O\left(\frac{n}{k}\right), \tag{7.36}$$

where n is the number of bits for the constant and k is the size of the pattern. Therefore, they cannot afford to search for large patterns. Their results use a maximum pattern size of six and they show that the vast majority of the benefits come from smaller patterns. They argue that this is due to the fact that FIR filter coefficients have a limited number of nonzero bits. While this is true, very large patterns (in the extreme case, patterns that span the entire constant) are frequent in real examples. In fact, in many linear systems, similar constants are repeated in several places. The four-point DCT gives an example of this phenomenon (see Section 7.3). Extracting such constants provides a large benefit that techniques that focus on extracting small patterns miss.

CSE algorithms for the MCM problem are typically performed after selecting a digit representation, which is often CSD, due to the fact the CSD has the minimum number of additions/subtractions for a single constant. This is a significant drawback to CSE approaches. Park and Kang [35] and Dempster and Macleod [36] show how using different representations for the constant encodings can lead to better results. However, the exponential number of representations further complicates a problem which itself is NP-complete. This suggests another weakness for CSE approaches which are themselves also NP-complete [37]. Even if the solution to the CSE problem is optimal, it does not necessarily provide an optimal solution to the MCM problem.

Graph-based algorithms iteratively construct a graph in a bottom-up manner that represents the multiplier block. Figures 7.2 and 7.4 provide some examples of these graphs. Heuristic algorithms construct the graph by determining the appropriate vertices to add to the graph. The nodes in the graph denote the coefficients. The edges are directed and represent values that are equal to the coefficients in the parent node shifted by some amount. The coefficient value that is stored at every node is obtained by adding up the values on the incoming edges to the node. Some examples of graph based algorithms include Bull and Horrocks [38], RAG-n [39], Bernstein [40] and Voronenko and Puschel [20].

The large majority of all of the aforementioned approaches attempt to minimize the number of additions/subtractions required to compute the constant multiplications. In fact, the problem is even more difficult than this. Every addition is not equivalent. The size and the speed of a specific addition highly depend on the numbers being summed. For example, consider summing $x + 4x$, where the variable x has two bits. Simply concatenating the variable x with itself will perform this addition. If $x = 01_2$, then $x + 4x = 0101_2$, which is simply the string "01" concatenated with itself, i.e., replicated twice. The higher-order two bits correspond to $4x$ and the lower two bits represent x. This requires no hardware and no delay for computation. Therefore, not all additions are the same; thus, it is possible to reorder additions to take advantage of this fact. The remainder of this chapter discusses this algorithmic nuance along with many others.

To provide some insight into the multiple-variable problem, consider first a simpler subproblem, where each constant is decomposed into an addition/subtraction of constant powers of two, e.g., $5x_0 + 3x_1 \rightarrow 4x_0 + x_0 + 2x_1 + x_1$. Furthermore, the focus is the area and the delay of three terms. Consider the expression $x_0 + 2x_1 + 4x_2$, as shown in Figure 7.5(a). In this case, a "dot" represents one bit of each variable (x_0, x_1, x_2), where each variable has four bits of precision. The variable x_1 is left shifted by one bit, corresponding to multiplication by 2. Similarly, x_2 is offset by two bit positions (multiplication by 4).

There are many possible implementations for this expression. Figure 7.5(a) shows one possible method using two stages of computation. The first stage uses half and full adders when necessary to compress the numbers into at most two Boolean values per bit position in the final result y_0. Notice that bit 0 of y_0 does not require an adder; the result is the least significant bit of x_0. Bit 1 requires a half

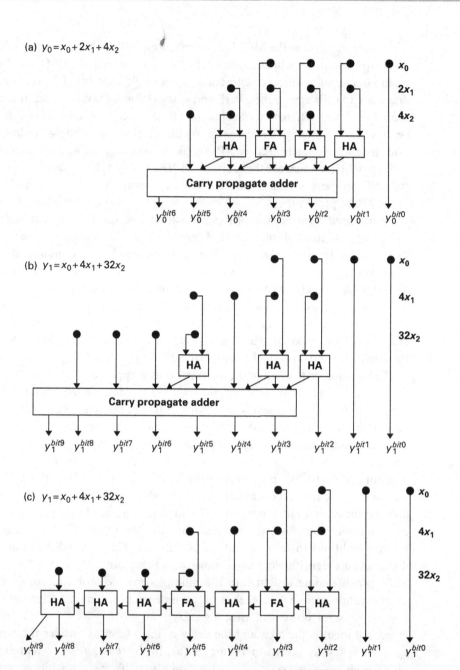

Figure 7.5 Depiction of the logic needed to implement two multi-variable three-term extractions. (a) The computation of $x_0 + 2x_1 + 4x_2$ using two full adders, two half adders and a four-bit CPA. (b) Three half adders and a six-bit CPA are required for computing $x_0 + 4x_1 + 32x_2$. (c) An optimized version of (b), which requires five half adders and two full adders.

Table 7.1 The synthesized area results from Synopsys Design Compiler Ultra, the minimum numbers of hand optimized half adders (HAs) and full adders (FAs), and corresponding hand optimized area for a variety of three term four-bit variables

Equation	Area	HA	FA	Area HA + FA
$x_0 + 2x_1 + 4x_2$	129.8	3	5	131
$x_0 + 4x_1 + 32x_2$	148.2	5	2	92.6
$x_0 + 4x_1 + 64x_2$	149.6	7	1	93.9
$x_0 + 2x_1 + 256x_2$	62.1	2	2	60.9
$x_0 + 4x_1 + 256x_2$	55	3	1	51.6
$x_0 + 8x_1 + 256x_2$	45.9	4	0	42.3

adder, bit 2 requires a full adder, and so on. The second stage uses a four-input CPA to compute the final answer.

One thing to note is that full functionality of the CPA is not always required. Consider the computation of the equation $y_1 = x_0 + 4x_1 + 32x_2$ shown in Figure 7.5(b). The CPA does not require the full functionality to compute bit 5 of y_1. It requires only a half adder because the first level has only one bit for this position. Similarly, bits 7 and 8 require only a half adder, not a full adder. It is relatively easy to locate these cases and optimize the CPA.

Even further reduction in area and delay is possible with optimization across two levels. Again, consider the expression for y_1. In particular, focus on bit 5 of the result. As noted before, the CPA requires only a half adder in this position. Combining the first stage half adder with the second stage half adder creates one full adder. The area and the delay for one full adder are less than those for two chained half adders.

Synopsys Design Compiler Ultra™ [16] uses transformations targeted towards constant multiplication including optimization of CSA trees to eliminate redundant half and full adders [41]. Table 7.1 shows six equations, the area results when they are synthesized by Synopsys Design Compiler Ultra™ [16] using a 90 nm TSMC™ [17] design library, and the results of multilevel optimization performed for minimizing the number of half and full adders. The HA and FA columns show the minimum number of half and full adders, and the final column, Area HA + FA, gives the resulting area. The areas for one full adder and one half adder are 19.9 and 10.6, respectively.

These results show several interesting trends. First, Synopsys Design Compiler Ultra™ does not always find the optimal solution, e.g., the results for $x_0 + 4x_1 + 32x_2$ and $x_0 + 4x_1 + 64x_2$ are off by a significant amount. This is not surprising since they utilize heuristic algorithms. However, the remaining four equations have area results close to those with the minimum number of half and full adders. Their architectures are generated in three stages: partial product generation, followed by a CSA tree, followed by a CPA [41]. This is similar to what is shown in Figure 7.5(a) and (b).

7.6   Overview of linear system optimizations

The linear system is formally described as a vector of inputs X multiplied by a transformation matrix A to obtain a vector of outputs Y, where each value of A is a constant:

$$\begin{bmatrix} Y_1 \\ Y_2 \\ \vdots \\ Y_m \end{bmatrix} = \begin{bmatrix} A_{1,1} & A_{1,2} & \cdots & A_{1,n} \\ A_{2,1} & A_{2,2} & \cdots & A_{2,n} \\ \vdots & \vdots & \vdots & \vdots \\ A_{m,1} & A_{m,2} & \cdots & A_{m,n} \end{bmatrix} \begin{bmatrix} X_1 \\ X_2 \\ \vdots \\ X_n \end{bmatrix}. \tag{7.37}$$

Methods that optimize for only one input, e.g., those algorithms that solve the MCM problem (Section 7.5), only consider part of the problem at a time. For example, the input variable X_1 is multiplied by the constants from the first column $(A_{1,1}, A_{2,1}, \ldots A_{m,1})$. This is also true for the other input variables. MCM can be used to multiply each of these input variables by the appropriate column of constants. Furthermore, the linear equation for each output variable can be viewed as an FIR filter (i.e., $Y_i = A_{i,1} \cdot X_1 + A_{i,2} \cdot X_2 + \cdots + A_{i,n} \cdot X_n$) and MCM can be used to optimize each of these equations individually. In both cases, the scope for optimization is limited, making it possible that the algorithm is not taking full advantage of the solution space.

As an illustration, consider the simple example shown in Figure 7.6. Figure 7.6(a) shows a simple linear system with two input and two output variables and a 2×2 constant matrix. The constants are encoded using simple binary representation though they could just as easily use any other number representation. Looking at the common digit patterns in the constants multiplying variable X_2 ($7 = $ "0111" and $12 = $ "1100"), the digit pattern "11" is detected and extracted. This results in a reduction of one operation as shown in Figure 7.6(c). However, if the scope of the

(a)

$$\begin{bmatrix} Y_1 \\ Y_2 \end{bmatrix} = \begin{bmatrix} 5 & 7 \\ 4 & 12 \end{bmatrix} \begin{bmatrix} X_1 \\ X_2 \end{bmatrix}$$

$5 = 0101_2$
$4 = 0100_2$
$7 = 0111_2$
$12 = 1100_2$

(b)

$Y_1 = X_1 + X_1 << 2 + X_2 + X_2 << 1 + X_2 << 2$
$Y_2 = X_1 << 2 + X_2 << 2 + X_2 << 3$

(c)

$D_1 = X_2 + X_2 << 1$
$Y_1 = X_1 + X_1 << 2 + D_1 + X_2 << 2$
$Y_2 = X_1 << 2 + D_1 << 2$

(d)

$D_1 = D_2 + X_2 << 1$
$D_2 = X_1 + X_2$
$Y_1 = D_1 + D_2 << 2$
$Y_2 = D_1 << 2$

Figure 7.6 An example that shows the benefit obtained by considering common subexpressions that span across multiple output variables: (a) the example linear system; (b) decomposing constant multiplications into shifts and adds; (c) extracting common bit patterns across constants multiplying a single output variable; (d) extending common subexpressions to include multiple output variables.

(a)

$$
\begin{bmatrix} Y_1 \\ Y_2 \\ Y_3 \end{bmatrix} = \begin{bmatrix} 0 & 1 & -1 & 0.33 \\ -1 & -0.66 & 0.33 & -0.33 \\ 1 & 0.33 & -0.66 & 0 \end{bmatrix} \begin{bmatrix} X_1 \\ X_2 \\ X_3 \\ X_4 \end{bmatrix}
$$

(b)

$$
\begin{bmatrix} Y_1 \\ Y_2 \\ Y_3 \end{bmatrix} = \begin{bmatrix} 1 & 0 & 0 \\ -1 & 1 & 1 \\ 0 & 0 & 1 \end{bmatrix} \begin{bmatrix} 0 & 1 & -1 & 0.33 \\ -2 & 0 & 0 & 0 \\ 1 & 0.33 & -0.66 & 0 \end{bmatrix} \begin{bmatrix} X_1 \\ X_2 \\ X_3 \\ X_4 \end{bmatrix}
$$

Figure 7.7 The constant matrix in (a) is split into two matrices in (b). This results in a reduction of multiplications for the overall system. Part (a) requires six multiplications corresponding to the six positive and negative values of 0.66 and 0.33. Part (b) only requires three multiplications for the two values of 0.33 and the one value of −0.66.

optimization is expanded to include multiple variables, the number of operations can be reduced even further as shown in Figure 7.6(d).

The works by Chatterjee *et al.* [42–44] use a combination of techniques including modifying the constant coefficient matrices and performing CSE. The modification of the coefficients is based on the fact that the complexity of the multiplier is dependent on the value of the coefficient and correspondingly transforms the linear system by splitting the constant matrices such that the overall area is reduced. The matrix decomposition technique splits the transformation matrix into the product of $2z + 1$ matrices $M = M_z \cdot M_{z-1} \cdot M_{z-2} \cdots M_0 \cdot M_{-1} \cdots M_{-z+1} \cdot M_{-z}$. The matrix is split through row and column transformations.

Figure 7.7 shows an example of matrix splitting in the linear system from [43]. The matrix is split with the intention of reducing the number of multiplications that are required. In the example in Figure 7.7(a) six multiplications are needed, one for each of the values not equal to 1 or −1. Figure 7.7(b) splits this matrix into two parts. As a consequence of this splitting, only three multiplications are now required, two multiplications for the two occurrences of 0.33 and one multiplication for −0.66. Note that the 1, −1, and −2 values can be converted to addition, subtraction, and shift, respectively. The matrix splitting is followed by a decomposition of the multiplications into shifts and additions along with an algorithm to eliminate common subexpressions. Chatterjee *et al.* proposed several algorithms for CSE. One was based on the bipartite matching technique from Potkonjak *et al.* [31] with an extension that enables it to find shifted forms of the bit patterns. The other algorithms are a greedy algorithm and one based on simulated annealing. While these techniques are focused on linear systems, they potentially miss optimization opportunities due to the fact that they consider the matrix splitting and the shift and add decomposition separately.

There are many works focused on the optimization of a specific transform. For example, countless hand optimizations exist for common transformations such as DCT and DFT. Section 7.7 presents general-purpose algorithms that are applicable to any linear system. The techniques are based on CSE and they are capable of optimizing across all the constants in the transformation matrix. Therefore, they search over a larger solution space than those algorithms that solve the MCM problem.

7.7   Transformation of a linear system into a polynomial expression

The following optimizations rely on transforming the linear system into a polynomial expression. This enables optimizations similar to those found in Chapter 6 to be used.

The first step models a single-constant multiplication, which is then extended to handle any general linear system. Given an integer constant c, the multiplication of that constant with a variable x can be transformed into a polynomial expression as shown below:

$$c \cdot x = \sum_i \pm (x \cdot L^i). \qquad (7.38)$$

Here L represents a left shift from the least significant digit and the index i corresponds to the digit position of the nonzero elements in the constant c where the position 0 denotes the least significant bit. Each term in the polynomial is positive or negative depending on the sign of the corresponding digit in the constant. For example, if $c = 6_{10} = (10\bar{1}0)_2$, then the transformation of $6 \cdot x$ is $x \cdot L^3 - x \cdot L$. A fixed point number can also be represented this way, but by using negative exponents of L instead. For example, the constant multiplication $(0.625_{10} \times x) = (0.101_2 \times x) = (x \cdot L^{-1} + x \cdot L^{-3})$.

A linear system is transformed into a polynomial simply by performing the previous expansion for each of the constant multiplications in the linear system. For example, consider the 4×4 integer transform used in the H.264 video encoding algorithm [45, 46], which is represented as

$$\begin{bmatrix} Y_1 \\ Y_2 \\ Y_3 \\ Y_4 \end{bmatrix} = \begin{bmatrix} 1 & 1 & 1 & 1 \\ 2 & 1 & -1 & -2 \\ 1 & -1 & -1 & 1 \\ 1 & -2 & 2 & -1 \end{bmatrix} \begin{bmatrix} X_1 \\ X_2 \\ X_3 \\ X_4 \end{bmatrix}. \qquad (7.39)$$

This is transformed into the following polynomial by expanding each of the constant multiplications as follows:

$$\begin{aligned} Y_1 &= X_1 + X_2 + X_3 + X_4, \\ Y_2 &= X_1 \cdot L + X_2 - X_3 - X_4 \cdot L, \\ Y_3 &= X_1 - X_2 - X_3 + X_4, \\ Y_4 &= X_1 - X_2 \cdot L + X_3 \cdot L - X_4. \end{aligned} \qquad (7.40)$$

7.8   Optimization for synthesis using two-operand adders

This section presents algebraic optimizations that can be used to eliminate common subexpressions in linear systems. These optimizations are based on techniques used in the domain of logic synthesis for multilevel optimization of Boolean logic to minimize the number of Boolean literals [47, 48]. These techniques can be modified to reduce the area and the power consumption of hardware implementations of linear system transforms.

The techniques for the optimization of Boolean expressions differ from the ones that will be described in this section in some fundamental ways:

(1) The Boolean methods work on a set of linear algebraic expressions. The optimizations described in this section consider linear systems transformed into a polynomial expression (as described in Section 7.7).
(2) The divisor extraction algorithm for Boolean expressions obtains divisors using a common literal support in every pair of cubes in the Boolean expression. The linear systems algorithm divides by a common shift factor between pairs of terms in the linear expressions. This is explained in more detail later in the section.
(3) The algorithms for Boolean expressions do not have a notion of subtraction, as the addition maps to Boolean OR and multiplication corresponds to Boolean AND. Linear systems will likely involve subtraction (especially when using CSD to encode constants) that must be taken into account in order to achieve the best optimization.

We next describe the concept and the generation of two-term algebraic divisors, and then present an algorithm for eliminating common subexpressions. The techniques are explained using the aforementioned H.264 transform as a running example (see Section 7.7). This technique of generating divisors and finding intersections among them is called concurrent arithmetic extraction (CAX).

7.8.1   The generation of two-term divisors

The optimization starts by translating the linear system into a polynomial expression as shown in Section 7.7. Then, the algorithm iteratively extracts the common subexpression corresponding to the best two-term divisor. The subsection starts with the definition of the terminology and then describes this process in detail.

A *two-term divisor* of a polynomial expression is a subexpression that is obtained by considering any pair of terms in the polynomial and dividing it by the smallest exponent of the variable L. Note that every term in the polynomial contains at most two variables, one of the input variables (e.g., X_1, X_2, X_3, X_4 in the H.264 example) and L, though sometimes L is implicit i.e., the exponent of L is zero. This is due to the fact that L denotes the amount of left shift for that input variable. Finding a two-term divisor is equivalent to factoring by the common left shift between two input variables. Therefore, the divisor must have at least one term

```
Divisors(P)
{
  // P = {pᵢ} : Set of expressions in polynomial form;
  D : Set of divisors and co-divisors = Φ;

  for (each polynomial pᵢ in P)
  {
    for (each two-term tuple (t₁, t₂) in pᵢ)
    {
      MinL = The minimum exponent of L in (t₁, t₂); // co-divisor
      t₁* = t₁/MinL;
      t₂* = t₂/MinL;
      d* = t₁* + t₂* ; // divisor;
      D = D ∪ (d* , MinL);
    }
  }
  return D;
}
```

Figure 7.8 Algorithm to generate two-term divisors.

where L has exponent equal to zero. A *co-divisor* is the exponent of L that is used to divide the terms to obtain the two-term divisor. Once a two-term divisor is selected as a common subexpression, the co-divisor is required to divide the original polynomial expression.

To illustrate divisors and co-divisors better consider the polynomial expression resulting from the output variable $Y_2 = X_1 \cdot L + X_2 - X_3 - X_4 \cdot L$ in the H.264 linear system. The minimum exponent of the two terms $X_1 \cdot L$ and $-X_4 \cdot L$ is L, which results in the divisor $(X_1 - X_4)$ with the corresponding co-divisor L. Other possible two-term divisors for Y_2 include $(X_1 \cdot L + X_2)$, $(X_1 \cdot L - X_3)$, $(X_2 - X_3)$, $(X_2 - X_4 \cdot L)$ and $(-X_3 - X_4 \cdot L)$. Each of these divisors has a co-divisor 1.

Figure 7.8 show the algorithm *Divisors* that is used to generate two-term divisors. The input of the algorithm is a linear system transformed into its polynomial form. The algorithm walks through each polynomial expression p_i, looks at every pair of terms, and finds the minimum exponent of L that divides the terms. This is the co-divisor. It then divides both terms by this minimum L value and stores this as the divisor along with the minimum L as the co-divisor in the set of possible divisors D. After iterating through all polynomial equations, it returns the set of all divisors.

Two-term divisors are important because they can be used to find any existing common subexpression in the set of polynomial expressions. Before discussing this more formally, some additional terminology must be defined.

Two divisors *intersect* if they are equal to each other or the negation of one divisor is equal to the other divisor. For example, the divisor $(X_2 - X_4 \cdot L)$ intersects both $(X_2 - X_4 \cdot L)$ and $(-X_2 + X_4 \cdot L)$. Two divisors *overlap* if they contain a common term. Consider the constant multiplication $21_{10}x = 10101_2 \cdot x$. Transforming this to a polynomial expression yields $x \cdot L^4 + x \cdot L^2 + x$. There are two instances of the divisor $(x \cdot L^2 + x)$. One corresponds to the second and third terms $(x \cdot L^2, x)$ with a co-divisor 1; the other corresponds to the first and second terms $(x \cdot L^4, x \cdot L^2)$ with a co-divisor L^2. These divisors intersect because both contain the second term of the polynomial expression, $x \cdot L^2$.

THEOREM *There exists a multiple-term common subexpression in a set of expressions if and only if there exists a nonoverlapping intersection among the set of divisors of the expressions.*

Proof

> If case: A nonoverlapping intersection among a set of divisors of an expression implies, by definition, that there is a nonoverlapping set of two-term subexpressions corresponding to the divisors.

> Only if case: Suppose there is a multiple-term common subexpression C, where C has the terms $\{t_1, t_2, \ldots, t_m\}$ that appear N times in the set of expressions. Take any $e = \{t_i, t_j\} \in C$. There are two cases to consider. First, if e satisfies the definition of a divisor, then there will be at least N instances of e in the set of divisors since there are N instances of C, assuming the divisor extraction procedure extracts all two-term divisors. In the second case, e does not satisfy the definition of a divisor, i.e., there are no terms in e that have an L with an exponent of zero. There must exist $e' = \{t_i', t_j'\}$, which is obtained by dividing t_i and t_j by the minimum exponent of L. This e' satisfies the definition of a divisor for every instance of e'. Since there are N instances of C, there are N instances of e, and hence there will be N instances of e' in the set of divisors. Therefore, in both cases, an intersection among the set of divisors will detect the common subexpression. *QED*

7.8.2 Concurrent arithmetic extraction (CAX) algorithm

This subsection presents the algorithm to eliminate common computations from linear systems. This reduces the area and the power consumption of hardware implementations of linear systems.

The algorithm proceeds by iteratively detecting and extracting two-term common subexpressions. Figure 7.9 provides a high-level overview of the algorithm. The input to the algorithm is a linear system transformed into a polynomial representation.

The first stage gathers statistical information on the available divisors and their corresponding co-divisors. This creates the set of all possible divisors along with the number of times they occur within the polynomial expressions, or equivalently, in the linear system. The function Divisors returns the set of all divisors and co-divisors of the expression. The algorithm scans these divisors while adding them to the set of all divisors D. If a divisor exists in a previous expression, then its frequency is updated. If the divisor is not present in a previous expression, it is added to the set D and its frequency is set to 1.

The second stage performs the selection and extraction of the two-term common subexpressions. The set D is scanned for the divisor that contains the

```
Two Term CAX(P)
{
    //P = {pᵢ} : Set of expressions in polynomial form;
    D = Set of divisors and co-divisors = Φ;

    //Stage1: Creating divisors, calculating their frequencies
    for (each polynomial pᵢ in P)
    {
        D_new = Divisors(pᵢ); // set of new divisors
        Update frequency statistics of divisors in D;
        D = D∪D_new;
    }

    // Stage 2: Iterative selection and elimination of the best divisor
    while(TRUE)
    {
        Find d = Divisor in D with the greatest number of non-overlapping intersections;
        if(d == NULL) break;
        Divide affected expressions in P by d;
        dʲ = set of intersecting instances of d;
        for (each instance i in dʲ)
          { Remove from D all instance of divisors formed using the terms in i; }
        Update frequency statistics of affected divisors;
        D_new = Set of new divisors corresponding to new terms added after division;
        D = D∪D_new
    }
}
```

Figure 7.9 Algorithm for performing two-term CAX.

largest number of nonoverlapping intersections. The number of nonoverlapping intersections is calculated from the set of all intersections using an iterative algorithm in which the current divisor that has the largest number of overlaps with other instances in the set is removed until no overlaps remain. After finding the divisor d with the largest number of nonoverlapping intersections, the expressions containing this divisor are divided by d. The other remaining divisors that contain a common term with d (i.e., they overlap) are removed from the set of possible extractable divisors D. This affects the frequency statistics of some of the divisors in D; the new statistics for these divisors are computed and recorded. Also, the extraction of the term creates new divisors. These new divisors are computed, along with their statistics and added to the set of divisors D. The algorithm continues until there are no remaining divisors in the set D.

The complexity of the algorithm is largely determined by the first stage, which computes the frequency statistics for the distinct divisors. The second stage is linear in the number of divisors due to the dynamic management of the set of divisors. Therefore, the first stage dominates the runtime of the algorithm. The worst-case complexity of the first stage for an $M \times M$ constant matrix occurs when every digit of each constant is nonzero. Assuming the constants contain N digits, each polynomial expression will have $O(MN)$ terms. Since the number of divisors

$$D_0 = X_0 + X_3 \qquad Y_0 = D_0 + D_1$$
$$D_1 = X_1 + X_2 \qquad Y_1 = D_2 + D_3L$$
$$D_2 = X_1 - X_2 \qquad Y_2 = D_0 - D_1$$
$$D_3 = X_0 - X_3 \qquad Y_3 = D_3 - D_2L$$

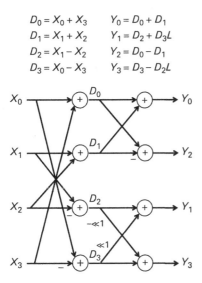

Figure 7.10 Using the two-term common subexpression technique to optimize the H.264 linear transform and the corresponding implementation.

is quadratic in the number of terms, the total number of divisors generated for each expression is $O(M^2N^2)$. This represents the upper bound on the total number of distinct divisors in the set D. Assuming a data structure for D that takes a constant time to search for a divisor with a given variable and exponent of L, the set of divisors D_{new} will have a maximum size of $O(M^2N^2)$ which will take $O(M^2N^2)$ time to compute the frequency statistics. This stage is done $M - 1$ times, yielding an overall complexity of $O(M^3N^2)$ for the first stage. This dominates the time of the second stage, and therefore the runtime of the algorithm is $O(M^3N^2)$.

Applying this algorithm to the 4×4 integer transform used in the H.264 video encoding example, results in the extraction of four common subexpressions, as shown in Figure 7.10, along with the implementation using these extractions. Note that the common subexpressions D_1 and D_2 occur in both their original and negated forms. The negated form of D_1 is found in the equation for Y_2 and that for D_2 in the equation for Y_3. It should be noted that this is the same implementation reported in [45] where the result is obtained manually.

7.9 FIR filter optimization

This section presents the performance of the optimization algorithm when used for FIR filters. FIR filters are commonplace in DSP and are prevalent in communication and multimedia systems. Since FIR filters continuously process incoming signals, their energy consumption and performance can have a major impact on the overall energy consumption and performance of the system. Thus, optimizing

FIR filters is of paramount importance, and consequently FIR optimization has received a lot of attention in practice and in the literature.

This section describes a number of common techniques targeted specifically at FIR filters. Note that FIR filters can be viewed as one-dimensional linear systems, while the techniques of the previous section can optimize more complex linear systems. The results for FIR optimization are presented first because they represent a simpler problem than full-blown linear system optimization.

7.9.1   FIR filter fundamentals

An L-tap FIR filter is an FIR filter whose output is the convolution of the last L input samples. In other words, L is the number of coefficients of the filter's impulse response (i.e., $h(k)$). Equation (7.41) represents an L-tap FIR filter whose input and output are x and y, respectively:

$$y[n] = \sum_{k=0}^{L-1} h[k] \times x[n-k]. \tag{7.41}$$

Note that this equation can be viewed as a one-dimensional transformation matrix:

$$y[n] = [h[L-1]\, h[L-2] \, \cdots \, h[1]\, h[0]] \begin{bmatrix} x[n-L+1] \\ x[n-L] \\ \vdots \\ x[n-1] \\ x[n] \end{bmatrix}. \tag{7.42}$$

Figure 7.11 shows the block diagram of the FIR filter of Equation (7.41). This is a direct implementation of Equation (7.41). Figure 7.3(a) shows the transposed form of this filter, which is obtained from the direct form by moving the latches outside the multiplier block. It performs L multiplications and $L-1$ additions to compute each sample of the output. A parallel implementation of this filter requires L multipliers and $L-1$ adders and would be fast, but its area may be prohibitively large for some applications, particularly those that use filters with a large number of taps. Filters that employ hundreds of taps are not uncommon. A purely serial implementation uses a single multiplier and a single adder and it requires L cycles to generate each output sample. Note the $O(L)$ area reduction of

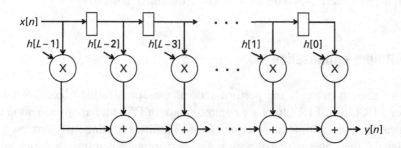

Figure 7.11 The direct form of an FIR filter.

the serial implementation comes at the price of the $O(L)$ reduction in the circuit's throughput. Instead of one multiplier and one adder, a single MAC block could be used. A MAC computes the product of two numbers and adds the product to an accumulator, i.e., $a = a + b \cdot c$. MAC functional units are common in DSP architectures.

An alternative implementation can be done using distributed arithmetic as described in Chapter 5. Distributed arithmetic is a bit-level rearrangement of constant multiplication, which replaces multiplication with a lookup table and a scaling accumulator. The distributed arithmetic architecture can tradeoff throughput for area by changing from a bit serial to a fully parallel implementation. In essence, this replicates the lookup tables, allowing parallel lookups, and therefore the multiplication of multiple bits is performed at the same time.

In Equation (7.41), coefficients ($h[k]$) are constant. Furthermore, the variable $x[n - k]$ can be written as a weighted sum of its bits as follows:

$$ x[n - k] = \sum_{b=0}^{B-1} x_b[n - k] \times 2^b \; x_0 \in [0, 1], \qquad (7.43) $$

where $x_b[n]$ is the bth bit of $x[n]$ and B is the input's bit width. Therefore, Equation (7.41) can be written in the following form:

$$ y[n] = \sum_{k=0}^{L-1} h[k] \times \left(\sum_{b=0}^{B-1} x_b[n - k] \times 2^b \right) = \sum_{k=0}^{L-1} \left(\sum_{b=0}^{B-1} h[k] \times x_b[n - k] \times 2^b \right) $$

$$ = \sum_{b=0}^{B-1} \left(\sum_{k=0}^{L-1} h[k] \times x_b[n - k] \times 2^b \right) = \sum_{b=0}^{B-1} 2^b \times \left(\sum_{k=0}^{L-1} h[k] \times x_b[n - k] \right). \qquad (7.44) $$

The term $h[k] \times x_b[n - k]$ can be computed by calculating the Boolean AND of the bit $h[k]$ with the bit $x_b[n - k]$. The AND gates and adders can be implemented using lookup tables (LUTs) as shown in Figure 7.12. The input is fed into a shift register. The output of the shift register is connected to a RAM-based shift register (the registers are not shown in the figure) [49]. The clock rate of the shift register is $B + 1$ times of the input sample rate, where B is the number of bits of input samples.

The data are stored in a particular address in the RAM-based shift register. The registered LUT outputs are added and saved in the scaling accumulator one bit at a time, from the least significant bit to the most significant bit. For a B-bit input, $B + 1$ clock cycles are needed to generate the filter's output. Thus, the number of clock cycles is not a function of the number of taps, but is rather a function of the precision of the input data.

The multiply–add and distributed arithmetic approaches differ in a fundamental way. The multiply–add approach computes the output one tap (coefficient) at a time. The distributed arithmetic approach computes the output one bit at a time. Consider a multiply–add implementation with a fixed number of resources (e.g., one adder and one multiplier). The latency of a 20-tap filter is twice that of a 10-tap filter (i.e., the sampling rate of the 20-tap filter is half that of the 10-tap

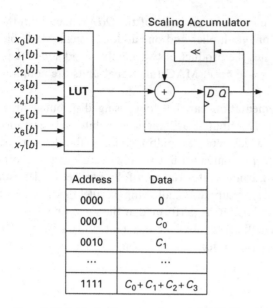

Figure 7.12 A block diagram of a serial FIR filter implemented using the distributed arithmetic technique.

filter). The latency of the distributed arithmetic implementation does not increase as the number of taps increases. However, the size of the LUTs does increase. The latency of the distributed arithmetic implementation is proportional to the size of the input data. For example, moving from 8-bit to 16-bit inputs doubles the latency (halves the sample rate) for a distributed arithmetic implementation. Doing the same on a multiply–add implementation requires a larger adder and multiplier, resulting in an increase in area, yet it does not decrease the sample rate. We note that this analysis is not 100% accurate, as a larger LUT in the distributed arithmetic approach would likely add latency in the first example, as would the larger adder and multiplier in the multiply–add approach in the second example. We are simply trying to point out the fundamental differences between these two techniques.

The serial distributed arithmetic architecture is area efficient, but it can process only one sample every $B + 1$ clock cycles. Furthermore, it can start processing the next input sample only when it finishes processing all bits of the current sample. Therefore, it has a limited performance. Using a parallel architecture instead of the serial architectures solves this problem.

Figure 7.13 shows a two-bit parallel distributed arithmetic FIR filter. The filter has a higher performance at the cost of larger area. This architecture reduces the number of clock cycles for processing each input sample by a factor of 2, which means the throughput also increases by a factor of 2. This improvement comes at the price of doubling the number of required LUTs and the size of the scaling accumulator, which is necessary to store the intermediate results.

The performance can be improved even further by increasing the number of input bits processed at each cycle. The best performance is achieved when all B bits

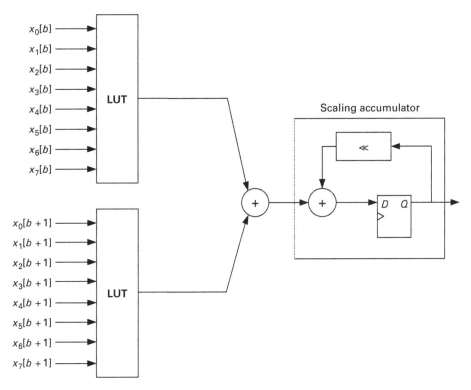

Figure 7.13 The block diagram of a two-bit parallel FIR filter implemented using the distributed arithmetic technique.

of the input are processed in a single cycle, but the area cost of this fully parallel implementation is prohibitively large.

Another technique for implementing FIR filters replaces the multiplications by a set of constants $\{h_k\}$, with a set of additions and shift operations that are optimized by sharing computation. Figure 7.14 shows this technique. Figure 7.14 is obtained from the transposed form of the FIR filter shown in Figure 7.3(b). The multiplier block is converted into a set of additions and hardwired shifts while sharing the common adders. The algorithms described in Section 7.8 can be used to transform the original multiplier block and factor out some common subexpressions and as a result to optimize the filter. Subsection 7.9.2 describes one such technique that minimizes the number of adders for the architecture shown in Figure 7.14. The performance of this filter is limited by the latency of the adder that has the largest number of bits and is the same as the performance of parallel distributed arithmetic, but with a significantly smaller area.

7.9.2   Filter architecture

The filter consists of two main blocks, the multiplier block and the delay block as illustrated in Figure 7.14. The multiplier block multiplies the current input

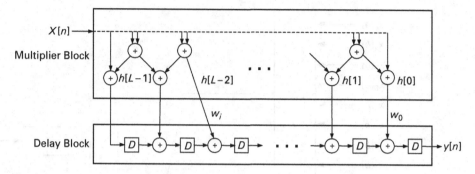

Figure 7.14 The FIR filter architecture consisting of adders and latches.

variable $x[n]$ with all coefficients of the filter and produces outputs w_i. The delay block delays outputs w_i and adds them to produce the filter output $y[n]$.

It is possible to optimize the additions and hardwired shifts performed inside the multiplier block in order to reduce the area of the filter. The additions are implemented using two-input adders configured in the fastest tree structure. The fastest tree structure for an expression is a tree in which each node of the tree is an adder. The tree is arranged such that the height of the tree is the minimum possible. Since registered adders[2] are used, the filter's performance is limited by the delay of the slowest adder only. Using CSE, the number of adders and, as a result, the area can be reduced. Because adders are registered, if the number of the adders of two paths differs, registers have to be inserted to synchronize all intermediate values generated during computation. Thus, using CSE may in some cases result in the addition of a significant number of registers to the circuit. Therefore, the overall area may increase.

As an example, consider the following two expressions that are part of a multiplier block:

$$F_1 = V + X + Y + Z,$$
$$F_2 = W + X + Y + Z.$$

Figure 7.15(a) shows the original unoptimized expression trees for F_1 and F_2. The critical delay paths of both expressions are equal to two addition cycles. The fastest implementation of these expressions requires six registered adders. Since $X + Y + Z$ is a common expression between F_1 and F_2, extracting this common subexpression optimizes the functions. Figure 7.15(b) shows the resulting structure.

Note that it requires two cycles to compute the expression $X + Y + Z$. Therefore, V and W must be delayed two cycles before they are added to $X + Y + Z$. Otherwise, it would not be possible to sample inputs at every cycle.

If an adder and a register have the same area, the area of the circuit in Figure 7.15(b) will be higher than the area of the circuit in Figure 7.15(a).

---

[2] A registered adder is an adder whose output is connected to a register.

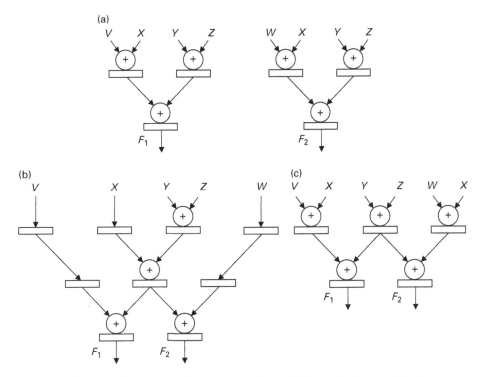

Figure 7.15 Reducing the number of registered adders: (a) the original unoptimized expression trees, (b) the trees optimized by extracting $(X + Y + Z)$ as the common subexpression, (c) the trees optimized by extracting $(Y + Z)$ as the common subexpression.

On the other hand, extracting the common subexpression $(X + Y)$, $(X + Z)$, or $(Y + Z)$ would decrease the number of adders by 1, without adding a register to the circuit as shown in Figure 7.15(c). Subsection 7.9.3 describes an algorithm for performing this optimization.

7.9.3 FIR filter optimization algorithm

The optimization algorithm reduces the area by extracting common subexpressions, using the two-term CAX algorithm explained in Sections 7.7 and 7.8. The algorithm first generates the polynomial formulation of constant multiplications introduced in Section 7.7 After that it calculates the minimum number of registers required for the FIR filter implemented in the architecture shown in Figure 7.14. This is accomplished by finding the fastest tree structure for the original expressions and inserting registers to give equal latency for different paths. For example, for the five-term expression $F = V + W + X + Y + Z$, the fastest tree structure has three addition steps and two extra registers to synchronize the intermediate values as shown in Figure 7.16. As a result of using two extra registers, the new values for inputs can be read in every clock cycle.

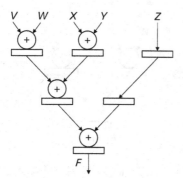

Figure 7.16 The fastest evaluation of expression F and inserted registers.

The next step generates all divisors of the expressions describing the filter and inserts them to a dynamic list of divisors. Then iteratively, the divisor with the greatest value is extracted. A divisor's value is defined as the number of additions saved by extracting the divisor minus the number of extra registers required. A registered adder and an extra (synchronizing) register are assumed to have the same cost when calculating the value.[3] After extracting the best divisor, the algorithm rewrites the expressions, generates new divisors corresponding to the new terms, and adds them to the list of divisors. Furthermore, the divisors corresponding to terms eliminated due to extracting the best divisor are removed from the list of divisors. The algorithm terminates when there is no divisor with positive value in the divisors' list (i.e., there is no divisor which can be extracted to further reduce the cost). Figure 7.17 shows the algorithm.

The example of Figure 7.15(a) needs six registered adders for the fastest evaluation of F_1 and F_2, and requires no additional registers. Selecting the divisor $d_1 = (X + Y)$ saves one addition without increasing the number of registers. Therefore, its value is 1. The value of each of the divisors $(X + Z)$ and $(Y + Z)$ is also 1. Arbitrarily selecting $(X + Y)$ and rewriting the expressions results in the following set of expressions:

$$d_1 = X + Y,$$
$$F_1 = d_1 + Z + V,$$
$$F_2 = d_1 + Z + W,$$

After rewriting the expressions, the algorithm generates new divisors and discards the old ones. In the next iteration, only divisor $d_2 = (d_1 + Z)$ remains. Selecting this divisor saves one adder, but increases the number of registers by five (see Figure 7.15(b)). Therefore, this divisor has a value of -4. Since there is no divisor

---

[3] Here, FPGA is the target architecture. Since most FPGAs have a D flip flop at the output of each LUT, it is easy and inexpensive to create registered adders. The results can be translated to other architectures (e.g., ASICs) with minor changes to the algorithm.

ReduceArea(P)
{
　// P : {p$_i$} = Set of expressions in polynomial form;
　D = Set of divisors and co-divisors = Φ;

　// Step 1: Creating divisors, calculating their frequencies and determining
　　the minimum number of registers required

　for (each polynomial p$_i$ in P)
　{
　　D$_{new}$ = **Divisors**(p$_i$); // set of new divisors
　　Update frequency statistics of divisors in D;
　　D = D ∪ D$_{new}$;
　　Calculate minimum registers required for fastest evaluation of p$_i$;
　}

　// Step 2: Iterative selection and elimination of the best divisor
　while(TRUE)
　{
　Find d = Divisor in D with greatest Value;
　// Value = Number of Additions reduced–Number of Registers Added;
　if (d == NULL) break;
　Rewrite affected expressions in p$_i$ using d;
　Remove divisors in D which have become invalid;
　Update frequency statistics of affected divisors;
　D$_{new}$ = Set of new divisors corresponding to new terms added after division;
　D = D ∪ D$_{new}$;
　}
}

Figure 7.17 The algorithm for reducing area.

with a positive value remaining, the algorithm terminates. Figure 7.15(c) illustrates the optimized expressions.

7.9.4　Experimental results

This subsection presents the experimental results of implementing the aforementioned FIR filter architectures using FPGAs. FPGA architectures primarily consist of a programmable logic fabric, which contains a large number of configurable logic blocks (CLBs). CLBs are composed of several bit-level LUTs; therefore, they are ideal for distributed arithmetic, and distributed arithmetic is a common method for implementing FIR filters on FPGA architectures. Note that many of the current generation FPGAs such as Xilinx Virtex II™ [50] have embedded multipliers, but the number of these multipliers is typically small and they operate on limited bit sizes, which restricts the computations' precision. Therefore, in many cases it is necessary to use some CLBs to implement multipliers. However, implementing multipliers in FPGAs requires a large number of CLBs. Since all

Table 7.2 The number of additions before and after optimization using various sizes of filters

Taps	Original additions	Optimized additions
6	16	6
10	15	10
13	48	13
20	56	15
28	86	24
41	128	34
61	179	42
71	112	28
119	352	65
152	462	80

Table 7.3 A comparison of the number of slices, LUTs, flip flops and performance (in million samples per second) for two filter architectures – the add and shift method and parallel distributed arithmetic

	Add and shift method				PDA			
Taps	Slices	LUTs	FFs	Performance (MSPS)	Slices	LUTs	FFs	Performance (MSPS)
6	264	213	509	251	524	774	1012	245
10	474	406	916	222	781	1103	1480	222
13	386	334	749	252	929	1311	1775	199
20	856	705	1650	250	1191	1631	2288	199
28	1294	1145	2508	227	1774	2544	3381	199
41	2154	1719	4161	223	2475	3642	4748	222
61	3264	2591	6303	192	3528	5335	6812	199
119	6009	4821	11551	203	6484	9754	12539	205
152	7579	6098	14611	180	8274	12525	15988	199

multiplications used in an FIR filter are constant multiplications, the area of multipliers can be greatly reduced by optimizing the constant multiplications.

Table 7.2 shows the results in terms of the number of additions when optimizing ten FIR filters using the techniques presented in Subsection 7.9.3. The first column shows the number of taps of the filters. The second column shows the original number of additions when the FIR filters are implemented using the two-term CAX method without extracting any common subexpressions. The third column shows the number of additions obtained using the modified two-term CAX algorithm described in Subsection 7.9.3.

Table 7.3 shows the results for the optimization algorithm after synthesis on a Xilinx Virtex II™ device. The table is divided into two sections. The first set of columns shows the results using the two-term CAX method while the second set shows the results using an architecture based on parallel distributed arithmetic (PDA). The first column shows the numbers of taps of the filters. Then, in each

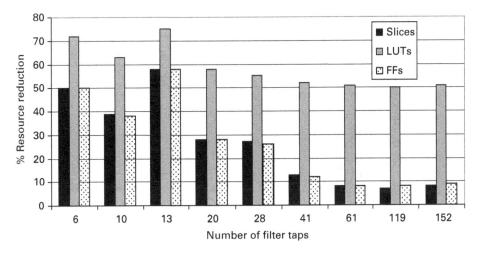

Figure 7.18 The reduction in slices, LUTs, and FFs of the shift and add method compared to the PDA architecture.

section the first column shows the numbers of slices of FPGA used for synthesizing the filters, while the second column shows the number of LUTs. The next two columns present the number of FFs and the performance in terms of million samples per second (MSPS) for each filter. The inputs are 12 bits, while the constants are 16 bits. The filters were synthesized for maximum performance using Xilinx Integrated Software Environment (ISE)™ on a Xilinx Virtex II™ device.

Figure 7.18 illustrates the reduction in the number of slices, LUTs and FFs. As one can see, on average the number of LUTs is 58.7% less for the filters optimized using the two-term CAX method. The reduction in the number of slices and FFs is about 25% on average. Although the algorithm reduces the number of operations and does not optimize performance, in many cases the synthesized circuits are faster than those produced by PDA. For example, for the 13-tap and 20-tap filters, the performance improves by about 26% because of using the optimization.

Figure 7.19 shows the power consumption for the method in Subsection 7.9.3 and the PDA method. As one can see, the two-term CAX method achieves up to 50% reduction in the dynamic power consumption. The reduction in the power consumption is due to the decrease in the number of LUTs and FFs required for implementing the filters.

FIR filters can be synthesized with embedded multipliers as well. Table 7.4 shows the results of this MAC-based method compared to the filters synthesized using the two-term CAX method. The table shows the number of slices and the performance in MSPS on the Virtex IV™ device [51]. As one can see, the MAC filter uses fewer slices compared to the two-term CAX method, but on the other hand it uses embedded multipliers. The number of required multipliers is equal to the number of taps of the FIR filter. Therefore, implementing filters with a large number of taps, such as the 61-tap filter, requires a high capacity device.

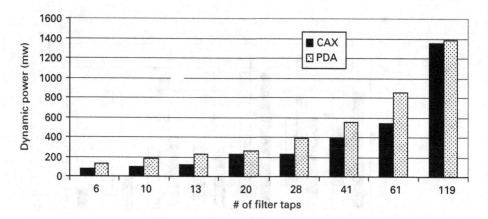

Figure 7.19 Comparison of the power consumption of CAX and the PAD method.

Table 7.4. Comparison with MAC-based FIR filter on the Virtex IV™ device

| Taps | CAX | | MAC filter | |
	Slices	MSPS	Slices	MSPS
6	264	296	219	262
10	475	296	418	253
13	387	296	462	253
20	851	271	790	251
28	1303	305	886	251
41	2178	296	1660	243
61	3284	247	1947	242
119	6025	294	3581	241
152	7623	294	7631	215

While the two-term CAX implementation uses only traditional logic slices of an FPGA, the MAC-based implementation requires both traditional and DSP slices of the FPGA. As a result the MAC-based implementation is slower due to the delay of MAC units and the delay of communication between traditional slices and DSP slices.

7.10   Synthesis for multiple-operand addition

It is possible to further optimize linear systems through the use of more complex adder trees. For example, if the delay is important, it is beneficial to use a CSA tree in conjunction with a summing CPA [52]. A CSA (see Figure 7.20 and also Subsection 5.4.5) is an adder with three inputs and two outputs. The final sum of the three inputs can be computed by adding the two outputs with a CPA.

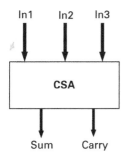

Figure 7.20 A CSA takes three input operands and reduces them to two output operands – a sum and a carry.

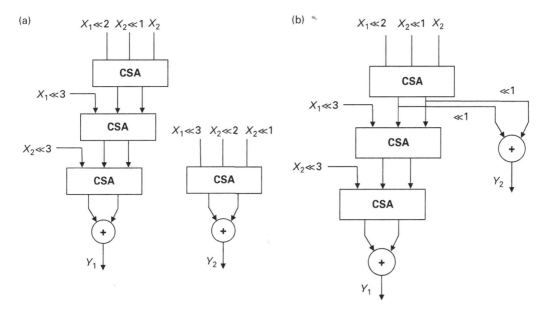

Figure 7.21 CSA trees: (a) original expressions, (b) optimized expressions.

The delay of a CSA is much less than the delay of a ripple carry adder (RCA). The reason is that the carry does not propagate in a CSA. Thus, in a circuit that uses CSAs to perform several additions, carry propagation is done only once when the final result is computed.

A CSA reduces three inputs to two outputs, representing the sum and carry bits. Thus, it is also called a [3:2] counter. The CSA's delay is equal to the delay of a single-bit full adder. Therefore, the delay of a CSA tree is a function of the tree's height. The delay for a CSA tree with height N is given by

$$\text{delay}(N) = \left\lceil \log_{1.5} \left\lceil \frac{N}{2} \right\rceil \right\rceil. \tag{7.45}$$

Figure 7.21 shows a circuit for computing two functions Y_1 and Y_2. The delay of the circuit is equal to the delay of three CSA adders and one ripple carry adder.

(a)
$$\begin{bmatrix} Y_1 \\ Y_2 \end{bmatrix} = \begin{bmatrix} 12 & 11 \\ 8 & 6 \end{bmatrix} \begin{bmatrix} X_1 \\ X_2 \end{bmatrix}$$

(b)
$$Y_1 = X_1 \ll 3 + X_1 \ll 2 + X_2 \ll 3 + X_2 \ll 1 + X_2$$
$$Y_2 = X_1 \ll 3 + X_2 \ll 2 + X_2 \ll 1$$

(c)
$$Y_1 = X_1 L^3 + X_1 L^2 + X_2 L^3 + X_2 L + X_2$$
$$Y_2 = X_1 L^3 + X_2 L^2 + X_2 L$$

Figure 7.22 A linear transform example: (a) the expressions in matrix form, (b) the expressions in linear form, (c) the expressions in polynomial form.

It is possible to reduce the delay of the critical path of a circuit by clustering arithmetic operators together. This is achieved through arranging arithmetic operators over logical operators by following certain rules [53]. These clustered arithmetic operators can be implemented using compressor trees consisting of CSAs followed by a final single CPA. This technique reduces the critical paths of circuits by as much as 46% [53].

It is also possible to use a modified version of the two-term CAX algorithm presented in Section 7.8 to minimize the number of CSAs required to implement an arithmetic function. Extracting three-term divisors that are suitable for computation using CSAs can minimize the arithmetic function. Extracting three-term divisors instead of two-term divisors reduces the total number of CSAs and the number of wires necessary to connect different adders. This algorithm is called the three-term CAX algorithm since it extracts three-term common subexpressions. The optimizations are done on expressions in the sum of products form corresponding to linear systems. The polynomial transform of Section 7.7 converts the linear expressions to polynomials. After that, the three-term CAX method generates all three-term divisors and a greedy algorithm iteratively selects the best divisor at each step and uses the divisor to simplify the expressions.

The example in Figure 7.22(a) shows a linear transform in matrix form. First, the constant multiplications are decomposed into additions and shift operations. Figure 7.22(b) shows the resulting expressions. Then, the expressions are transformed into the polynomial form as illustrated in Figure 7.22(c). Implementing the original linear system using CSAs requires four CSAs as shown in Figure 7.21(a).

7.10.1   Three-term divisor extraction algorithm

This algorithm generates all divisors of an expression by considering every combination of three terms and dividing each of them by the minimum exponent of L. For example, in Figure 7.22(c), the minimum exponent of L for the terms in the expression Y_2 is L. Dividing the terms by L results in the divisor $d = X_1 L^2 + X_2 L + X_2$.

Divisors-3(p$_i$)
{
   // p$_i$: An expression in polynomial form
   D = Set of divisors and co-divisors = Φ;

   for (each 3-term tuple (t$_1$, t$_2$, t$_3$) in p$_i$)
   {
     MinL = The minimum exponent of L in (t$_1$, t$_2$, t$_3$); // co-divisor
     t$_1$* = t$_1$/MinL;
     t$_2$* = t$_2$/MinL;
     t$_3$* = t$_3$/MinL;
     d* = (t$_1$* + t$_2$* + t$_3$*); // divisor;
     D = D$\cup$(d*, MinL);
   }
   return D;
}

Figure 7.23 Algorithm for extracting three-term divisors.

An expression with N terms has $\binom{N}{3}$ three-term divisors. Figure 7.23 shows the algorithm for extracting three-term divisors.

The following theorem illustrates the significance of three-term divisors.

THEOREM *A common three-term subexpression exists if and only if a nonoverlapping intersection exists among the set of three-term divisors.*

A few definitions are required to understand the proof to this theorem. Two divisors **intersect** if their absolute values are equal. For example, $X_1 + X_2L^2 + X_2$ intersects with $X_1 + X_2L^2 + X_2$. Two divisors **overlap** if there is a common term among the terms from which they are derived. For example, consider the expression $Y = X_1L^3 + X_1L^2 + X_1L + X_1$. Dividing the first three terms by L yields the divisor $d_1 = X_1L^2 + X_1L + X_1$. The last three terms yield the divisor $d_2 = X_1L^2 + X_1L + X_1$. Divisors d_1 and d_2 intersect since they have the same terms; they also overlap since two of the terms from which they are obtained are common.

Proof

   If case: If there exist N divisors in the set of all divisors, which intersect and are nonoverlapping, there are N instances of the same three-term common subexpression among the set of expressions.

   Only if case: Assume there exist N nonoverlapping instances of the same three-term expression $d = t_1 + t_2 + t_3$ among the set of expressions. If the minimum exponent of L among the terms in d is 0, then d is a divisor. Since the divisor generation algorithm extracts all possible three-term divisors, d represents N nonoverlapping divisors. If the minimum exponent of L among the terms in d is not 0, d does not satisfy the definition of divisor. Then there

Three-term CAX(P)
```
{
    // P:{pᵢ} = Set of expressions in polynomial form;
    D = Set of divisors = Φ;

    //  Step 1. Creating divisors and their frequency statistics
    for (each polynomial pᵢ in P)
    {
        Dₙₑw = Divisors-3(pᵢ); // set of new three-term divisors
        Update frequency statistics of divisors in D;
        D = D ∪ Dₙₑw;
    }

    //  Step 2. Iterative selection and elimination of best divisor
    while (TRUE)
    {
        d = divisor in D with highest number (frequency) of nonoverlapping intersections;
        if (d == NULL) break;
        Rewrite affected expressions in P using d;
        Remove divisors in D which have become invalid;
        Update frequency statistics of affected divisors;
        Dₙₑw = Set of new divisors corresponding to new terms added after division;
        Update frequency statistics of divisors in D;
        D = D ∪ Dₙₑw;
    }
}
```

Figure 7.24 The three-term extraction algorithm.

exists $d^* = t_1^* + t_2^* + t_3^*$ which is derived by dividing each term in d by the minimum exponent of L; d^* satisfies the definition of divisor. Thus, there will be N nonoverlapping divisors represented by d^*. *QED*

7.10.2   Iterative CAX algorithm

Figure 7.24 shows the three-term CAX algorithm. First, the algorithm finds and stores the frequencies of all distinct divisors. A divisor's frequency is the number of instances of the divisor. To compute the frequencies, the algorithm generates all three-term divisors of each expression D_{new} and finds their intersections with the existing set D.

If there is an intersection between divisor d_1 in D and divisor d_2 in D_{new}, the algorithm updates the frequency of divisor d_1 and adds the matching divisor d_2 to the list of divisors that intersect with d_1. The algorithm then adds divisors in D_{new} that do not intersect with any divisor in D to D as distinct divisors.

In the next step, the algorithm iteratively selects the best three-term divisor and uses it to optimize the expressions. The best divisor is defined as the divisor with the highest number (frequency) of nonoverlapping divisor intersections. Then, the algorithm rewrites the expressions that contain this best divisor. Since the three-term divisors are implemented with CSAs and each CSA has two outputs, a sum and a carry, each divisor also produces two numbers corresponding to the two outputs.

$$D_1 = X_1 \ll 2 + X_2 \ll 1 + X_2$$
$$Y_1 = X_1 \ll 3 + X_2 \ll 3 + (D_1^S + D_1^C)$$
$$Y_2 = (D_1^S + D_1^C) \ll 1$$

Figure 7.25 Expression rewritten after extracting a three-term common subexpression.

Figure 7.25 shows the expressions after the selection of the subexpression $D_1 = X_1 \ll 2 + X_2 \ll 1 + X_2$. Here D_1 is the extracted divisor; D_1^S and D_1^C are the sum and the carry outputs of D_1, respectively.

After selecting the best divisor, the divisors that overlap with it no longer exist. Thus, the algorithm removes such overlapping divisors from the dynamic list of divisors D. As a result, the frequencies of some divisors in D are affected. Thus, the frequencies must be recomputed. Furthermore, adding new terms to expressions means some new divisors corresponding to new terms may exist; thus, new divisors are generated and added to the dynamic set of divisors D and the frequencies are recomputed.

The algorithm stops when no useful divisor is left. For the example of Figure 7.25, after rewriting the expressions and updating the set of dynamic divisors D, the algorithm finds no useful divisor and terminates. Figure 7.21(b) shows the optimized circuit.

ALGORITHM COMPLEXITY The first step of the algorithm, which computes the frequencies of distinct divisors, is the most time-consuming step. The number of three-term divisors for an expression with N terms is $\Theta(N^3)$. Therefore, if there are M expressions, the complexity of the first step is $\Theta(MN^3)$. The second step iteratively selects a divisor, which reduces the number of terms in the affected expressions by 1. In the worst case, for each expression, the number of terms from N, the original value, reduces to two. This requires $N - 2$ steps for each expression. For M expressions, the number of steps would be $\Theta(MN)$. Therefore, the overall complexity of the algorithm is $\Theta(MN^3) + \Theta(MN) = \Theta(MN^3)$.

7.10.3 Experimental results

Table 7.5 presents the area of several circuits before optimization and after optimization using two different versions of the three-term CAX algorithm described in Subsections 7.10.1 and 7.10.2. CAX–Bin works on the binary representation of the constants, while CAX–CSD works on the CSD representation.

The circuits correspond to the 4×4 integer transform used in H.264 video encoding, DCT, IDCT, DFT, DHT, DST, a 20-tap FIR filter, and a 41-tap FIR filter. They are all linear transforms implemented in the sum of products form. The circuits were synthesized in mmi25.db, which is a 0.25 m technology library, using compile_ ultra option in the Synopsys Design Compiler™. The Synopsys Designware™ library was used for the datapath components [16]. The coefficients' bitwidths are 16 for the first six examples and 24 for the two FIR filters. The inputs are 12 bits for all examples.

Table 7.5 The areas of the original expressions and the expressions optimized using three-term extraction with binary (Bin) and CSD number representations for the constants

Benchmark	Bitwidth	Original	CAX–Bin (% improvement over original)	CAX–CSD (% improvement over original)
H.264	16	202 020	199 370 (1.31%)	172 810 (14.46%)
DCT8	16	659 190	618 940 (6.11%)	526 180 (20.18%)
IDCT8	16	579 900	558 490 (3.69%)	488 780 (15.71%)
DFT8	16	608 140	532 740 (12.40%)	500 110 (17.76%)
DST8	16	682 070	637 830 (6.49%)	550 470 (19.29%)
DHT8	16	767 230	813 230 (−6.00%)	636 100 (17.09%)
FIR20	24	124 700	132 540 (−6.29%)	110 550 (11.35%)
FIR41	24	282 490	278 350 (1.47%)	238 720 (15.50%)
Average	N/A	488 217	471 436 (3.44%)	402 965 (16.42%)

The third column of the table shows the areas of the original circuits. The fourth and the fifth columns show the area of the circuits and the percentage of improvement over the original circuits for circuits optimized using the three-term CAX algorithm with the coefficients encoded in binary and CSD, respectively. As one can see, the three-term CAX–Bin algorithm increases the area in two cases, but it achieves 3.44% reduction in the area on average. On the other hand, the three-term CAX–CSD algorithm reduces the area in all cases. Furthermore, it achieves better results than the CAX–Bin algorithm in all examples.

The circuits of Table 7.5 were synthesized using tight timing constraints. The H.264 example used a constraint of 7 ns. For DCT, IDCT, DFT, DHT, and DST, the timing constraints were set to 8 ns, while for the two FIR filters, they were set to 5 ns. All circuits were able to meet the timing constraints. Furthermore, the lengths of the critical paths of all circuits of the same example were within 1% of each other.

The area reduction reported in Table 7.5 is due to the reduction in the number of logic gates used for implementing functions only; it does not factor in the area reduction due to the reduction in the number of wires, which can be calculated after detailed placement and routing. While reduction in the number of wires can further reduce the area, some high-fanout nets corresponding to the extracted common subexpressions may cause congestion in the layout; this might offset some of the area reduction due to the reduction in wiring.

7.11   Delay-aware optimization

While decreasing the number of operations required to compute a set of arithmetic expressions can reduce the circuit area and its energy consumption, it may increase the delay of the critical path. Therefore, care must be taken when optimizing expressions when the delay is important.

This section discusses the delay-aware CAX algorithm. It provides optimization techniques for linear arithmetic expressions that can be changed to take into account the delay while reducing the number of operations. This is demonstrated for two cases: the first considers two-input adders and the second uses CSAs for synthesis.

7.11.1 Delay-aware two-term CAX

The redundancy elimination algorithm can be modified to consider the delay of the critical path while performing optimization. As a result, subexpressions and their delay are concurrently optimized. This is in contrast with conventional high-level synthesis techniques that separately apply the redundancy elimination transformation and the delay minimization transformation. In conventional techniques, the tree height reduction (THR) algorithm is typically used for delay minimization [54]. The THR algorithm uses extensive backtracking to search the solution space, thus it is very expensive in terms of CPU time.

The technique presented in this subsection can be used for optimizing expressions involving multiple variables with different arrival times. As a motivational example, consider the evaluation of the expression $F = a \ll 3 + a \ll 2 + a + b \ll 3 + b \ll 2 + b + c \ll 2 + c + d + e$. Assume that all of the inputs are available at time $t = 0$, except for input a, which is available at time $t = 1$. Figure 7.26(a) shows the evaluation of the expression. In the figure, each edge of the graph shows the arrival times of various signals in the DFG. The expression consists of nine additions. The length of the critical path is four additions when using the fastest tree structure. There are two common subexpressions $d_1 = a + b$, and $d_2 = a + b + c = d_1 + c$. Factoring out these common subexpressions results in the implementation in Figure 7.26(b), which requires only six additions and its critical path consists of four additions. Note the delay has increased because now input a is on the critical path. Since the arrival time of variable a is $t = 1$, this means the delay of the new circuit is one unit more than the delay of the original circuit. The delay-aware common subexpression method solves this issue. In this case, only the common subexpression $d_1 = a + b$ is extracted. The result requires seven additions, but the length of the critical path does not increase as shown in Figure 7.26(c).

7.11.1.1 Problem formulation

The minimum latency of a linear system can be achieved when there is no limit on the resources (i.e., the number of adders) that can be used during synthesis. If all inputs arrive at the same time, $t = 0$, then the latency can be calculated using:

$$\text{min\_latency} = \lceil \log_2 N_{max} \rceil, \tag{7.46}$$

where N_{max} is the maximum number of terms in any of the expressions in the set.

If the signal arrival times are different, N_{max} in Equation (7.46) has to be modified to take into account the difference in the arrival times of inputs. Here it is assumed the arrival times are integer numbers and the delay of an adder/subtractor is one unit. A term with arrival time $i > 0$ can be viewed as being

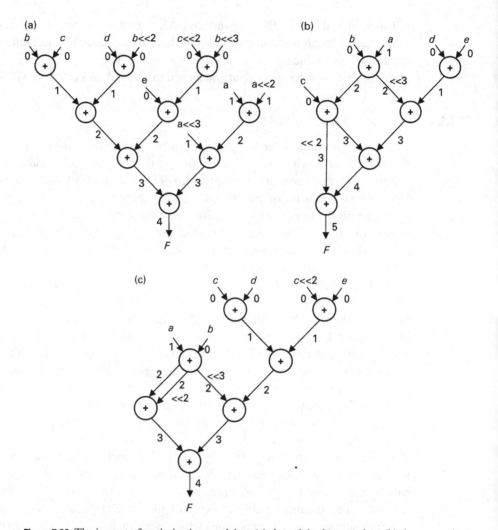

Figure 7.26 The impact of optimization on delay: (a) the original expression, (b) the expression after eliminating common subexpressions, (c) the expression after using delay-aware CAX.

produced by the summation of 2^i dummy terms available at time $i = 0$ because the summation's delay will be i. This increases the number of terms of the expression by $2^i - 1$.

For example, consider the expression shown in Figure 7.26(a). This expression has ten terms, three of which have arrival times equal to 1. Therefore, the number of terms is assumed to be $10 + 3 \times (2^1 - 1) = 13$. The minimum delay of the expressions calculated from Equation (7.46) is four units.

A recursive common subexpression is a subexpression that contains a variable corresponding to another common subexpression. For example, consider the constant multiplication $(1010\bar{1}01010\bar{1}) \times X$ shown in Figure 7.27(a). The common subexpression $d_1 = X{<}{<}2 + X$ in Figure 7.27(b) is nonrecursive

(a)
$F = (1010\overline{1}01010\overline{1}) \times X$
$F = X \ll 10 + X \ll 8 - X \ll 6 + X \ll 4 + X \ll 2 - X$

(b)
$d_1 = X \ll 2 + X$
$F = d_1 \ll 8 + d_1 \ll 2 - X \ll 6 - X$

(c)
$d_1 = X + X \ll 2 + X$
$d_2 = d_1 \ll 2 - X$
$F = d_2 \ll 6 + d_2$

Figure 7.27 Recursive and nonrecursive common subexpressions: (a) the original expression, (b) the expression optimized using nonrecursive CSE, (c) the expression optimized using recursive CSE.

and it reduces the number of additions by one. The common subexpression $d_2 = d_1 \ll 2 - X$ is recursive since it contains the variable d_1 which corresponds to a previously extracted common subexpression. Extracting d_2 leads to the elimination of one more addition.

PROBLEM STATEMENT Given a multiplierless realization of a linear system, the objective is to minimize the number of additions/subtractions such that the latency does not exceed a given threshold. For simplicity, assume this threshold is equal to the minimum possible latency given by Equation (7.45). The problem can use both recursive and nonrecursive common subexpressions to give the maximum reduction in the number of additions/subtractions without violating the delay constraint.

7.11.1.2 Delay-aware CAX algorithm

The *delay-aware CAX algorithm* takes into account the delay of a circuit while performing optimization. The algorithm reduces the number of additions/subtractions as much as possible while maintaining the latency under a specified threshold. At each step, the algorithm only considers subexpressions/divisors whose extractions will not increase the delay of the expressions beyond the given threshold.

The following describes the algorithm used for calculating the delay of an expression. This is followed by the description of the main algorithm that uses the delay calculation algorithm to optimize expressions without increasing their delays. For simplicity we assume unit delay of a single addition/subtraction and the arrival times of all variables are integer numbers.

The arrival time of a variable is the earliest its value is available. There is an arrival time corresponding to each divisor's output. To handle variables with different arrival times, assume that each term available at time $t = i$ is covered by 2^i dummy terms available at time $t = 0$. This has no impact on the quality of the final solution, but it helps to simplify the delay calculation formula, as explained later.

Consider the expression F as shown in Figure 7.28, which shows the arrival times of the variables as superscripts. The figure shows the calculation of the arrival times of divisor outputs and the original terms covered by the divisors.

$F = a^{(0)} + b^{(1)} + c^{(2)} + d^{(0)}$

$d_1 = b^{(1)} + c^{(2)}$
Arrival time $(d_1) = 3$
Terms covered $(d_1) = 2^1 + 2^2 = 6$

$d_2 = d_1 + a$
Arrival time $(d_2) = 4$
Terms covered $(d_2) = 6 + 1 = 7$

Figure 7.28 The divisor information for an example expression.

i = the number of instances of divisor D in the expression
t = delay in terms of addition steps necessary for in computing divisor D

T_{cov} = the terms covered by i instances of D
$T_{not-cov}$ = the terms not covered by instances of $D = T - T_{cov}$

nc = the number of values in $T_{not-cov}$ still available for computation after time t

Total values available after time $t = i + nc$
Delay of the expression after extracting all instances of divisor
        D of expression $= \log_2\lceil(i + nc)\rceil$

Figure 7.29 The procedure for calculating delay.

Figure 7.29 shows the procedure for the calculation of an expression's delay after a divisor contained in the expression is extracted. The algorithm partitions the terms of the expression into the terms covered by the divisor, T_{cov}, and the remaining terms, $T_{not-cov}$.

The algorithm calculates the delay from the number of values available for computation after time t, which is the time taken to compute the divisor under investigation. Among T_{cov} terms, there will be i values available corresponding to the i instances of the divisor. The value of nc, the number of values from $T_{not-cov}$ available after time t, has to be calculated. In general, the terms in $T_{not-cov}$ have to be scheduled to get this information. However, scheduling for every candidate divisor even using a simple algorithm such as ASAP [55], which requires quadratic time in the number of terms is expensive. In many cases, nc, the number of values, can be calculated using a simple formula.

Let $T_{not-cov-orig}$ be the number of original terms corresponding to the terms in $T_{not-cov}$. Then nc can be calculated using

$$nc = \left\lceil \frac{T_{not\_cor\_orig}}{2^j} \right\rceil \tag{7.47}$$

if one of the following holds

(1) if none of the terms in $T_{not-cov}$ has been covered by any divisor;
(2) some terms in $T_{not-cov}$ are covered by divisors covering 2^j original terms, where j is an integer, and the divisor is implemented by using the fastest tree structure, i.e., 2^j original terms are covered by a divisor whose delay is j.

(a)
$$F = aL^3 + aL^2 + a + bL^3 + bL^2 + b + cL^2 + c + d + e$$

$d_1 = a^{(1)} + b^{(0)}$ → delay(d_1) = $t = 2$
i = instances of d_1 in $F = 3$
$T_{cov} = \{aL^3, aL^2, a, bL^3, bL^2, b\}$
$T_{not\text{-}cov} = \{cL^2, c, d, e\}$
$nc = 1$
Delay = $2 + \lceil \log_2(3+1) \rceil = 4$

$d_1 = a + b$
$$F = d_1L^3 + d_1L^2 + d_1 + cL^2 + c + d + e$$

(b)

$d_2 = d_1^{(2)} + c^{(0)}$ → delay(d_2) = $t = 3$
i = instances of d_2 in $F = 2$
$T_{cov} = \{d_1L^2, d_1, cL^2, c\}$
$T_{not\text{-}cov} = \{d_1L^3, d, e\}$
$nc = 1$
Delay = $3 + \lceil \log_2(2+1) \rceil = 5$

$d_2 = d_1 + c$
$d_1 = a + b$
$$F = d_2L^2 + d_2 + d_1L^3 + d + e$$

Figure 7.30 The delay calculation for an example expression: (a) selecting $d_1 = a + b$, (b) selecting $d_2 = d_1 + c$.

Equation (7.47) helps to significantly speed up the delay calculation. Additionally, if the divisor under investigation covers 2^j terms, where j is an integer, and the divisor is implemented in the fastest tree structure, i.e., 2^j terms are covered by a divisor whose delay is j, then extracting the divisor does not increase the overall delay of the expression. If none of the above is satisfied, then nc has to be calculated using ASAP scheduling [55].

Figure 7.30 illustrates the delay calculation for the example expression. Figure 7.30(a) shows the delay calculation for divisor $d_1 = a + b$. The divisor's delay is two units. The expression tree corresponding to the selection of this divisor is shown in Figure 7.26(c). As one can see, four values are available for computation after computing $d_1 = a + b$. Three of the terms correspond to the three uses of the divisor d_1 ($i = 3$), and one of them ($nc = 1$) is from $T_{not\text{-}cov}$, i.e., the terms other than those covered by d_1. The delay is calculated to be 4 by using the procedure in Figure 7.29.

Figure 7.30(b) shows the delay calculation when $d_2 = d_1 + c$ is extracted. The delay of the divisor d_2 is three units. Figure 7.26(b) shows the expression tree with the selection of d_2. The number of values available for computation after $t = 3$ steps is three; two of which (since $i = 2$) correspond to the two uses of divisor d_2 and the other one (note $nc = 1$) corresponds to d and e. Using the procedure in Figure 7.29, the delay is calculated to be five units. Figure 7.26(b)shows the expression tree.

```
Find_True_Value(d, MaxDelay)
{
    {d_instances} = Set of instances of divisor d
    P = {p_i} = Set of expressions containing any of the instances in {d_instances}
    Allowed_instances = ϕ;

    for (each expression p_i in P)
    {
        Valid_d_i = Set of non-overlapping instances that can be extracted from
                    p_i without making its delay greater than MaxDelay
        Allowed_instances = Allowed_instances ∪ Valid_d_i;
    }

    True_value = |Allowed Instances|;
    return True_value;
}
```

Figure 7.31 The algorithm for finding a divisor's true value.

The delay-aware optimization algorithm is based on the two-term CAX algorithm described in, Section 7.8. The difference is that in the delay-aware optimization algorithm, instead of calculating the number of additions saved by the divisor, the true value of the divisor is calculated. The true value of a divisor is the number of instances of the divisor that can be selected without increasing the delay beyond the maximum specified delay (*MaxDelay*). The delay of an instance of a divisor is calculated using the method described previously. Figure 7.31 shows the algorithm used for finding the true value of a divisor.

For each divisor d, the procedure in Figure 7.31 is called to calculate the true value of the divisor for a given limit on the maximum delay (i.e., *MaxDelay*). The procedure collects the set of all expressions containing instances of divisor d in the set $P = \{p_i\}$. Then for each expression p_i in the set, the algorithm finds the number of nonoverlapping instances of divisor d whose extraction do not increase the delay of the critical path of p_i beyond *MaxDelay*. The true value of the divisor is equal to the sum of the number of such instances over all expressions in $\{p_i\}$.

7.11.1.3 Experimental results

This subsection presents the results of the comparison between the delay-aware optimization algorithm with the original algorithm and the Nonrecursive CSE Algorithm [56]. Table 7.6 shows the total number of additions and the number of additions on the critical path for a set of examples optimized by three algorithms. All examples are FIR filters; therefore, they are single-variable expressions. The number of taps for each filter is shown in the second column of the table. All coefficients of the filters are 24-bit integers. The table shows the results of nonrecursive CSE, delay-ignorant and delay-aware CAX algorithms.

As one can see, the delay-ignorant method achieves the least number of additions compared to the other methods, but this comes at the price of increasing the delay of the critical path in two cases (filters 3 and 4). The delay-aware optimization algorithm achieves the fastest implementation in all cases, but at the expense

Table 7.6 Results of optimizing FIR filters using nonrecursive CSE (NRCSE), delay ignorant, and delay aware algorithms (A is area and CP is the critical path in terms of the number of adder stages required to compute the output)

Filter	Taps	Original A	CP	NRCSE A	CP	Delay-ignorant A	CP	Delay-aware A	CP
1	20	106	4	59	4	23	4	23	4
2	41	238	4	146	4	54	4	54	4
3	401	1540	4	921	3	239	4	254	3
4	401	2002	4	1,184	4	316	5	317	4
Average		971.5	3.75	577.5	3.75	158	4.25	162	3.75

Table 7.7 Results for multi-variable DSP transforms (A is area and CP is the critical path in terms of the number of adder stages required to compute the output)

Transform	Original A	CP	Delay-ignorant A	CP	Delay-aware A	CP
DCT	2033	8	946	8	946	8
IDCT	1784	7	861	8	923	7
DFT	1761	7	853	8	925	7
DST	2066	8	949	8	949	8
DHT	2174	8	1013	8	1013	8
Average	1963.6	7.6	924.4	8	951.2	7.6

of requiring a few extra additions compared to the delay-ignorant algorithm [57]. The nonrecursive CSE algorithm also achieves the fastest implementation in all cases, but it misses many opportunities for reducing the number of additions. Since the delay-aware method explores recursive common subexpressions in addition to nonrecursive ones, it achieves a further reduction of 67.4% in the number of additions over the nonrecursive CSE algorithm.

Table 7.7 presents the results for some DSP transforms with multiple variables. The optimized transforms are the DCT, IDCT, DFT, DST, and DHT [58]. All transforms are eight-point, therefore, they have eight inputs and eight outputs; furthermore, each transform requires a total of 64 constant multiplications to perform its calculation. All coefficients have 24 bits of precision. The results assume that the arrival times of inputs $\{X_0, X_1, \ldots, X_7\}$ are $\{0, 0, 1, 1, 2, 2, 3, 3\}$, respectively.

The table shows the total number of additions/subtractions and the number of additions/subtractions on the critical path for each transform before optimization and after optimization by the delay-ignorant and the delay-aware algorithms. The nonrecursive CSE algorithm [56] is unable to optimize multiple-variable examples such as these transforms. As one can see, the delay-ignorant algorithm produces the smallest number of additions/subtractions for all examples, but at the cost of increasing the latency in some cases. On the other hand, the delay-aware optimization algorithm achieves the fastest implementation, but at the cost of a 3% increase in the number of additions compared to the delay-ignorant algorithm. Note that the delay-aware algorithm still reduces the number of additions on average by 45.6% compared to the original unoptimized examples.

7.11.2   Delay-aware three-term CAX

It is possible to make the three-term CAX algorithm delay-aware as well. In order to do this, the minimum delay achievable for each expression is calculated before starting the optimization. The three-term extraction presented in Figure 7.24 is modified to calculate the effect of each divisor on the delay and selects only the divisors that do not increase the delay. The result is a reduction in the number of adders while the minimum possible delay is maintained. This subsection presents the delay model used to calculate the expression delays followed by the algorithm and the experimental results.

7.11.2.1   Delay model

As in the delay model used in [59], the delay of a CSA adder is assumed to be 1 (i.e., both the sum and the carry outputs are assumed to have a single unit delay). Further, it is assumed that the arrival times of all signals of the circuit are integers. The generalization to handle noninteger arrival times is straightforward.

The iterative algorithm [59] can find the minimum delay of an expression, which is an optimal polynomial time algorithm for finding the fastest CSA tree for every expression. At each step, the algorithm sorts the terms of the expressions according to their nondecreasing availability times and allots the first three terms to a CSA. The algorithm stops when there are fewer than three terms.

This algorithm finds the minimum delay of expressions under the assumed delay model. Then, each step of the optimization selects an expression whose extraction would not increase the delay of expressions.

Consider the evaluation of the following arithmetic expressions,

$$F_1 = a + b + c + d + e,$$
$$F_2 = a + b + c + d + f.$$

Assume that all variables are available at time $t = 0$, except variable a, which is available at time $t = 2$. Using the optimal CSA allocation algorithm [59], the minimum delays for both F_1 and F_2 are calculated as $3 + Delay(Add)$, where $Delay(Add)$ is the delay of the final two-input adder.

Figure 7.32 shows the evaluation of the two expressions after performing the delay-ignorant extraction. The arrival times of signals are shown along the edges of the circuit. This example first extracts the subexpression $d_1 = a + b + c$. After

$d_1 = a + b + c$
Delay$(d_1) = 3$
$F_1 = d_1^S + d_1^C + d + e$
$F_2 = d_1^S + d_1^C + d + f$

Delay$(F_1, F_2) = 5 +$ Delay(Add)

$d_2 = d_1^S + d_1^C + d$
Delay$(d_2) = 4$
$F_1 = d_2^S + d_2^C + e$
$F_2 = d_2^S + d_2^C + f$

Delay$(F_1, F_2) = 5 +$ Delay(Add)

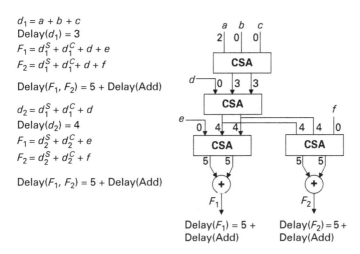

Delay$(F_1) = 5 +$ Delay$(F_2) = 5 +$
Delay(Add)   Delay(Add)

Figure 7.32 The delay-ignorant three-term CAX.

$d_1 = b + c + d$
Delay$(d_1) = 1$
$F_1 = d_1^S + d_1^C + e + a$
$F_2 = d_1^S + d_1^C + f + a$

Delay$(F_1, F_2) = 3 +$ Delay(Add)

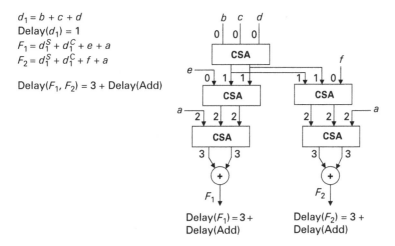

Delay$(F_1) = 3 +$ Delay$(F_2) = 3 +$
Delay(Add)   Delay(Add)

Figure 7.33 The delay-aware three-term CAX.

that the subexpression $d_2 = d_1^s + d_1^c + d$ is extracted. This leads to an implementation with only four CSAs, but the delay of the circuit is now $5 + Delay(Add)$, which is two units more than the optimum delay.

Figure 7.33 shows the result of the delay-aware extraction. Here, the subexpression $a + b + c$ is not extracted because by doing so the delay will increase. The divisor $d_1 = b + c + d$ does not increase the delay so it is extracted. After rewriting the expressions, the common subexpression $d_1^s + d_1^c + a$ is considered, but is not selected because it increases the delay. The delay-aware extraction results in one more CSA than the delay-ignorant one, but the circuit would have the minimum delay.

Table 7.8 Comparison of the results of the delay-ignorant three-term extraction and the delay-aware three-term extraction algorithm

Example	Delay-ignorant			Delay-aware		
	CSAs	Delay	CPU time (s)	CSAs	Delay	CPU time (s)
H.264	78	9	0.2	79	8	1.95
DCT8	222	14	8.5	232	13	44.9
IDCT8	34	14	3.3	201	13	20.9
6-tap FIR	11	5	0.01	15	4	0.03
20-tap FIR	34	6	0.04	45	5	0.16
41-tap FIR	79	6	0.26	91	5	0.7
Average	103.2	9	2.05	110.5	8	11.4

7.11.2.2   Algorithm

The delay-aware optimization algorithm is based on the original algorithm shown in Figure 7.24. In the new algorithm, when searching for the divisor with the most nonoverlapping instances, only the divisors that do not increase the minimum delay are considered. Thus, the delay must be calculated for every candidate divisor.

The complexity of the delay calculation for an expression is quadratic in the number of terms of the expression when using the algorithm in [59].

7.11.2.3   Experimental results

Table 7.8 compares the results of the original three-term extraction algorithm and the delay-aware version. As expected, the original algorithm results in fewer CSAs, but it increases the delay in all examples. The delay-aware algorithm results in the minimum delay, but because of the additional constraint added to the optimization problem, the number of CSAs increases by an average of 15.5% over the delay-ignorant algorithm. Despite this, the number of CSAs is still 31.1% less than the number of CSAs of the original unoptimized expressions.

Calculating the delay of each candidate divisor at every iteration increases the CPU time of the algorithm substantially. The average CPU time of the delay-aware algorithm is five times the average CPU time of the original algorithm.

7.12   Software optimization

The previous discussion has primarily focused on the hardware implementation of linear systems. In this case, the decomposition of the constant multiplication results in significant gains, as shown in the experimental results. However, it is possible to perform optimizations that enhance the runtime of linear systems running as software on a microprocessor. This section discusses such techniques.

(a)
$$Y_1 = 17X_1 + 22X_2 + 17X_3 + 10X_4$$
$$Y_2 = 17X_1 + 10X_2 - 17X_3 - 22X_4$$
$$Y_3 = 17X_1 - 10X_2 - 17X_3 + 22X_4$$
$$Y_4 = 17X_1 - 22X_2 + 17X_3 - 10X_4$$

(b)
```
int C[4][4] = {17, 22, 17, 10, 17, 10, -17, -22, 17, -10, -17, 22, 17, -22, 17, -10}
for (int i = 1; i ≤ 4; i++) {
   Y[i] = 0;
   for(int j = 1; j ≤ 4; j++)
     Y[i] += C[i][j] * X[j];
}
```

(c)
$$D_1 = 17X_1; \quad D_2 = 17X_3$$
$$D_3 = 22X_2 + 10X_4; \quad D_4 = 10X_2 - 22X_4$$
$$D_5 = D_1 + D_2; \quad D_6 = D_1 - D_2$$
$$Y_1 = D_5 + D_3$$
$$Y_2 = D_6 + D_4$$
$$Y_3 = D_6 - D_4$$
$$Y_4 = D_5 - D_3$$

Figure 7.34 Optimization of the 4×4 VC-1 video codec: (a) the input linear system; (b) a software implementation for the linear system; (c) the optimized software for the linear system using the two-term CAX technique described in Section 7.8.

7.12.1 Optimization without constant expansion

It is possible to use the two-term CAX algorithm from Section 7.8 to optimize a linear system without performing binary or CSD expansion. In this case, the algorithm finds common subexpressions among various terms of a linear system. Note that linear systems very often repeat their constants. As such, these optimizations are typically very useful and important in the overall optimization, even in the case of the software implementation.

Figure 7.34(a) shows the equations of a 4×4 linear integer transform used in VC-1 video codec standard [60]. Figure 7.34(b) shows a straightforward software implementation of the transform. While this implementation is compact and easy to write, it is very inefficient in terms of execution time and energy consumption. Figure 7.34(c) shows the optimized equations. Calculating the original equations implemented in Figure 7.34(b) requires 16 multiplications and 12 additions/subtractions, whereas only 6 multiplications and 8 additions/subtractions are necessary to calculate the optimized equations.

Note that CSE algorithms may also find a solution similar to that above. The impact of this optimization on the number of clock cycles will be presented for the 4×4 transform in the next subsection.

As another example, H.264 video compression standard uses a 6-tap filter with coefficients $(1, -5, 20, 20, -5, 1)/32$ for Luma interpolation. In Figure 7.35(a)

(a)

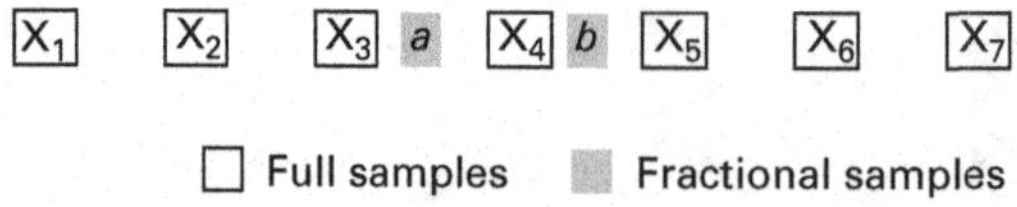

$\boxed{X_1}$ $\boxed{X_2}$ $\boxed{X_3}\ a$ $\boxed{X_4}\ b$ $\boxed{X_5}$ $\boxed{X_6}$ $\boxed{X_7}$

☐ Full samples   ▨ Fractional samples

(b)

$a = \text{Clip}(X_1 - 5X_2 + 20X_3 + 20X_4 - 5X_5 + X_6 + 16) \gg 5)$
$b = \text{Clip}(X_2 - 5X_3 + 20X_4 + 20X_5 - 5X_6 + X_7 + 16) \gg 5)$

$$\text{Clip}(x) = \begin{cases} 0 & \text{if } x < 0 \\ x & \text{if } 0 \leq x \leq MAX \\ MAX & \text{if } x > MAX \end{cases}$$

(c)

$D_1 = X_2 + X_5$
$D_2 = X_3 + X_4$
$D_3 = X_3 + X_6$
$D_4 = X_4 + X_5$
$a' = X_1 + X_6 - 5D_1 + 20D_2$
$b' = X_2 + X_7 - 5D_3 + 20D_3$
$a = \text{Clip}((a'+16) \gg 5)$
$b = \text{Clip}((b'+16) \gg 5)$

Figure 7.35 Luma interpolation which plays an integral part in H.264 video compression. (a) The computation consists of six full samples and two fractional samples. (b) The pseudo code describing the original, unoptimized computation of the fractional samples a and b. (c) The optimized code for the fractional samples using CAX without binary or CSD expansion.

X_1–X_7 are full samples and a and b are fractional samples whose values are estimated from the values of full samples. Figure 7.35(b) shows the equations which are used to estimate the values of a and b.

While 8 multiplications, 12 additions/subtractions and 2 shifts are necessary to compute the equations in their original forms, the optimized equations in Figure 7.35(c) can be computed using 4 multiplications, 12 additions/subtractions and 2 shifts.

7.12.2   Optimization after constant expansion

It is possible to use conventional binary or CSD representations to expand constant multiplications appearing in a linear system and optimize the resulting set of equations. Note that expanding the terms breaks them into simpler terms that are easier to calculate, but there will be a larger number of terms, for example, $21 \times X$ can be expanded to $16X + 4X + X$. While the original term can be computed using one multiplication, the expanded term requires two shift operations and two additions. When implemented in software, this means that the processor executes more instructions. While each instruction consumes different amounts of

$D_0 = X_3 - X_1$

$D_1 = X_3 + X_1$

$D_2 = X_0 + X_2$

$D_3 = X_0 - X_2$

$D_4 = X_1 \ll 2 + D_0$

$D_5 = D_1 \ll 2 - X_3$

$D_6 = D_0 + D_4 \ll 2$

$D_7 = D_1 + D_5 \ll 2$

$D_8 = D_2 \ll 4$

$D_9 = D_3 \ll 4$

$D_{10} = D_6 \ll 1$

$D_{11} = D_7 \ll 1$

$D_{12} = D_2 + D_8$

$D_{13} = D_3 + D_9$

$Y_0 = D_{12} + D_{10}$

$Y_1 = D_{13} + D_{11}$

$Y_2 = D_{13} - D_{11}$

$Y_3 = D_{12} - D_{10}$

Figure 7.36 The VC-1's 4×4 linear integer transform equations optimized after performing CSD expansion.

energy, the energy consumption is not a strong function of the instruction type. Therefore, this transformation not only reduces the performance but also increases the energy consumption of the processor. On the other hand, if a large overlap exists among the terms generated due to the binary or CSD expansions, it is possible to improve the overall performance and reduce the energy consumption.

As an intermediate solution, binary or CSD expansion can be performed selectively for some terms of the linear system in which a large overlap exists. Alternatively, it is possible to use binary or CSD expansions and optimize the equations and heuristically replace some shift and add operations that are performed on the same variable, with multiplications if such opportunities exist. Figure 7.36 shows the optimized equations for the 4×4 linear integer transform used in VC-1 shown in Figure 7.34(a).

As one can see, the optimized equations can be computed using 14 additions/ subtractions and 8 shifs, while 16 multiplications and 12 additions/subtractions were necessary to compute the equations in their original forms.

As another example, consider Luma interpolation equations in Figure 7.35. Optimizing equations after performing CSD expansion results in the equations in Figure 7.37. In this case, 14 additions/subtractions and 7 shifts are required to compute the equations.

$$D_\emptyset = X_3 \ll 2 - X_2$$
$$D_1 = X_6 - X_5 \ll 2$$
$$D_2 = D_4 + D_0$$
$$D_3 = D_4 - D_1$$
$$D_4 = X_4 \ll 2$$
$$a' = X_1 - X_5 + D_1 + D_2 \ll 2 + D_2$$
$$b' = X_7 - X_3 - D_\emptyset + D_3 \ll 2 + D_3$$
$$a = Clip((a' + 16) \gg 5)$$
$$b = Clip((b' + 16) \gg 5)$$

Figure 7.37 The H.264's Luma interpolation equations optimized after performing CSD expansion.

7.13   Summary

This chapter focused on the optimization of linear systems for both hardware synthesis and software compilation. It discussed solutions that viewed the problem in many different ways. For example, it described several problems relating to constant multiplication, including the optimization of a variable multiplied by a constant (i.e., the single-constant multiplication problem), as well as the multiplication of a variable by a set of constants (i.e., the multiple-constant multiplication problem). It showed that these two problems are a subset of the linear system optimization problem; while they can be used to solve the linear system optimization problem, they potentially miss opportunities for finding optimum solutions. The chapter provided a framework for linear system synthesis based upon the transformation of the linear system into a set of polynomial equations. This allowed using techniques similar to those presented in Chapter 6, which focused on the synthesis of polynomial expressions. Furthermore, it was shown that the optimizations are easily extended to handle different types of underlying arithmetic architectures (e.g., those based on CSAs rather than CPAs). Finally, it was shown how the techniques could be applied to software implementations of linear systems.

References

[1] P. J. Schneider and D. H. Eberly, *Geometric Tools for Computer Graphics*, New York, NY: Elsevier Science Inc.
[2] R. Tolimieri, M. An, and C. Lu, *Algorithms for Discrete Fourier Transforms and Convolution*. New York, NY: Springer, 1997.
[3] K. Beauchamp, *Applications of Walsh and Related Functions*. New York, NY: Academic Press, 1984.
[4] G. D. Bergland, A fast Fourier transform algorithm for real-valued series, *Communications of the ACM*, **11**(10), 703–10, 1968.
[5] R. N. Bracewell, Discrete Hartley transform, *Journal of the Optical Society of America*, **73**(12), 1832–5, 1983.

[6] K. R. Rao and P. Yip, *Discrete Cosine Transform: Algorithms, Advantages, Applications*. New York, NY: Academic Press Professional, Inc., 1990.

[7] S. A. Martucci, Symmetric convolution and the discrete sine and cosine transforms, *IEEE Transactions on Signal Processing*, **42**(5), 1038–51, 1994.

[8] S. M. Henrique, *Signal Processing with Lapped Transforms*. Norwood, MA: Artech House, Inc., 1992.

[9] L. R. Rabiner and B. Gold, *Theory and Application of Digital Signal Processing*, Englewood Cliffs, NJ: Prentice-Hall, Inc., 1975.

[10] M. Vetterli and J. Kovačević, *Wavelets and Subband Coding*. Upper Sadde River, NJ: Prentice-Hall, Inc., 1995.

[11] JPEG Standard (JPEG ISO/IEC 10918–1 ITU-T Recommendation T.81). htpp://www.ıtu.int/rec/T-REC-T.81/en

[12] I. E. G. Richardson, *H.264 and MPEG-4 Video Compression*, John Wiley and Sons, 2003.

[13] P. Cappello and K. Steiglitz, Some complexity issues in digital signal processing, *IEEE Transactions on Acoustics, Speech and Signal Processing*, **32**(5) 1037–41, 1984.

[14] D. E. Knuth, *The Art of Computer Programming*, Vol. **2**, *Seminumerical Algorithms*. Reading, MA: Addison Wesly, 1997.

[15] W. Huapeng and M. A. Hasan, Closed-form expression for the average weight of signed-digit representations, *IEEE Transactions on Computers*, **48**(8), 848–51, 1999.

[16] Synopsys Datasheet, Design Compiler Ultra-Design Compiler® at its Best, http://www.synopsys.com

[17] TSMC Design Document, TSMC 90 nm Technology Platform, http://www.tsmc.com

[18] A. G. Dempster and M. D. Macleod, Constant integer multiplication using minimum adders, *IEE Proceedings on Circuits, Devices and Systems*, **141**(5), 407–13, 1994.

[19] O. Gustafsson, A. G. Dempster, and L. Wanhammar, Extended results for minimum-adder constant integer multipliers, *IEEE International Symposium on Circuits and Systems, 2002*, Vol. **1**, pp. I-73–I-76. Washington, DC: IEEE Computer Society, 2002.

[20] Y. Voronenko and M. Puschel, Multiplierless multiple constant multiplication, *ACM Transactions on Algorithms*, **3**(2), 11, 2007.

[21] M. D. Ercegovac and T. Lang, *Digital Arithmetic*. San Francisco, CA: Morgan Kaufmann Publishers, 2004.

[22] J. O. Coleman, Cascaded coefficient number systems lead to FIR filters of striking computational efficiency, *International IEEE Conference in Electronics, Circuits and Systems, 2001*. Washington, DC: IEEE Computer Society, 2001.

[23] S. S. Muchnick, *Advanced Compiler Design and Implementation*, San Francisco, CA: Morgan Kaufmann Publishers, 1997.

[24] P. Briggs, K. D. Cooper, and L. T. Simpson, Value numbering, *Software – Practice and Experience*, **27**(6), 701–24, 1997.

[25] R. Sethi and J. D. Ullman, The generation of optimal code for arithmetic expressions, *Journal of the ACM*, **17**(4), 715–28, 1970.

[26] W. M. McKeeman, Peephole optimization, *Communications of the ACM*, **8**(7), 443–4, 1965.

[27] A. S. Tanenbaum, H. van Straven, and J. W. Stevenson, Using peephole optimization on intermediate code, *ACM Transactions on Programming Languages & Systems*, **4**(1), 21–36, 1982.

[28] C. N. Fischer and R. J. LeBlanc Jr., *Crafting a Compiler*, Menlo Park, CA: Benjamin/Cummings, 1991.

[29] P. Briggs and K. D. Cooper, Effective partial redundancy elimination, *Proceedings of the ACM SIGPLAN Conference on Programming Language Design and Implementation, 1994*, pp. 159–70. New York, NY: ACM, 1994.

[30] A. V. Aho, S. C. Johnson, and J. D. Ullman, Code generation for expressions with common subexpressions, *Journal of The ACM*, **24**(1), 146–60, 1977.

[31] M. Potkonjak, M. B. Srivastava, and A. P. Chandrakasan, Multiple constant multiplications: efficient and versatile framework and algorithms for exploring common subexpression elimination, *IEEE Transactions on Computer Aided Design of Integrated Circuits and Systems*, **15**(2), 151–65, 1996.

[32] M. Mehendale, S. D. Sherlekar, and G. Venkatesh, Synthesis of multiplier-less FIR filters with minimum number of additions, *International Conference on Computer-Aided Design, San Jose, 1995*, pp. 668–71. Washington, DC: IEEE Computer Society, 1995.

[33] R. I. Hartley, Subexpression sharing in filters using canonic signed digit multipliers, *IEEE Transactions on Circuits and Systems II: Analog and Digital Signal Processing*, **43**(10) 677–88, 1996.

[34] R. Pasko, P. Schaumont, V. Derudder, V. Vernalde, and D. Durackova, A new algorithm for elimination of common subexpressions, *IEEE Transactions on Computer Aided Design of Integrated Circuits and Systems*, **18**(1), 58–68, 1999.

[35] I.-C. Park and H.-J. Kang, Digital filter synthesis based on an algorithm to generate all minimal signed digit representations, *IEEE Transactions on Computer Aided Design of Integrated Circuits and Systems*, **21**, 1525–9, 2002.

[36] A. G. Dempster and M. D. Macleod, Using all signed-digit representations to design single integer multipliers using subexpression elimination, *IEEE Symposium on Circuits and Systems, Vancouver, 2004*. Washington, DC: IEEE Computer Society, 2004.

[37] M. R. Garey and D. S. Johnson, *Computers and Intractability: a Guide to the Theory of NP-completeness*, San Francisco, CA: W. H. Freeman, 1979.

[38] D. R. Bull and D. H. Horrocks, Primitive operator digital filters, *IEE Proceedings on Circuits, Devices and Systems*, **138**(3), 401–12, 1991.

[39] A. G. Dempster and M. D. Macleod, Use of minimum-adder multiplier blocks in FIR digital filters, *IEEE Transactions on Circuits and Systems II: Analog and Digital Signal Processing*, **42**(9), 569–77, 1995.

[40] R. L. Bernstein, Multiplication by integer constants, *Software – Practice and Experience*, **16**(7), 641–52, 1986.

[41] R. Zimmermann and D. Q. Tran, Optimized synthesis of sum-of-products, *Asilomar Conference on Signals, Systems and Computers, Pacific Grove, 2003*. Washington, DC: IEEE Computer Society, 2003.

[42] A. Chatterjee, R. K. Roy, and M. A. d'Abreu, Greedy hardware optimization for linear digital systems using number splitting and repeated factorization, *IEEE Transaction on Very Large Scale Integrated Systems*, **1**, 423–31, 1993.

[43] H. T. Nguyen and A. Chatterjee, Number-splitting with shift-and-add decomposition for power and hardware optimization in linear DSP synthesis, *IEEE Transactions on Very Large Scale Integrated Systems*, **15**(2), 419–24, 2000.

[44] N. Huy and A. Chatterjee, OPTIMUS: a new program for OPTIMizing linear circuits with number-splitting and shift-and-add decompositions, *Conference on Advanced Research in VLSI, Chapel Hill, 1995*, pp. 258–71. Washington, DC: IEEE Computer Society, 1995.

[45] H. S. Malvar, A. Hallapuro, M. Karczewicz and L. Kerofsky, Low-complexity transform and quantization in H.264/AVC, *IEEE Transactions on Circuits and Systems for Video Technology*, **13**(7), 598–603, 2003.

[46] T. Wiegand, G. J. Sullivan, G. Bjontegaard *et al.*, Overview of the H.264/AVC video coding standard, *IEEE Transactions on Circuits and Systems for Video Technology*, **13**(7), 560–76, 2003.

[47] R. K. Brayton, A. L. Sangiovanni-Vincentelli, C. T. McMullen, and G. D. Hachtel, *Logic Minimization Algorithms for VLSI Synthesis*. Norwell, MA: Kluwer Academic Publishers, 1984.

[48] J. Vasudevamurthy and J. Rajski, A method for concurrent decomposition and factorization of Boolean expressions, *Proceedings of the IEEE International Conference on Computer-Aided Design, Santa Clara, 1990*, pp. 510–13. Washington DC: IEEE Computer Society, 1990.

[49] http://www.xilinx.com/ipcenter/catalog/logicore/docs/ram_shift.pdf

[50] Xilinx Inc., *Virtex II Platform FPGA Handbook*, 2000.

[51] Xilinx Inc., *Virtex-4 Handbook*, 2004.

[52] N. Weste and D. Harris, *CMOS VLSI Design – A Circuits and Systems Perspective*, 3rd edn. Boston, MA: Addison Wesley Publishing Company, 2004.

[53] I.-C. Park and H.-J. Kang, Digital filter synthesis based on an algorithm to generate all minimal signed digit representations, *IEEE Transactions on Computer-Aided Design of Integrated Circuits and Systems*, **21**, 1525–9, (2002).

[54] J. Um, T. Kim, and C. L. Liu, A fine-grained arithmetic optimization technique for high-performance low-power data path synthesis, *Proceedings of the 37th Design Automation Conference (DAC)*, pp. 98–103. New York, NY: ACM, 2000.

[55] G. D. Micheli, *Synthesis and optimization of digital circuits*, first edition, Boston, MA: McGraw-Hill Higher Education, 1994.

[56] J. Um and T. Kim, Layout-aware synthesis of arithmetic circuits, *Proceedings of the 39th Design Automation Conference (DAC)* pp. 207–12. New York, NY: ACM, 2002.

[57] A. G. Dempster and M. D. Macleod, Use of minimum-adder multiplier blocks in FIR digital filters, *IEEE Transactions on Circuits and Systems II: Analog and Digital Signal Processing*, **42**, 569–77, 1995.

[58] T. G. Noll, Carry-save arithmetic for high-speed digital signal processing, *Proceedings of the IEEE International Symposium on Circuits and Systems*, pp. 982–6. Washington, DC: IEEE, 1990.

[59] O. Gustaffson, A. G. Dempster, and L. Walhammar, Extended results for minimum-adder constant integer multipliers, *Proceedings of the IEEE International Symposium on Circuits and Systems, 2002*, Vol. **1**, I-73–I-76. Washington, DC: IEEE, 2002.

[60] SMPTE 421M, *VC-1* Compressed Video Bitstream Format and Decoding Process. htpp://www.smpte.org

Index

Numbers in *italics* indicate figures.
Numbers in **bold** indicate tables.

Printed in the United States
by Baker & Taylor Publisher Services